NUTCA

EVIDENCE

AUSTRALIA
Law Book Company
Sydney

CANADA and USA
Carswell
Toronto

NEW ZEALAND
Brookers
Wellington

SINGAPORE and MALAYSIA
Sweet & Maxwell Asia
Singapore and Kuala Lumpur

NUTCASES

EVIDENCE

FIRST EDITION

by

MICHAEL STOCKDALE
Senior Lecturer in Law
Northumbria University

REBECCA MITCHELL
Principal Lecturer in Law
Northumbria University

NATALIE WORTLEY
Barrister, Senior Lecturer in Law
Northumbria University

ADAM JACKSON
Barrister, Lecturer in Law
Northumbria University

London ● Sweet & Maxwell ● 2007

*Published in 2007 by Sweet & Maxwell Limited of
100 Avenue Road, London NW3 3PF
www.sweetandmaxwell.co.uk
Typeset by LBJ Typesetting of Kingsclere
Printed in the Netherlands by Krips of Meppel*

No natural forests were destroyed to make this product.
Only farmed timber was used and replanted.

A CIP catalogue record for this book is available
from the British Library.

ISBN 978-1-84703-060-3

CONTENTS

TABLE OF CASES

TABLE OF STATUTES

1. BURDEN AND STANDARD OF PROOF

Civil Proceedings

Key Principle: The party to civil proceedings who asserts the existence (or non-existence) of a fact in issue, the existence (or non-existence) of which forms an essential element of that party's claim, bears the legal burden of proving the existence (or non-existence) of the fact.

Wakelin v London and South Western Railway Company 1886
This case concerned the death of the appellant's husband as a result of being hit by a train. Henry Wakelin lived near a railway line that was intersected by a footpath on a level crossing. The crossing was guarded by hand gates. There was a watchman at the gates during the day, but not during the night. Mr Wakelin's body was found at night on the railway line near the crossing. Trains on the line did have headlights but did not give any warning when approaching the crossing. The deceased's widow, Jane Wakelin, brought an action in negligence against the railway company. She was initially successful, however, on appeal this verdict was set aside. The case eventually reached the House of Lords.

Held: (HL) Appeal dismissed. It was for the plaintiff to prove that her husband's death was caused by the negligent act or omission of the defendants. This she had failed to do, because there was no evidence as to how the accident occurred.

Commentary
The facts established by the evidence in *Wakelin* were equally consistent with the negligence of the plaintiff's husband as they were with the negligence of the defendants and, consequently, the plaintiff had failed to prove that her husband's death had been caused by the defendants' negligence.

Key Principle: It may be difficult to determine which party to

civil proceedings bears the legal burden of proving (or disproving) a fact in issue in circumstances in which it is not
clear whether proving (or disproving) the fact forms an
essential element of the claimant's cause of action or of the
defendant's defence or is a matter that can be relied upon by
the claimant in rebuttal of a defence that the defendant has
established.

Joseph Constantine Steamship Line Limited v Imperial Smelting Corporation 1941

The appellants, Joseph Constantine Steamship Line Limited,
owned a steamship called the Kingswood. The respondents,
Imperial Smelting Corporation, chartered the ship to sail from
Port Pirie, South Australia to Europe with a cargo of ores and
concentrates. The vessel was anchored outside Port Pirie when
an explosion occurred on board. The damage caused by the
explosion rendered the vessel unable to fulfil the charter
requirements and sail to Europe. The appellants gave notice to
this effect to the respondents, who claimed damages for breach
of contract. The appellants, in defence, claimed that the contract
had been frustrated by the explosion. The respondents claimed
that the defence of frustration did not prevent the appellants
from being in breach of contract unless they could prove that
the frustrating event occurred without any fault on their part.
The appellants argued that, once the frustrating event was
proved, the respondents must prove fault on their part in order
to deprive the appellants of their defence of frustration. Atkin-
son J. found for the appellants. On appeal to the Court of
Appeal, this decision was reversed.

Held: (HL) Appeal allowed. The appellants were not required
to prove absence of fault on their part in order to rely on the
defence of frustration.

Commentary

Where a defendant to civil proceedings relies on a defence which
merely amounts to a denial of facts asserted by the claimant's claim
and, thus, does not assert the existence (or non-existence) of any
new facts in issue, this does not place any legal burden of proof on
the defendant. Where, however, a defence does involve asserting
the existence (or non-existence) of facts the existence (or non-
existence) of which was not asserted by the claimant, then, the
existence (or non-existence) of the relevant facts forming an
essential element of the defendant's defence, the defendant bears

the legal burden of proving (or disproving) the existence of those facts. The problem in the *Joseph Constantine* case was that it was unclear whether proving absence of fault on the part of the defendant formed an essential element of the defence of frustration, in which case the legal burden of proving the absence of fault would be borne by a defendant who relied upon the defence of frustration, or whether fault on the part of the defendant was a matter that could be relied upon by a plaintiff in rebuttal of the defence of frustration, in which case the legal burden of proving fault on the part of the defendant would be borne by a plaintiff who wished to rebut the defence. The House of Lords held that the latter position was correct. Consequently, in circumstances in which the evidence established the existence of the supervening event but was insufficient to determine whether or not the supervening event was a result of default on the part of the defendant, the plaintiff had failed to satisfy the legal burden of rebutting the defence of frustration.

Key Principle: **Where a party to civil proceedings bears the legal burden of proving (or disproving) a fact in issue, the party only discharges that burden by proving that the fact is more likely to be true (or false) than not, it not being sufficient to assert an improbable explanation that is more likely to be true that that relied on by the other party.**

Rhesa Shipping Co SA v Edmunds 1985

In this case a cargo ship, *Pop M*, sank off the coast of Algeria with its cargo of sugar. The shipowners, who had two similar insurance policies for the vessel with the defendants, sought to recover for their loss. Both policies required proof that loss was caused by "perils of the sea" to be recoverable. Water had entered the ship through a large hole in the ship's plating. The plaintiff shipowners blamed the loss on collision with an unidentified, moving, submerged submarine. The submarine did not surface, was not seen and had not been detected. The defendant insurers contested this explanation for the sinking of the vessel, and asserted that wear and tear had resulted in the plating opening up under the ordinary action of the sea. At the original trial, the judge regarded the plaintiffs' submarine theory as extremely improbable but regarded the defendants' wear and tear theory as virtually impossible and, thus, held that the cause of the loss had been a collision with a submerged submarine. The defendants' appeal was dismissed by the Court of Appeal.

Held: (HL) On appeal from the Court of Appeal, the House of Lords held that the burden of proving, on a balance of proba- bilities, that the ship was lost by perils of the sea was with the shipowners throughout. The only conclusion which could be reached on the facts was that the reason for the loss of the ship in calm weather was in doubt. The shipowners had therefore failed to discharge the burden of proof.

Commentary
The standard of proof in civil proceedings is proof on the balance of probabilities. This requires the evidence to be such that the judge can say "more probable than not" (*Miller v Minister of Pensions* 1947). In *Rhesa Shipping*, the House of Lords emphasised that: the burden of proof was borne by the plaintiffs; the standard of proof was proof on a balance of probabilities; the defendants were under no obligation to attempt to prove that the ship was lost other than by perils of the sea; if the defendants' attempted to prove that the ship was lost other than by perils of the sea they were not obliged to prove this on a balance of probabilities; and, it was open to the court to conclude, on a balance of probabilities, that the cause of the ship's loss remained in doubt, in which case the plaintiffs would have failed to discharge the burden of proof. In *Rhesa Shipping*, the trial judge had erroneously regarded himself as bound to choose between the theories advanced by the plaintiffs and the defendants and had not considered that it was open to him to decide that, since he was unable to make a finding concerning the cause of the hole in the ship's plating, the plaintiffs had failed to discharge the burden of proving that the ship was lost by perils of the sea. Proof on the balance of probabilities required the judge to be satisfied that it was more likely than not that an event had occurred before he found that the event had occurred; it did not accord with common sense for a judge, having concluded that it was extremely unlikely that an event had occurred, to find that it was more likely to have occurred than not.

Key Principle: **Where serious allegations are made in civil proceedings, the standard of proof remains proof on the balance of probability, but the more serious the allegation the**

less likely it is to be true and the stronger the evidence that
will be required to prove that it is true.

Re H and others (Minors) (Sexual Abuse: Standard of Proof) 1996

This case concerned an appeal by a local authority against
orders made in the County Court dismissing applications by the
local authority for care orders in respect of a number of
children. R, who lived with their mother and was father to the
two youngest children, had been charged with rape after the
eldest of the children alleged he had sexually abused her. The
local authority then sought care orders under s.31(2) of the
Children Act 1989. Section 32(2) of the Children Act 1989
provides that a court can only make a care order if it is satisfied
that the child concerned is suffering or is likely to suffer
significant harm, and that this harm is attributable to the care
the child is receiving or likely to receive or the child is beyond
parental control. Although R was acquitted of rape, the local
authority application for care orders was based solely on the
rape allegation by the eldest child. In the county court, the judge
decided that the local authority had not sufficiently established
that the abuse of the eldest child, which formed the basis for
their application for care orders for the younger children, had
occurred. He was, however, suspicious and felt there was a real
possibility that abuse may have occurred. On appeal to the
Court of Appeal, the local authority was unsuccessful.

Held: (HL) Appeal dismissed, Lord Browne-Wilkinson and
Lord Lloyd of Berwick dissenting. The burden of proving facts
leading to the criteria set out in s.32(2) of the Children Act 1989
being met rested on the applicant for care orders. The appropriate standard of proof was the ordinary civil standard of balance
of probability. When applying the civil standard, the court
would bear in mind that the more serious the allegation the less
likely the alleged event was to have occurred and, thus, the
stronger the evidence that would be required before the court
could conclude that the allegation had been proved on the
balance of probability. Upon the facts of the case, sexual abuse
not having been proved, there were no facts upon which the
county court judge could properly have concluded that there
was a likelihood of harm to the other children.

Commentary

The House of Lords in *Re H* indicated that where serious
allegations are raised in civil proceedings, this does not mean that

the court should apply a higher standard of proof. Rather, the court should still apply the civil standard of proof on a balance of probabilities but, in applying the civil standard, the court should take the inherent probability or improbability of the alleged event into account, stronger evidence being required to prove the occurrence of a more improbable event on the balance of probabilities. Thus, for example, a stepfather is normally less likely to have raped his stepdaughter than to have slapped her in a fit of temper, and physical injury is normally less likely to have been caused deliberately rather than accidentally.

It should be noted that in *R. (McCann and Others) v Crown Court at Manchester and another* 2002, the House of Lords held that, even though proceedings under s.1 of the Crime and Disorder Act 1998 (re the making of anti-social behaviour orders) were civil proceedings to which the civil standard of proof should apply, in order to make the task of magistrates under s.1 of the 1998 Act less complicated, they should apply the criminal standard of proof rather than adopting the approach of the House of Lords in *Re H*.

Criminal Proceedings

Key Principle: **In criminal proceedings, subject to the common law defence of insanity and any statutory provisions which place the legal burden of proving (or disproving) a fact in issue on the accused, the legal burden of proving (or disproving) the facts in issue is borne by the prosecution.**

Woolmington v The Director of Public Prosecutions 1935
Reginald Woolmington was convicted of the wilful murder of his wife on December 10, 1934 and sentenced to death. He and his wife had been married for a short time when she left him and went to live with her mother. Reginald was apparently anxious for her to return to him. He went to visit her at her mother's house with a sawn-off shotgun. Reginald claimed that he took the gun with the purpose of frightening her into coming back to him by threatening to commit suicide. During the visit to his estranged wife, a gun was heard to go off and Reginald was seen leaving the property by a neighbour, who was also his wife's aunt. Reginald claimed that the gun going off was an accident. During the trial, the judge in summing up the case told the jury that the killing of a human was homicide and that all homicide was presumed to be malicious and murder, unless the

contrary was proved. If the fact of killing had been proved, the defendant had to prove that there were circumstances of accident, necessity or infirmity which proved the absence of malice and alleviated the crime so that it was only manslaughter. The defendant's appeal to the Court of Criminal Appeal was unsuccessful, however, an appeal was allowed to the House of Lords.

Held: (HL) The appeal was allowed. Subject to the defence of insanity and any statutory exceptions, it was for the prosecution to prove the guilt of the accused. If there was a reasonable doubt, created by prosecution or defence evidence, as to whether the prisoner killed the deceased with a malicious intention, the prosecution had not made out the case and the prisoner was entitled to an acquittal.

Commentary
In criminal proceedings, the "*Woolmington* principle" is that the legal burden of proving the guilt of the accused beyond reasonable doubt is borne by the prosecution. Thus, the prosecution must prove that the accused committed the *actus reus* of the offence with which he is charged while possessing the requisite *mens rea*. Moreover, with the exception of the common law defence of insanity and any statutory provisions that place a legal burden of proof on the accused (such as s.2 of the Homicide Act 1957, which places the legal burden of proving diminished responsibility on the accused), the prosecution must also disprove the accused's defences. Thus, for example, the prosecution bears the legal burden of disproving common law defences, such as self-defence, duress and provocation, beyond reasonable doubt.

Key Principle: **The legal burden of proving the common law defence of insanity in criminal proceedings is borne by the accused.**

M'Naghten's Case 1843
Daniel M'Naghten was charged with the murder of Edward Drummond. M'Naghten had shot Drummond in January 1843. He pleaded not guilty and evidence was given that he was not of sound mind when the shooting took place. At the original trial, the jury returned a verdict of not guilty on the ground of insanity. The House of Lords debated this verdict and decided

to take the opinion of all the judges on a number of questions of law in such cases, including the proper questions to be put to the jury where a person charged with a crime is alleged to suffer from insane delusion and insanity is relied on as a defence, and in what terms ought the question to be left to the jury as to the person's state of mind when the act was committed.

Held: (HL) The jury ought to be told that every man is to be presumed sane and to be responsible for his crimes until the contrary is proved to the satisfaction of the jury. To establish the defence of insanity it must be clearly proved that, when the act was committed, the accused was afflicted by such a defect of reason, due to disease of the mind, as not to know the nature of the act he was doing, or not to know that what he was doing was wrong.

Commentary
M'Naghten established that the legal burden of proving the defence of insanity is borne by the accused. This is the only common law defence which imposes a legal burden of proof upon the accused in criminal proceedings.

Key Principle: **Where the prosecution bears the legal burden of disproving a defence which raises a new issue, the judge should only leave the defence to the jury if the evidence before the jury is capable of raising the defence (i.e. if the evidential burden of raising the defence is satisfied).**

R. v Lobell 1957
The accused was charged with wounding with intent to cause grievous bodily harm. There was evidence of self-defence, and the judge directed the jury to the effect that the burden of proof in relation to the defence of self-defence was borne by the accused.

Held: (CCA) The legal burden of rebutting the defence of self-defence was borne by the prosecution, but the defence should only be left to the jury if there was evidence from which a jury would be entitled to find in favour of the accused in relation to that issue. If, on the evidence, the jury was left in doubt as to whether the killing or wounding might have been in self-defence, the proper verdict was not guilty. Upon the facts of the *Lobell* case there was material on which the jury might have made a finding of self-defence. The judge had stressed several times when summing up that the burden of proof lay on the accused and the Court of Appeal was not satisfied that the jury would have convicted if it had been directed correctly. Thus, the accused's conviction was quashed.

Commentary
Where a defence, such as the common law defences of self-defence, provocation or duress (indeed, such as any common law defence except insanity) raises issues that do not form essential elements of the prosecution case but does not fall within an exception to the "*Woolmington* principle", the prosecution will bear the legal burden of disproving the defence beyond reasonable doubt if there is evidence before the jury which is capable of raising the defence. Thus, the accused is sometimes said to bear the "evidential burden" of raising such a defence but, in reality, regardless of which party adduces the evidence, if there is evidence before the court in support of such a defence which is capable of putting a reasonable doubt in the minds of the jury then the defence should be left to the jury and it should be directed that the legal burden of disproving it is borne by the prosecution.

Key Principle: **There is an "exception" to the principle that the prosecution bears the legal burden of proof in criminal proceedings which applies in the case of enactments which prohibit the performance of an act other than in specified circumstances, or by persons who belong to specified classes or who possess specified qualifications, or with the licence or permission of specified authorities.**

R. v Edwards 1974
In October 1973, the defendant, Errington Edwards, was convicted of selling intoxicating liquor without a justices' licence, in contravention of the Licensing Act 1964. He leased property in Brixton, the basement of which was found to be full of people drinking alcohol, following a search under warrant by police officers. The basement was fitted up as a bar. Mr Edwards was not present during the search of the property. At his trial, Mr Edwards made an unsworn statement to the effect that he had

not been in occupation of the property. Mr Edwards appealed against conviction on the ground that the prosecution had omitted to call any evidence to prove that there was no justices' licence granted to him.

Held: (CA) The appeal was dismissed. The common law had evolved an exception to the fundamental rule of criminal law that the prosecution must prove every element of the offence charged. This exception was limited to offences arising under enactments prohibiting the performance of an act other than in specified circumstances, or by persons who belonged to specified classes or who possessed specified qualifications, or with the licence or permission of specified authorities. It was for the court to determine whether, upon its true construction, an enactment fell within the exception. Upon the facts of *Edwards*, it had been for the defendant to prove that he was the holder of a justices' licence allowing the sale of liquor, not for the prosecution to prove that no such licence had been granted to him.

R. v Hunt 1986

The appellant was convicted of being in unlawful possession of a Class A drug contrary to s.5(2) of the Misuse of Drugs Act 1971. The drug had been found at his home following a search, under warrant, by police officers. The drug was in white powder form and was contained in a folded piece of paper under an ashtray in the bedroom of the house. The appellant told the police that the powder was amphetamine sulphate. Evidence at the trial included a report of an analyst that the powder was not amphetamine sulphate but in fact contained morphine mixed with atropine and caffeine. Section 5(2) of the Misuse of Drugs Act 1971 provided that it was an offence for a person to have a controlled drug in his possession in contravention of s.5(1). Section 5(1) provided that, subject to any regulations under s.7 of the Act, it was not lawful for a person to have a controlled drug in his possession. Section 7 allowed regulations to be made which excepted specified controlled drugs from the provisions of s.5(1). The Misuse of Drugs Regulations 1973, reg.4(1) provided that s.5(1) of the Misuse of Drugs Act 1971 did not have effect in relation to controlled drugs specified in Schedule 1 of the regulations. Paragraph 3 of the schedule essentially included preparations of medicinal opium or of morphine containing not more than 0.2 per cent morphine compounded with active or inert ingredients such that the morphine could not be recovered by readily applicable means. The prosecution had adduced no evidence concerning the proportion of morphine in the powder, but the judge had ruled against a defence submission of no case to answer and the appellant had then changed his plea to not guilty.

On appeal, the Court of Appeal held that the burden lay on the appellant to prove, on the balance of probabilities, that the preparation of morphine in the appellant's possession fell within the relevant exception found in the Misuse of Drugs Regulations 1973.

Held: (HL) The prosecution were required, as an essential element of the offence, to prove the possession of a prohibited substance and the burden therefore lay upon the prosecution to prove not only that the powder contained morphine but also that it was not morphine in the form permitted under the Misuse of Drugs Regulations 1973, reg.4(1) and Sch.1. Appeal allowed.

Commentary

As was indicated above in the commentary to *Woolmington v DPP*, the principle that the prosecution bears the legal burden of proving (or disproving) the facts in issue in criminal proceedings is subject both to the common law defence of insanity and to statutory provisions which place a legal burden of proof on the accused. As the House of Lords recognised in *R. v Hunt* 1987, a statutory provision (like s.2 of the Homicide Act 1957) may place a legal burden of proof on the accused expressly or, alternatively, a statutory provision, like the provision which the *Edwards* case concerned, may, on its true construction, place a legal burden of proof upon the accused even though it does not do so expressly. It should be noted that the common law "exception" recognised by the Court of Appeal in *Edwards* is effectively embodied, for the purposes of summary trial, in s.101 of the Magistrates' Courts Act 1981.

The House of Lords in *Nimmo v Alexander Cowan and Sons Ltd* 1968 had indicated that where the linguistic construction of a statute did not make clear where the burden of proof lay, the courts should take into account other considerations including the mischief to which the statute was directed and the ease or difficulty that the parties faced in discharging the burden of proof. The House of Lords in *Hunt* regarded the ease or difficulty faced by the respective parties in discharging the burden of proof as a consideration of great importance. Their Lordships in *Hunt* did not regard the "exception" that the Court of Appeal had identified in *R. v Edwards* as an exception to the general rule that the legal burden of proof in criminal proceedings is borne by the prosecution. Rather, they regarded the formula laid down by the Court of Appeal in *Edwards* as "an excellent guide" to the construction of statues. As regards the construction of the provisions which *Hunt*'s case concerned, reg.4 dealt with the definition of the essential ingredients of the offence and, consequently, the legal burden of proving what amounted to an essential element of the offence with which the accused was charged was borne by the prosecution. Their Lordships indicated that the prosecution would normally have had the substance analysed and, thus, would normally have no difficulty in adducing evidence to satisfy the legal burden of proving that the substance did not fall within Schedule 1. In contrast, their Lordships indicated that had the burden of proof been placed on the accused, the accused might have encountered real difficulties in discharging it; i.e. the accused was not entitled to a proportion of the substance that the police had seized and by the time they had had it analysed there might have been little of it left.

Key Principle: **The criminal standard of proof is proof beyond reasonable doubt, but a judge may find it more straightforward to direct a jury to the effect that they must be "satisfied so they feel sure" of the accused's guilt.**

R. v Summers 1952

This case concerned a man convicted of stealing copper, for which he was sentenced to five years' imprisonment. In summing up, the chairman of quarter sessions (the case was heard at Surrey Quarter Sessions) told the jury that they should acquit the man if they had reasonable doubt as to his guilt. The chairman went on to elaborate upon what he meant by reasonable doubt, suggesting that it was the sort of judgment that the ordinary man of the world brought to bear on his own affairs and that if they concluded on the evidence that "this might have happened, or it might not", that amounted to a reasonable doubt.

Held: (CCA) The Court of Criminal Appeal dismissed the accused's appeal, concluding that no jury hearing the chairman's words would have thought that the chairman was saying any more than that they were required to acquit if they had a doubt. Their Lordships went on to indicate that it was better not to use the expression "reasonable doubt", because attempts to define it tended to result in confusion, and that it would be better to direct a jury that they must be satisfied so that they can feel sure.

Commentary

The criminal standard of proof is proof beyond reasonable doubt. This does not require proof beyond a shadow of a doubt, and remote or fanciful possibilities do not prevent a case from being proved beyond reasonable doubt, but proof beyond reasonable doubt does require a high degree of probability (*Miller v Minister of Pensions* 1947). In practice, a judge may find it more straightforward to direct a jury to the effect that they must be "satisfied so that they feel sure" of the accused's guilt rather than that they must be "satisfied beyond reasonable doubt". It should be noted that where the defence bears the legal burden of proving a fact in issue in criminal proceedings the standard of proof is proof on a balance of probabilities (*R. v Carr-Briant* 1943).

Key principles: **Where the statutory imposition of a legal burden of proof upon the accused would violate Art.6(2) of the European Convention on Human Rights it may be necessary to read the provision, under s.3(1) of the Human Rights Act 1998, as merely imposing an evidential burden upon the accused.**

R. v Lambert 2001

The appellant, Lambert, was convicted of possession of a controlled drug with intent to supply, contrary to s.5 of the Misuse of Drugs Act 1971. In his defence at the original trial, the appellant relied on s.28(3)(b)(i) of the Misuse of Drugs Act 1971 claiming that he did not believe or suspect, or have reason to suspect, that he was in possession of a controlled drug. The drug, cocaine, had been found in a bag in his possession. The judge directed the jury that the prosecution had only to prove that Lambert had and knew that he had the bag in his possession and that the bag contained a controlled drug. To rely on the defence provided by s.28(3) of the Misuse of Drugs Act 1971, Lambert had to prove, on the balance of probabilities, that he did not know that the bag contained a controlled drug. Effectively, s.28 imposed a legal rather than a merely evidential burden on Lambert. Following his conviction, Lambert appealed to the Court of Appeal, but was unsuccessful. There then followed an appeal to the House of Lords. By this time, the Human Rights Act 1998 had come into force. The House of Lords had three issues to address. The first related to the nature of the offence under s.5 of the Misuse of Drugs Act 1971, the second related to the direction given to the jury at the original trial concerning the nature of the burden of proof that was imposed upon the accused in relation to the defence under s.28 of the Act and the third was whether the appellant could rely on an alleged breach of his rights under the European Convention for the Protection of Human Rights and Fundamental Freedoms, Art.6(2) the presumption of innocence, by the investigating or prosecuting authority when the original trial had taken place before the Human Rights Act 1998 had come into force.

Held: (HL) Appeal dismissed. The appellant could not rely on provisions in the Human Rights Act 1998 to challenge the direction given to the jury by the original trial judge. The offence under s.5 of the Misuse of Drugs Act 1971 required the prosecution to prove that the accused had a bag in his possession containing a controlled drug. The prosecution did not have to prove that the accused knew that the bag contained a controlled drug. Rather, where the prosecution proved that the accused had a bag in his possession containing a controlled drug, the accused could seek to establish one of the defences provided by s.5(2) or s.28 of the 1971 Act. However, once an accused was entitled to rely on provisions of the Convention (Art.6(2)), then s.28 would, in accordance with s.3(1) of the Human Rights Act 1998, have to be read as imposing only an evidential burden, and not a legal burden of proof, on the accused. Upon the facts of Lambert's case, even if the trial judge had directed the jury that the accused bore only an evidential burden in establishing a defence under s.28 of the 1971 Act, the jury would have reached the same verdict.

Commentary
Article 6(2) of the European Convention on Human Rights provides that "Everyone charged with a criminal offence shall be presumed innocent until proved guilty in accordance with law." Section 3(1) of the Human Rights Act 1998 essentially requires that, so far as possible, primary legislation is read and given effect

to in a way which is compatible with the Convention. The House of Lords in *Lambert* held that, once the Human Rights Act 1998 was in force, if the legal burden of proving Lambert's defence was borne by the accused, this would give rise to a violation of Art.6(2). This was so because while Art.6(2) did not prevent the imposition of a rebuttable presumption upon the accused provided that it fell within reasonable limits (*Salabiaku v France* 1988) and while there were reasons for imposing the legal burden of proof upon the accused (e.g. discouraging the distribution of drugs), these reasons had to be balanced against the rights of the accused, and the imposition of a legal burden of proof could not be justified when one took into account what the accused potentially had at stake (i.e. a possible maximum sentence of life imprisonment). Their Lordships also held, however, that, in accordance with s.3(1) of the 1998 Act, it was possible to read s.28(2) of the 1971 Act in a convention compatible way, such that it merely imposed an evidential burden upon the accused, and that s.28(2) should be read in this way once the 1998 Act was in force. Essentially, as the House of Lords recognised in *Sheldrake* (considered later) an evidential burden is the burden of adducing evidence which raises an issue which is fit for consideration by the jury or the magistrates, the prosecution bearing the legal burden of disproving a defence so raised beyond reasonable doubt. Thus, where a provision which appears to impose a legal burden of proof upon the accused is "read down" so as only to impose an evidential burden upon the accused, the result is that the legal burden of disproving the defence will be borne by the prosecution, though there must be evidence before the court to raise the defence before the prosecution's duty to disprove it arises.

Key principles: **The imposition of a legal burden of proof upon the accused will not necessarily violate Art.6(2) of the European Convention on Human Rights.**

R. v Johnstone 2003

The appellant was charged with having committed offences under s.92 of the Trade Marks Act 1994. During a search of his home, hundreds of compact discs and cassettes were found, which were bootleg recordings, that is, copies of an unlawful recording of a live performance. One of the defences relied on by the appellant was the defence provided by s.92(5), which, essentially, provided that it was a defence for the accused to show that he believed on reasonable grounds that the use of the sign was not an infringement of the registered trade mark.

Held: (HL) In order to determine the appeal before the House of Lords it was not necessary to determine the incidence of the legal burden of proof in relation to the s.92(5) defence but since the Court of Appeal had expressed conflicting views on the point, the House of Lords decided to state its views in relation to the issue. Their Lordships held that the burden of proof placed on an accused using the s.92(5) defence was compatible with Art.6(2) of the Convention. The Convention required that a reasonable balance had to be held between the public interest and the interests of the individual. For a reverse burden of proof to be acceptable there had to be a compelling reason why it was fair and reasonable to deny the accused the protection of the normal presumption of innocence. There were compelling reasons present in the case of s.92(5).

Commentary

The House of Lords recognised that the Art.6(2) presumption of innocence did not prevent the existence of presumptions that operated against the accused provided that they were kept within reasonable limits which took into account the importance of what was at stake and maintained the rights of the defence (*Salabiaku v France* 1988). There were compelling reasons for placing the legal burden of proof on the accused. Persons who dealt in branded goods were aware of the need to guard against counterfeit goods, to deal with reputable suppliers and to keep records, and were aware of the risks if they failed to do these things. Furthermore, since persons who supply counterfeit goods to traders, if they can be traced at all, are unlikely to cooperate with an investigation, if the prosecution was required to prove that traders acted dishonestly, there would be fewer investigations and fewer prosecutions. Taking into account both how important and difficult it was to combat counterfeiting and the relative ease for an accused of raising the issue of his honesty, it was fair and reasonable to require a trader, where the need arose, to prove the defence on the balance of probabilities.

Key principles: **The imposition of a legal burden of proof** upon the accused may violate Art.6(2) of the European Convention on Human Rights but will not necessarily do so.

Sheldrake v Director of Public Prosecutions; Attorney General's Reference (No.4 of 2002) 2004

The House of Lords was considering here an appeal by the Director of Public Prosecutions in a case concerning a contravention of s.5(1)(b) of the Road Traffic Act 1988 and a reference from the Attorney General in a case concerning offences under s.11(1) of the Terrorism Act 2000. Both the Road Traffic Act 1988 s.5(2) and the Terrorism Act 2000 s.11(2) imposed on the defendant the burden of proving specified matters in order to escape liability, that is reverse burdens of proof. The s.5(2) defence essentially required the accused to prove that at the time when he was alleged to have been in charge of a motor vehicle after consuming so much alcohol that the proportion of alcohol in his breath exceeded the prescribed limit, there was no likelihood of his driving the vehicle while the proportion of alcohol in his breath remained likely to exceed the limit. The s.11(2) defence essentially required the accused to prove both that the proscribed organisation of which he was alleged to have been a member, or to have professed to have been a member, was not proscribed when he became a member, or began to profess to be a member, and to prove that he had not taken part in any of the organisation's activities while it was proscribed. These reverse burdens were challenged as being incompatible with Art.6(2) of the European Convention for the Protection of Human Rights and Fundamental Freedoms 1950 (Human Rights Act 1998, Sch.1) which established a presumption of innocence in criminal proceedings. The questions for the House of Lords were whether these provisions did infringe Art.6(2) and, if they did, whether, in accordance with s.3 of the Human Rights Act 1998, the court was required to read them down as imposing only an evidential burden on the defendant in order to ensure compatibility with Art.6(2).

Held: (HL) Before the Human Rights Act 1998 came into force, the statutory provisions that the case concerned would clearly have been interpreted as imposing a legal burden of proof upon the accused. The case law under the European Convention on Human Rights concerning the Art.6(2) presumption of innocence established, among other matters, that presumptions against the accused, while not outlawed, were to be kept within reasonable limits and must not be arbitrary and that relevant considerations when determining the reasonableness or proportionality of such a presumption included: the opportunity that the accused was given to rebut the presumption; the maintenance of the accused's rights; the flexibility of the presumption's application; the retention by the court of a power to assess the evidence; the importance of what was at stake; and the difficulty that the prosecution might face if the presumption did not exist. The Court of Appeal in *Attorney-General's Reference (No.1 of 2004)* had preferred the approach of the Lord Nicolls in the House of Lords in *R. v Johnstone* 2003 to that of Lord Steyn in the House of Lords in *R. v Lambert* 2001, but both were recent decisions of the House of Lords which bound the lower courts. Nothing said in *Johnstone* had suggested an intention to modify *Lambert*, which was not to be treated as superseded or overruled and differences between *Johnstone* and *Lambert* could be explained by reference to their different subject matter. The task of the court was not that of deciding whether a reverse burden should be imposed on a defendant but, rather, was that of assessing whether a burden that Parliament had enacted unjustifiably infringed the Art.6(2) presumption of innocence. It was, however, questionable whether, as had been indicated by the Court of Appeal in *Attorney-General's Reference (No.1 of 2004)*, the presumption was that Parliament would not have created an exception to the presumption of innocence without good reason, as this could lead the court to give too much weight to the statute and too little weight both to the presumption of innocence and to the court's obligation under s.3 of the Human Rights Act 1998. The House of Lords in *Sheldrake* was inclined to agree with the conclusions that the Court of Appeal had reached in *Attorney-General's Reference (No.1 of 2004)* in relation to the cases before it, but the House of Lords did not endorse the general guidance that the Court of Appeal had given in *Attorney-General's Reference (No.1 of 2004)* except to the extent that it accorded with the opinions of the House of Lords in *Lambert* and *Johnstone*, which continued to be the leading domestic cases in relation to reverse burdens of proof.

(1) Although the defence in s.5(2) of the Road Traffic Act could be assumed to infringe the presumption of innocence in Art.6(2), the provision was directed at a legitimate object, i.e. the prevention of death, injury and damage caused by someone driving a vehicle when unfit to do so. The burden of proof placed on the defendant was not unreasonable or arbitrary. The defendant had a

full opportunity to prove facts within his own knowledge, which were far more appropriate for him to prove on the balance of probabilities than for the prosecution to prove beyond reasonable doubt. If a driver tried and failed to establish a defence under s.5(2), the resulting conviction should not be regarded as unfair.

(2) Parliament had clearly intended to impose a legal burden of proof on the defendant in s.11(2) of the Terrorism Act 2000 and s.11(1), (2) clearly had a legitimate end in deterring people from joining and becoming involved in the activities of certain proscribed terrorist organisations. However, s.11(2) was to be read and given effect as imposing on the defendant an evidential burden only. A person innocent of any blameworthy or criminal conduct could fall within the provisions of s.11(1) of the Terrorism Act 2000. To require that such a person could only exonerate themselves under s.11(2) on the balance of probabilities created a real risk of unfair conviction. To impose this legal burden on the defendant was not a justifiable and proportionate legislative response.

Commentary

Sheldrake demonstrates that the imposition of a legal burden of proof upon the accused will not necessarily give rise to a violation of Art.6(2) of the European Convention on Human Rights, but that it may do so. With reference to the case law of the European Court of Human Rights, their Lordships indicated that whether an infringement of the Art.6(2) presumption of innocence was justifiable would depend upon an examination of the facts and circumstances of the statutory provision in question as it was applied upon the facts of the specific case before the court. In *Attorney-General's Reference (No.1 of 2004)*, the Court of Appeal had provided general guidance to the lower courts. Among other matters, their Lordships had indicated that the courts should discourage the citation of authority other than *R. v Johnstone* and that where the exception to the presumption of innocence was proportionate with the objective of the reverse burden, it was sufficient that the exception was reasonably necessary in the circumstances, the assumption being that Parliament would not create an exception to the presumption of innocence without a good reason. The House of Lords in *Sheldrake* held, however, that *Lambert* and *Johnstone* were not inconsistent, that the decisions in those cases were different because they concerned different subject matters and that the guidance given by the Court of Appeal in *Attorney General's Reference (No.1 of 2004)* was not to be followed to the extent to which it was inconsistent with *Lambert* and *Johnstone*.

2. COMPETENCE AND COMPELLABILITY

Key Principle: **At common law, a witness is competent to give evidence if the witness sufficiently appreciates the seriousness of the occasion and realises that taking the oath involves more than the duty of telling the truth in ordinary life.**

R. v Bellamy 1985

The appellant was convicted of rape in July 1984. Both he and the victim were of low mental ability and suffered significant mental handicap. The trial judge thought it correct to investigate the competence of the victim as a witness given her low mental ability. He listened to evidence from the appellant's social worker and the appellant and questioned her as to her belief and knowledge in God, her understanding generally and of the importance of telling the truth. The judge ruled that the victim was competent to give evidence but that, given her lack of belief in God, she should not take an oath but should make an affirmation. The defendant appealed on the ground that the judge was not entitled to cause the victim to affirm and that the fact that the key evidence in the trial was given in this unauthorised manner vitiated his conviction.

Held: (CA) Appeal dismissed. The judge had been correct in investigating the competence of the complainant as a witness but should not have also investigated her belief or otherwise in God. In order for a witness to be sworn, it was no longer necessary for the witness to be aware of the divine sanction of the oath, rather, the decisions of the Court of Appeal in *R. v Hayes* 1977 and *R. v Campbell* 1983 had demonstrated that what was necessary was that the witness sufficiently appreciated the seriousness of the occasion and realised that taking the oath involved more than the duty of telling the truth in ordinary life. Upon the facts of *Bellamy*, the complainant had realised that she could ''be put away'' if she told a lie, and it was, thus, evident that she did realise that taking the oath involved more than the duty of telling the truth in ordinary life. Since the judge had concluded that the complainant was a competent witness, and if she had no objection to being sworn, he should have allowed her to be sworn. However, the irregularity in this aspect of the trial, i.e. that the witness had affirmed rather than taking the oath, had not been of a material nature and could not have affected either the complainant's evidence or the jury's appreciation of it.

Commentary

At common law, the test of competence to give evidence is, essentially, whether the witness sufficiently appreciates the solemnity of the occasion and the particular responsibility of telling the truth that taking the oath involves. Where a witness passes this test, the witness may give sworn evidence, either by taking the oath or by making a solemn affirmation. Where the witness fails this test, the witness is not competent and, thus, may not testify. In *Bellamy* the complainant, having passed this test, was entitled to be sworn and should have been permitted to take the oath unless she objected to taking it, in which case she should have been permitted to make a solemn affirmation under s.5 of the Oaths Act 1978.

The common law principles encountered in *Bellamy* in the context of criminal proceedings continue to govern the competence of witnesses in the context of civil proceedings, subject to the exception that where a person under 18 does not understand the nature of the oath, the child may still be competent to give unsworn evidence in civil proceedings under s.96 of the Children Act 1989 (see *C v C* 2001, below).

In the criminal context, however, the competence of a witness to give evidence is no longer governed by the ability of the witness to understand the nature of the oath. Rather, the test of competence is that which is laid down by s.53(3) of the Youth Justice and Criminal Evidence Act 1999, under which a person is not competent to give evidence in criminal proceedings if the person cannot understand questions put to him as a witness and give answers to them which can be understood. Where a witness fails the s.53(3) test, the witness will not be competent to give evidence in criminal proceedings. Where the witness passes the s.53(3) test, however, the presumption under s.55 of the 1999 Act is that the witness may give sworn evidence. Where a party adduces evidence to this effect, however, a witness who has passed the s.53(3) test will not be entitled to give sworn evidence if the witness does not sufficiently appreciate the solemnity of the occasion and the particular responsibility of telling the truth that taking the oath involves. Moreover, s.55 also provides that a witness who is under 14 years of age cannot give sworn evidence. Where a witness who is under 14 years of age or who does not sufficiently appreciate the solemnity of the occasion and the particular responsibility of telling the truth that taking the oath involves passes the s.53(3) test, the witness may give unsworn evidence in criminal proceedings under s.56 of the 1999 Act.

Key Principle: **In criminal proceedings the test of competence is whether a person can understand questions put to him as a witness and can give answers to them which can be understood.**

R. v MacPherson 2005

This case concerned a conviction for the indecent assault of a four-and-a-half-year-old child. At the original trial, which took place shortly after the incident had occurred, counsel for the defendant submitted that the child was not a competent witness. The judge ruled that the child was a competent witness, having watched her video-recorded interview and having seen the child himself, accompanied by counsel for both sides, and asked her questions of a general nature. The defendant appealed on the grounds that the judge erred in determining whether or not the child was competent on the basis of the video-recorded interview alone; that the judge had no or insufficient regard to the requirement that he should assess her ability to understand and answer questions as a witness and that in reaching his decision regarding competence the judge had no or insufficient regard to the child's ability to participate meaningfully in cross-examination.

Held: (CA) Appeal dismissed. The judge plainly did not make a decision on the competence of the witness based solely on the memorandum video; he had also interviewed the child himself. Once the issue of the competence of a witness was raised, it was for the party calling the witness to satisfy the court that, on the balance of probabilities, the witness was competent. This would usually be determined before the witness was sworn. In this type of case, the judge should watch the video-recorded interview and/or ask the child appropriate questions. The test of competence in the Youth Justice and Criminal Evidence Act 1999, s.53 required that the witness was able to understand questions put to him or her as a witness and give answers that could be understood by the court. Put to him as a witness simply meant asked of him in court. Upon the facts of the instant case (the Court of Appeal having viewed the video recorded interview) the child had understood the questions and had given intelligible answers. There was no requirement that the witness should be aware of his or her status as such, questions of credibility and reliability going to the weight of the witness's evidence, not to the competence of the witness. In this case, the judge had set himself the right test and had reached the right conclusion as to the competence of the child.

Commentary

As was indicated in the commentary to *Bellamy*, above, the test of competence in criminal proceedings is now that laid down by s.53(3) of the Youth Justice and Criminal Evidence Act 1999, i.e. a person is not competent to give evidence in criminal proceedings if the person cannot understand questions put to him as a witness and give answers to them which can be understood. Re the admissibility of video-recorded evidence under a special measures direction, see Chapter 5, below.

Key Principle: **A witness who cannot totally understand questions or who cannot give answers that can be totally understood may still be competent to give evidence in criminal proceedings.**

R. v Sed 2004

This case concerned an allegation of rape made by an 81-year-old women suffering from Alzheimer's disease. A video-taped interview was conducted by the police, during which the allegation was made. Prior to the trial, the judge heard an application from the prosecution that at the trial the complainant's evidence should be put to the jury via the medium of the video-taped interview. Two psychiatrists gave evidence at the hearing that the complainant was suffering from moderate to severe Alzheimer's disease at the time of the alleged rape. Both expressed the view that, both at the time when she gave her video-recorded interview and thereafter, the complainant had not been fit to give evidence in court due to this condition. The judge decided that the complainant's evidence should be admitted, in video-taped form, at the trial and that the evidence satisfied the test of competence in s.53 of the Youth Justice and Criminal Evidence Act 1999.

Held: (CA) Appeal dismissed. The judge had not found that the complainant had understood all questions put to her or that all of her answers were understandable, but had found that her understanding of questions and the intelligibility of her answers was sufficient to enable a jury to evaluate her evidence. Section 53 of the 1999 Act did not require 100 per cent understanding of questions or 100 per cent intelligibility of answers. The judge, in determining the issue of competence, was required to take into account the overall performance of the witness, it being for the jury to determine the reliability and cogency of the evidence. The judge had been entitled to determine that the witness was competent.

Commentary

As has already been demonstrated above, the test of competence in criminal proceedings is now laid down by s.53(3) of the Youth Justice and Criminal Evidence Act 1999, thus a person is not competent to give evidence in criminal proceedings if the person cannot understand questions put to him as a witness and give answers to them which can be understood. The decision of the Court of appeal in *Sed* demonstrates that, in order for a witness to pass this test, 100 per cent ability to understand questions and 100 per cent intelligibility of answers is not required, and that where a witness is competent, the credibility of the witness and the reliability of the witness's evidence are matters for the jury.

Key Principle: **The prosecution may compel the accused's unmarried partner to give evidence against him.**

R. v Pearce 2001

The defendant Pearce was convicted of murder in June 2000. He had stabbed his brother three times in the chest. Both men were drunk at the time of the incident. At the original trial, the judge allowed the prosecution to treat both the defendant's daughter and Loveina Pearce, the women with whom the defendant had lived for 19 years, and with whom he had had three children, as hostile witnesses, and to cross-examine them on statements they had made to the police following the incident. The defendant appealed against conviction, arguing that if they had been married, his partner would not have been a compellable witness, that the reason for such a rule was to protect family relationships and that the modern concept of family, and the provisions of Art.8 of the European Convention on Human Rights, required that his partner should not have been a compellable witness.

Held: (CA) Appeal dismissed. The relevant provisions relating to the compellability of a wife or husband were found in s.80(1) of PACE. The section referred to the "wife or husband of a person charged". Loveina Pearce was not married to the defendant. The words of the statute were clear and were not capable of being extended to cover the relationship in question. The provisions of Art.8 of the Convention concerning a proper respect for family life did not require that a co-habitee of a defendant, whether or not married to him, should not be compelled to give evidence. This was an area where the interests of the family had to be weighed against those of the community. The fact that a concession had been made to husbands and wives in a statutory provision did not mean that a similar concession had to be made to those not in the position of a husband or a wife.

Commentary

In general, where a witness is competent to give evidence in criminal (or civil) proceedings the witness is also compellable, i.e. the court can require the witness to give evidence. There are, however, exceptions to this general rule, the main exceptions being that the accused in criminal proceedings is never a compellable witness while he remains in danger of conviction (Criminal Evidence Act 1898, s.1(1)) and that there are limitations upon the compellability of the accused's spouse (i.e. the accused's husband or wife).

The compellability of the accused's spouse or civil partner in criminal proceedings is governed by s.80 of PACE. Essentially, under s.80, the accused's spouse or civil partner is compellable to give evidence on behalf of the accused but is not compellable to give evidence on behalf of the prosecution or a co-accused unless the offence with which the accused is charged is a "specified offence" (i.e. an offence involving an assault, injury or threat of injury to the spouse or civil partner, such an offence or a sexual offence on a person under 16 or attempting to commit, or aiding and abetting the commission of such an offence). The spouse or civil partner of the accused is not compellable by any party to the proceedings, however, if the spouse or civil partner is charged with an offence in the proceedings. Moreover, where former spouses or former civil partners have been divorced, the former spouse or civil partner is compellable by any party to the proceedings just as though the former spouse or civil partner and the accused had never been married/just as though the civil partnership had never existed.

Key Principle: **Under s.96 of the Children Act 1989, a child is competent to give unsworn evidence in civil proceedings if the child understands that it is his duty to speak the truth and has sufficient understanding to justify his evidence being heard.**

C v C 2001
The facts of this case are considered in Chapter 10, below.

Held: (CA) The decision in this case is considered in Chapter 10, below.

Commentary
Section 96 of the Children Act 1989 applies in the context of civil proceedings to persons under 18 years of age who do not sufficiently appreciate the solemnity of the occasion and the particular responsibility of telling the truth that taking the oath involves. Thus, in the context of civil proceedings, a "child" may give sworn evidence at common law if it understands the nature of the oath. If this is not the case, the child may still give unsworn evidence if it passes the s.96 test. It is submitted that, in line with the general common law principle that a party who seeks to adduce evidence bears the burden of proving that the conditions of admissibility are satisfied (*R. v Yacoob* 1981), where a party seeks to call a child witness in civil proceedings, it will be for the party who wishes to call the witness to satisfy the legal burden of proving that the s.96 test is satisfied.

3. CORROBORATION AND SUPPORTING EVIDENCE, IDENTIFICATION EVIDENCE AND LIES TOLD BY THE ACCUSED

Corroboration and Supporting Evidence

Corroborative evidence must be independent of the witness whose evidence requires corroboration. It must also connect the accused to the offence by confirming both that an offence was committed and that the accused was the person who committed it (*R. v Baskerville* 1916). In general, corroboration is not required in English law, that is the accused may be convicted on the evidence of a single witness. Certain statutes do impose corroboration requirements. For example, under s.89 of the Road Traffic Regulation Act 1984, the accused cannot be convicted on the evidence of a single witness. Other areas where corroboration is still required by statute are speeding and treason, but these are exceptional as a number of the statutory provisions that formerly required corroboration have been repealed and corroboration is not required at common law.

Prior to the relevant provisions of the Criminal Justice Act 1988 and the Criminal Justice and Public Order Act 1994 coming into force, a judge was, at common law, required to direct the jury of the danger of convicting on the uncorroborated evidence of certain categories of witness, namely children, accomplices and sexual offence complainants. Although these corroboration warning requirements were abolished by the 1988 and 1994 Acts, it appears that some form of warning to the jury will still be required where there is an evidential basis for suggesting that a witness is unreliable (see *R. v Makanjuola* below).

Key Principle: **Where there is an evidential basis for suggesting that a witness is unreliable, the judge should give the jury an appropriate warning.**

R. v Makanjuola 1995
The defendant was convicted of indecently assaulting the complainant when they were alone in the storeroom of the restaur-

ant where they both worked. The defendant denied the offence in interview and did not give evidence at trial. The complainant was cross-examined on the basis that she had made up her account because she was angry with the defendant over an incident that had occurred several days earlier. The judge did not warn the jury to treat her evidence with caution.

Held: (CA) There was no evidential basis for regarding the complainant as inherently unreliable and the conviction was safe. However, where a witness was shown to be unreliable, a judge might consider it necessary to urge the jury to treat her evidence with caution. Whether the giving of a warning was necessary and, if so, what form of warning should be given was a matter for the judge's discretion.

Commentary
Although the former common law corroboration warning requirements that related to children, accomplices and sexual offence complainants have been abolished by statute, it may still be desirable for the judge to warn the jury about the evidence of potentially unreliable witnesses. The Court of Appeal in *Makanjuola* held that a witness was no longer to be regarded as unreliable merely because he fell within one of the categories of witness in respect of whom a corroboration warning was previously required (children, sexual offence complainants and accomplices). However, where there is some evidential basis for suggesting that the witness is unreliable, it appears that the judge may still find it necessary to urge the jury to exercise caution before relying upon his evidence. In a stronger case, for example where the witness has lied, made previous false complaints or bears a grudge against the defendant, the judge may need to warn the jury that they should look for some supporting evidence. In *Makanjuola* itself, the defendant did not testify and the points made in cross-examination were not supported by any other evidence. There was therefore no evidential basis for regarding the complainant as inherently unreliable.

Key Principle: **The approach of the Court of Appeal in *Makanjuola* is also applicable in circumstances in which, prior to the abolition of the corroboration warning requirements, the judge was not required to give a corroboration warning** but was required to advise the jury to exercise caution or take care in relation to the evidence of a witness.

R. v Muncaster 1999

The police discovered a quantity of LSD in an envelope in a hire car being driven by the accused. The car had been hired by his co-accused and her fingerprints were found on the envelope. The co-accused later attended the police station with further drugs, claiming that she had been to see the accused in prison and that he had told her that there were further drugs in her house, where he had been staying, and that he had asked her to dispose of them for him. She gave evidence to this effect at trial. The judge did not give a corroboration warning but referred to the co-accused as "having an axe to grind".

Held: (CA) Appeal dismissed. Formal corroboration warnings had been abolished by statute and the observations of the Court of Appeal in *Makanjuola* (see above) also applied in circumstances in which the court, while not required to give a corroboration warning, would formerly have been required to warn the jury to exercise caution in relation to the evidence of a witness. It was a matter for the judge what type of warning to give and how much detail to go into.

Commentary
Prior to the statutory abolition of the common law corroboration warning requirements, judges were at times required to warn the jury to exercise caution in relation to the evidence of certain witnesses even though a full corroboration warning was not required (for example where the mental condition and criminal connection of a witness made the giving of a warning appropriate, *R. v Spencer* 1987; where there was material to suggest that a witness's evidence might have been tainted by an improper motive, *R. v Beck* 1982; or where one co-accused gave evidence against another, *R. v Cheema* 1994). Following the abolition of the corroboration warning requirements, the Court of Appeal in *Muncaster* held that the approach of the Court of Appeal in *Makanjuola* now applies in such circumstances. Examination of subsequent case law suggests that a warning should, in general, be given whenever one co-accused gives evidence against another (*R. v Petkar* 2004). Moreover, there are other areas in which a judge would be well advised in practice to give the jury a warning. Thus, for example, in *R. v Stone* 2005, the Court of Appeal, with reference to the decision of the Privy Council in *Benedetto and*

Labrador v R. 2003, indicated that, in general, a warning will be required in the context of a cell confession (that is a confession allegedly made to another prisoner who is yet to be tried). Their Lordships also indicated, however, that a warning will not be required in every such case (for example where the confession would not have been easy to invent there is no point in requiring the judge to tell the jury that confessions can be easy to concoct).

Identification Evidence

Key Principle: **Where a case depends wholly or substantially on disputed identification evidence, the jury should be warned that there is a special need for caution.**

R. v Turnbull 1976
The defendants planned to burgle a bank. In order to avoid the difficulty of gaining access to the safe, they nailed the night safe shut from the outside and pinned up a notice claiming that the safe was broken and asking customers to post their deposits through the letterbox in the front door. Another notice saying "Night Safe Here" was stuck above the letterbox. The police were alerted to the scheme by a suspicious customer and were lying in wait. A police officer driving home saw a man removing the notices from the night safe and the letterbox. The man glanced sideways and the officer recognised him as the defendant Turnbull.

Held: (CA) Although the police officer only caught a fleeting glimpse of the defendant from a moving car at night time, there was ample other evidence which went to support the correctness of the identification. The appeal was dismissed.

Commentary
In 1976 a Departmental Committee was set up under Lord Devlin following two high profile miscarriages of justice caused by honest but mistaken identification evidence. In *Turnbull*, the Court of Appeal, adopting most of the recommendations contained in the Devlin Committee's report, laid down guidelines to be followed in all cases that depend wholly or substantially on disputed identification evidence:

1. The judge must warn the jury of the special need for caution in identification cases and instruct them that a mistaken witness can be a convincing witness.

2. The jury must be instructed to examine closely the circumstances of the identification, including: length of the observation; distance; lighting; whether the witness's view was impeded in any way; whether the witness had seen the accused before; the length of time between the original observation and the subsequent identification of the accused to the police; and, any discrepancy between the original description given by the witness and the actual appearance of the accused.

3. If the identification evidence is of good quality, it can be left to the jury.

4. If the identification evidence is of poor quality, for example where the witness had only a fleeting glimpse of the offender, the judge must withdraw the case from the jury unless there is other evidence capable of supporting the correctness of the identification.

Key Principle: **The jury must be warned that there is a special need for caution in identification cases and that a convincing witness may nevertheless be mistaken. This is so even where the case is a recognition case.**

R. v Bentley 1994

The defendant and the victim, who were known to each other, both attended a club to watch a televised boxing match. An altercation took place, following which the victim had a glass pushed into his face and was severely wounded. He identified the defendant as being the person responsible.

Held: (CA) Although the judge reminded the jury of the weaknesses in the evidence, such as the fact that the victim was under the influence of alcohol, the conviction was unsafe because there was no warning as to the dangers of identification evidence or that a convincing witness may nevertheless be a wrong witness.

Commentary

The Court of Appeal in *Bentley* indicated that recognition cases (that is cases where the witness purportedly identifies someone he knows) are not necessarily straightforward, as the witness may have made a mistake. Even in a case like the instant case, it was still advisable to alert the jury both as to the possibility that an honest mistake had been made and as to the dangers of identification evidence and the reason why such evidence is dangerous.

Key Principle: **The judge must tell the jury that the special need for caution in identification cases arises because miscarriages of justice have occurred in the past.**

R. v Nash 2004
The defendant was arrested, along with a number of others, on suspicion of violent disorder and assault following a fight near a car park in a residential area. The defendant admitted that he had been present in the area at the time of the fight but denied that he had participated in any violence. The judge gave the jury a *Turnbull* warning but failed to explain why there was a special need for caution in identification cases.

Held: (CA) Appeal allowed. The judge should have told the jury that the need for caution in identification cases arises as a result of the courts' actual experience of miscarriages of justice.

Commentary
It appears that in order to convey the "*full force*" of the *Turnbull* direction, the jury should be told that the courts' concern about identification evidence is based on actual experience of wrongful convictions obtained from such evidence. It has been suggested that this aspect of the direction is an important part of the process of educating the jury about the dangers of identification evidence (*R. v Pattison and Exley* 1995).

Key Principle: **The trial judge must outline for the jury any specific weaknesses in the identification evidence.**

R. v Stanton 2004
Two 12-year-old girls were indecently assaulted by a man at a public swimming pool. They telephoned their mother and then reported the offence to the assistant manager. They identified the defendant, who was swimming in the pool with his two

children, as being responsible. A number of discrepancies arose during the course of the girls' evidence. The mother also gave evidence that they had told her that they would be unable to recognise the man who had molested them. In summing up, the judge failed to outline to the jury the specific features that might undermine the identification evidence.

Held: Appeal allowed. It was the judge's duty to draw the jury's attention to any specific features that might undermine the identification.

Commentary
This case shows that even where the trial has been short and the issues are straightforward, it is not enough for the judge to simply direct the jury that they must consider any discrepancies in the evidence. Rather, he must point out to them any specific weaknesses in the identification. It appears that where he directs the jury that they must look for supporting evidence, the judge must also identify what evidence he considers is capable of supporting the correctness of the identification. In *Stanton* it was said that a discussion should take place between the judge and counsel prior to summing up in every case where a *Turnbull* direction may be required.

Key Principle: **The correctness of an identification by one witness can be supported by the identification evidence of other witnesses.**

R. v Weeder 1980
The victim was attacked by two men near his home. He fell to the ground and turned to see one of his assailants wielding a bat. He later identified the defendant as the man with the bat during a street identification procedure. A witness looking out of the window of a nearby house also saw the assault and identified the two men responsible, both of whom were known to her. The judge directed the jury that they could take each witness's identification evidence into account as supporting the identification by the other.

Held: (CA) Appeal dismissed. A judge is entitled to direct the jury that an identification by one witness can constitute support for the identification by another provided that he warns them clearly that even a number of honest witnesses can all be mistaken.

Commentary
The Court of Appeal in *Turnbull* indicated that supporting evidence need not amount to corroboration provided that its effect is to make the jury sure that the identification witness was not mistaken. Supporting evidence may take a variety of forms other than the evidence of other identification witnesses. Thus, for example, the Court of Appeal in *Turnbull* recognised that where the jury reject the accused's alibi, this may, potentially, amount to supporting evidence. Their Lordships indicated, however, that in such circumstances the jury would have to be directed that sometimes a person might put forward an alibi to bolster a genuine defence. It was only if the jury were satisfied that the sole reason for putting forward a false alibi was to deceive that they could rely on it to support the identification evidence.

Key Principle: **A *Turnbull* warning is required in cases where the witness purports to recognise the accused, as well as in cases involving the identification of someone unknown to the witness. It would be wholly exceptional to dispense with a *Turnbull* warning completely.**

Shand v R. 1996
A man was shot and killed in a piazza in Jamaica. Another man was also shot but survived. The surviving victim and another eye witness had known the defendant for five and four years respectively, identified him as the gunman. The defendant raised an alibi and maintained that the witnesses were lying. No *Turnbull* warning was given. The defendant was convicted of murder and sentenced to death.

Held: (PC) A *Turnbull* warning is required in cases of recognition as well as pure identification cases. Nevertheless, the conviction was safe because the identification evidence was exceptionally good.

Commentary
Their Lordships accepted that in some cases, such as those involving pure recognition where the issue is the credibility of the

witness, it might be appropriate to give a shorter version of the usual *Turnbull* warning. However, the court emphasised that cases in which a warning could be entirely dispensed with must be wholly exceptional. In *Beckford v R.* 1993, it was suggested that such exceptional circumstances might arise where, for example, the accused was a workmate of the witness who he had known for 20 years and he had been conversing with him face to face in a room for half an hour. In *Shand* it was suggested that even in such exceptional cases, a judge would be wise to tell the jury to consider whether they were satisfied that the witness was not mistaken in view of the danger of mistake referred to in *Turnbull*.

Key Principle: **A Turnbull warning may not be required where the accused claims that the witness is deliberately lying in order to frame him.**

R. v Cape 1996

The defendants were convicted of causing grievous bodily harm with intent and violent disorder after a young man had his ear bitten off in a public house. The licensee, who was a former police officer, testified that five or six men held the victim down and beat him and that someone was chanting *"bite it off"*. The licensee identified the three defendants, who were known to him, as being part of the group of assailants. The defendants admitted being in the public house but denied participating in any violence. Their defence was that the licensee was lying and was motivated by malice. No *Turnbull* warning was given.

Held: The conviction was safe. A *Turnbull* direction was not required because the defendants were not claiming that this was a case of mistaken identification.

Commentary

The basis for this decision seems to be that the *Turnbull* warning is designed for cases where there is a danger of mistaken identification. In this case, the witness was either deliberately lying or he was not and there was no room for mistake. However, at least in the case of the defendant Cape, the witness was cross-examined about the circumstances of the identification, including the lighting conditions in the public house, suggesting that mistake was put forward as a secondary line of defence. It is submitted that, in these circumstances, a *Turnbull* warning would have been appropriate.

This decision is also somewhat difficult to reconcile with the Privy Council's decision in *Shand*. In *Shand*, the defendant suggested that the witnesses were lying and that one of them might be motivated to do so by political differences, yet the Court held that a *Turnbull* direction should have been given.

Key Principle: **A Turnbull warning is not required where the accused admits presence at the scene of the crime but denies participation in the offence.**

R. v Slater 1995

The victim was punched to the face in a nightclub and sustained a broken jaw. He described his attacker to the police and the defendant, an unusually tall man of heavy, muscular build, was arrested a month later. The defendant admitted being present in the nightclub at or about the time of the offence but denied being involved in any assault. No identification parade was held and the judge did not give a *Turnbull* warning.

Held: Appeal dismissed. The judge did not need to give a *Turnbull* warning because there was no possibility of mistaken identification.

Commentary

It appears that where the issue is not the defendant's presence at or near the scene of an offence but what he was doing there, it does not automatically follow that a *Turnbull* direction is required. Here there was no possibility that one person had been mistaken for another because of the defendant's wholly unusual size. There was no evidence to suggest that anyone else was present who remotely resembled him. An identification parade was not mandatory in this situation for the same reason. Presumably, where the accused is not unusual looking and has no particular distinguishing features, both an identification parade and a *Turnbull* direction will be required.

Key Principle: **An identification procedure should normally be held whenever a suspect disputes an identification.**

R. v Forbes 2001
The defendant was convicted of attempted robbery. After withdrawing £10 from a cashpoint machine, the victim was approached by a man asking for money. When he refused, the man became aggressive and revealed what looked like the handle of a knife. The victim escaped to his friend's car. As they drove off, he saw the man who had tried to rob him and made eye contact with him. The man spat at the car. The victim called the police on his mobile telephone. The police arrived a short time later and drove him round the streets in a police car to look for the man. In due course, the victim identified the defendant, who was arrested. The defendant denied the offence in interview. He asked for an identification parade but none was held.

Held: (HL) There should have been an identification parade but the identification evidence was compelling and the conviction was safe.

Commentary
Identification procedures are governed by Code D of the codes of practice issued under the Police and Criminal Evidence Act 1984 (PACE). The identification of the accused by a witness in the street in circumstances such as those in *Forbes* is commonly referred to as a "street identification". It is clear from the judgment in *Forbes* (and from amendments made to Code D since the case was decided) that a street identification must be followed by a formal identification procedure.

The current version of Code D provides that an identification procedure shall be held where the suspect is known to the police and available and either (i) the witness has previously identified the suspect prior to a formal identification procedure taking place or (ii) there is a witness available who purports to be able to identify the offender or there is a reasonable prospect of the witness being able to do so. Although decided under an old version of Code D, *Forbes* is authority for the proposition that the wording of the Code makes an identification procedure mandatory, save where the suspect is well known to the witness or in other exceptional circumstances.

Code D sets out three main types of identification procedure, namely video identification, identification parades and group identification. Video identification replaced the identification parade as the preferred procedure following amendments to the Code in 2004.

It appears from *Forbes* that the failure to hold an identification procedure could lead to the exclusion of identification evidence under s.78 of PACE. Alternatively, if the evidence is not excluded, the judge should direct the jury that the breach of Code D has deprived the accused of the opportunity to test the reliability of the witness's identification and that they should take account of that fact in their assessment of the case, giving it such weight as they think fair.

Key Principle: **A witness should not normally be invited to identify the accused when he is in the dock at trial.**

R. v Fergus 1992
A man was stabbed during a disturbance at a party at the defendant's house. The victim claimed that he had seen the man who stabbed him once before and that someone else had told him that the man's name was Fergus. At trial, the victim was asked whether the man he knew as Fergus was in court and he pointed out the defendant, who was in the dock.

Held: (CA) Appeal allowed. An identification parade should have been held.

Commentary
The courts have long recognised the dangers inherent in dock identifications (*R. v Cartwright* 1914). A properly conducted identification procedure preserves important safeguards for the defendant. It is usually carried out nearer to the time of the actual offence, while events are fresh in the witness's memory, whereas a dock identification at trial is likely to take place some considerable time later. An identification procedure also places the accused among a number of others of similar appearance, thereby reducing the risk that the witness will simply pick out someone who looks similar to the offender. Conversely, a dock identification gives rise to the danger that the witness will be influenced by the very fact that the accused is in the dock. Although the judge possesses the discretion to allow a dock identification, in practice, given that Code D makes formal identification procedures mandatory, it is difficult to conceive of circumstances in which a dock identification might be permitted in the Crown Court.

Case law suggests that a dock identification is more likely to be admissible in the magistrates' courts (*Barnes v Chief Constable of Durham* 1997). The basis for this appears to be that Code D only requires the police to hold an identification procedure where identification is in dispute. Where an offence is minor, it will often be the case that the accused is not interviewed and the police will have no way of knowing whether he disputes identification. However, the Criminal Procedure Rules now require the defence to indicate the issues in a case prior to trial. Where the defence indicate in advance that identification is in dispute, it may be that it will be inappropriate for the prosecution to rely on a dock identification.

Key Principle: **Where the jury members themselves make an identification from a video recording or photographs, a full *Turnbull* warning is not required.**

R. v Blenkinsop 1995
A peaceful demonstration by a group of hunt saboteurs evolved into an attack on the home of the kennel huntsman. The defendant was one of 24 people charged with violent disorder. The issue was whether the defendant merely took part in the demonstration or whether he joined in the violence. The prosecution relied upon photographs of the incident that were taken by police. The photographs showed a man in a green waxed jacket participating in the violence and the prosecution invited the jury to conclude that this was the defendant.

Held: A *Turnbull* warning was not necessary as the jury members themselves were making the identification.

Commentary
It was established in *R. v Dodson* (1984) that a jury can be invited to identify the defendant from photographs or video footage from their own observations of the defendant in court, without the assistance of a witness. It appears that, although a full *Turnbull* direction will not be required in such a case, the jury should be warned of the risk of mistaken identification and advised of the need to exercise particular care when making an identification themselves. Factors that the jury should be directed to consider will include the quality of the picture and any change in the

physical appearance of the accused between the date that the photograph or video was taken and the date of trial.

Key Principle: **The Turnbull principles apply equally to identification by voice.**

R. v Hersey 1998

Two men robbed a shop wearing balaclavas. The shopkeeper recognised the voice of one of the men as being that of the defendant, who was a regular customer. The police assembled a voice "identification parade", in which 11 men plus the defendant each read out a passage of text. The shopkeeper was able to pick out the defendant's voice. An application to exclude evidence of the voice identification procedure under s.78 of PACE was refused.

Held: Appeal dismissed. There is nothing wrong in principle with identification by voice provided that the judge directs the jury in terms similar to those set out in *R. v Turnbull.*

Commentary

In *R. v Davies* (2004), the Court of Appeal accepted that voice identification or voice recognition evidence should be approached with even greater care than visual identification evidence. However, despite hearing conflicting expert evidence about the reliability of voice identification, the Court declined to hold that it was inadmissible.

Lies Told by the Accused

Key Principle: **Where the accused has told lies either in interview or at trial, the judge must direct the jury that they can only take the lies into account as evidence of guilt if satisfied beyond reasonable doubt both that the accused did lie and that he did not lie for an innocent reason.**

R. v Burge and Pegg 1996

The defendants planned to burgle a bed-sit belonging to a 74-year-old retired Iranian colonel. They forced entry to his room wearing masks and carrying sticking tape and twine. They gagged and bound him and stole a watch and chain. They left their victim tied up and he subsequently died of asphyxia. In interview the defendants each blamed the other for going too far. At their trial for murder, they claimed that the deceased was alive when they left and that their friend, who lived upstairs and was a prosecution witness, must have killed him after they left. The judge gave the jury a warning about the lies told to the police. The defence argued on appeal that he should also have given a warning in relation to lies told from the witness box.

Held: The warning given was adequate as it conveyed the message that the jury could not take lies into account unless they were sure both that the defendants did lie and that they lied because the were guilty and not for some other reason. The appeal was dismissed.

Commentary
Where the accused tells lies, either in court or out of court, the judge should warn the jury that they may properly take his lies into account in deciding his guilt only if they are sure first, that he did in fact lie and second, that he did not lie for an innocent reason. This warning is commonly known as a *Lucas* direction (*R. v Lucas* (1981)). In *Burge and Pegg*, the Court of Appeal confirmed that a Lucas direction will be required in four situations:

1. where the accused relies on evidence of alibi;
2. where the judge directs the jury that the accused's lies may be supporting evidence;
3. where the prosecution rely on a lie as evidence of guilt; and
4. where there is a real danger that the jury may treat the lie as evidence of guilt.

Key Principle: **A *Lucas* direction is not necessary where the lies told by the accused relate to the central issue in the case.**

R. v Ball 2001
The defendant was charged with dangerous driving following a police chase. He initially told the police that he was driving the car but later claimed to have been a passenger in the vehicle. He named another man as being the driver. At trial he continued to assert that he was the passenger. The trial judge did not give a *Lucas* direction.

Held: Appeal dismissed. A *Lucas* direction was not required because the question of who was the driver was the very issue that the jury had to resolve.

Commentary

It appears that where the accused lies about peripheral matters, whether prior to trial or while giving evidence, a *Lucas* direction will be required. However, where the matters that the jury might regard as lies relate to the central issue in the case, a warning is not required. In *Ball*, for example, if the jury were sure that the defendant was lying about being the passenger, they had no other choice but to convict him of being the driver. Where the lie relates to the central issue in the case in this way, a *Lucas* direction would be otiose and would only confuse the jury. The defendant is adequately protected by the standard direction on the burden and standard of proof.

Key Principle: A *Lucas* direction is not required if there is no danger that the jury might treat lies as evidence of guilt.

R. v Middleton 2001

In the early hours of the morning a house was burgled and property, including a set of car keys, was stolen. The owner's BMW which was parked outside was also taken. The defendant was stopped driving the stolen vehicle less than 12 hours later. Property from the burglary was found at his mother's house. The defendant claimed in interview that he had been paid by someone to drive the car out of London and that the property from the burglary had been in the boot. He maintained this account at a trial. The judge agreed to give a *Lucas* direction but then failed to do so.

Held: (CA) Appeal dismissed. If the jury concluded that the defendant had lied when giving an innocent explanation for his possession of the car, they had to convict him. A *Lucas* direction would only confuse and complicate the issue.

Commentary

The Court reiterated that the purpose of a *Lucas* direction is to prevent the jury from adopting what has been described as "forbidden reasoning", namely equating lies with guilt. Where there was no risk that the jury would adopt this line of reasoning, a warning would not be required. The Court thought it inherently unlikely that a warning would be appropriate in relation to lies told in evidence, as the consequence of the jury rejecting the defendant's evidence will usually be covered by directions concerning the burden and standard of proof. However, it is submitted that this will only be the case where lies concern the central issue or issues that the jury have to decide. Where the accused lies in evidence about peripheral or collateral matters, a *Lucas* direction is likely to be necessary to prevent the jury from concluding that he must also be lying about the central issues in the case.

Key Principle: **Where the lie relates to an alibi, the judge should give a "failed alibi warning".**

R. v Khalique 2005

The defendant was convicted of a series of assaults on his wife which were committed shortly after their marriage. His defence to one of the charges was alibi. He claimed that he had been staying with his brother at the relevant time. The defendant's brother gave evidence confirming his alibi but the defendant's niece contradicted it. The judge did not give any particular warning to the jury.

Held: (CA) Where the defence is alibi, the judge must warn the jury that the burden of proof is on the prosecution to disprove the alibi and that a false alibi may be given for an innocent reason.

Commentary

The Court recognised that there is a danger that, because an alibi is inevitably raised by the defence, the jury will assume that the burden of proof is on the defendant. It is therefore crucial that the judge directs the jury on the burden and standard of proof specifically in relation to the alibi (*R. v Preece* 1992). The jury should also be directed that a false alibi may be invented to bolster a genuine defence. It appears that the specimen direction on alibis should be followed closely.

4. THE ACCUSED'S RIGHT OF SILENCE

The Common Law

Key Principle: Adverse inferences may be drawn from the accused's failure to respond to an accusation made by someone who is not a person in authority.

Parkes v R. 1976
The defendant was convicted of the murder of a young woman. He and the victim lived in separate rooms of the same house. The victim's mother arrived at the house to find her daughter in her room bleeding from two stab wounds. She found the appellant in the back yard of the property with a knife. She accused the appellant of stabbing her daughter and he made no reply. The judge instructed the jury that they could infer from this that the defendant accepted the truth of the accusation.

Held: (PC) The parties were speaking on even terms. The jury were therefore entitled to draw adverse inferences from the appellant's reaction to the accusation, including his silence.

Commentary
Before the provisions of the Criminal Justice and Public Order Act 1994, which permit the drawing of inferences from silence in certain specified circumstances came into force, it was possible to draw an inference at common law that the accused had, by his words, his conduct, his action or his demeanour, accepted the truth of a statement that was made in his presence (*R. v Christie* 1914). The provisions of the 1994 Act do not preclude the drawing of inferences from the accused's silence or reaction at common law and, consequently, the common law principles continue to apply in appropriate circumstances. The Court of Appeal in *R. v Collins* 2004 indicated that the position at common law is that: the jury must determine whether the statement that was made in the accused's presence calls for a response from him; if the statement calls for a response from the accused and the accused does not respond, the statement is only evidence against the accused if the jury decide that the accused accepted the statement by his reaction; silence can only be used against the accused if the accused was on equal terms with the person who

made the accusation. So far as the role of the judge is concerned, where the defence challenges the admissibility of such evidence, the Court of Appeal in *R. v Osbourne* (*The Times*, November 17, 2005) indicated that the judge must consider: whether a properly directed jury could conclude that the accused had adopted the statement; whether the matter was sufficiently relevant to justify its introduction in evidence; and whether admitting the evidence would have such an adverse effect on the fairness of the proceedings that it ought not to be admitted.

Criminal Justice and Public Order Act 1994

Section 34—Silence when Questioned or Charged

Essentially, where the accused was not denied access to legal advice, s.34 of the 1994 Act permits the tribunal of fact to draw adverse inferences where the accused relies in his defence upon a fact that he failed to mention when questioned or charged, provided that the fact was one that he could reasonably have been expected to mention in the circumstances existing at the time.

Key Principle: **Adverse inferences can only be drawn where the accused relies at trial upon a fact that he did not mention when questioned or charged.**

R. v Knight 2003
The defendant was convicted of indecently assaulting his friend's ten-year-old daughter. At the beginning of the interview, his solicitor read out a prepared statement giving an account wholly in line with his later testimony at trial. He declined to answer further police questions on the advice of his solicitor. At trial, the judge directed the jury that they could infer that he did not answer police questions because he did not think that his account would stand up to police scrutiny.

Held: (CA) Appeal allowed. There was no room for adverse inferences where the appellant's prepared statement was complete and accurate and he did not depart from it by raising new facts at trial.

Commentary

It is clear from the wording of s.34 that the accused's silence in interview is not itself a ground for drawing adverse inferences. It is only where the accused relies at trial upon a fact that he failed to mention in interview that adverse inferences can be drawn under s.34. Thus where the accused fails to give evidence at trial, an inference will not usually be available under s.34 as he has failed to rely on any fact at trial (but see *Webber* below). The jury will, of course, be entitled to draw inferences from his failure to give evidence (see s.35 below).

It appears from *Knight* that where the accused gives a prepared statement (i.e. a written account that is read out on tape at the start of his police interview) and then remains silent for the remainder of the interview, no inference can be drawn from the mere refusal to answer questions. An adverse inference will only be available if the accused subsequently relies at trial on a new fact or facts that he failed to mention in his prepared statement.

This is perhaps surprising given that s.34 specifies that inferences are available as a result of a failure to answer questions. A prepared statement is read out at the start of an interview and not in response to any questions. However, the Court of Appeal in *Knight* felt that s.34 required the suspect to disclose his account but that it did not require the suspect to subject himself to police cross-examination, which was a significantly greater intrusion into the general right of silence than the requirement to disclose his factual defence.

The court did emphasise that the prepared statement is not in itself an antidote to later adverse inferences as it may be inaccurate or incomplete. If the accused departs from the prepared statement and gives evidence of new facts at trial, adverse inferences will be available.

Key Principle: **The accused relies on a fact at trial where he gives evidence of it himself or where his counsel puts it to other witnesses in cross-examination.**

R. v Webber 2004

The defendant was convicted of conspiracy to murder. The prosecution case was based on three separate incidents involving attacks on the victim. When interviewed by the police, the defendant denied presence at the scene of two of the incidents and denied participation in any conspiracy. At trial, his counsel put a number of facts to prosecution witnesses that had not been raised in interview, including an allegation that the victim had planned to ambush the defendant. The defendant did not give evidence. The judge directed the jury that the putting of assertions to prosecution witnesses amounted to reliance on facts that the defendant had failed to mention in interview and that they could therefore draw adverse inferences against him.

Held: (HL) Appeal dismissed. A defendant relied on a fact or matter in his defence not only when he gave or adduced evidence of it but also when his counsel put the fact or facts to prosecution witnesses.

Commentary
Previous cases had queried whether the mere putting of a fact to a witness in cross examination could amount to reliance on that fact for the purposes of s.34 (*R. v Chenia* (2002)). In *Webber* the House of Lords concluded that an accused person could rely on a fact in his defence, even though neither he nor any party called on his behalf had given direct evidence of that fact, where his counsel put a specific and positive case to prosecution witnesses as opposed to asking questions merely intended to probe or test the prosecution case. Thus a defendant who fails to give evidence risks both a s.34 and s.35 inference (see below for inferences under s.35).

Key Principle: **A theory or speculation is not a fact for the purposes of s.34.**

R. v Nickolson 1999
A nine-year-old girl alleged that her stepfather had sexually assaulted her. The police searched her house and recovered her nightdress. Stains on the nightdress were examined and found to contain traces of the defendant's semen. When asked to account for this at trial, the defendant suggested that the complainant could have visited the lavatory after he had masturbated and picked up the staining from the lavatory seat. The judge invited the jury to draw adverse inferences from his failure to mention this possibility to the police in interview. At the time of the interview, the police were not aware of the results of the examination of the nightdress.

Held: (CA) Appeal allowed. A s.34 direction was not appropriate because the defendant was putting forward a speculative theory or a possibility rather than relying on a fact.

Commentary
It appears that s.34 will not operate where an accused fails to mention a speculative theory in interview and that there is a distinction between theories and facts. However, it is submitted that the better argument for suggesting that adverse inferences ought not to be drawn is that inferences are only available where the fact is one that the accused could reasonably have been expected to mention in the circumstances existing at the time. In *Nickolson*, for example, the defendant was not aware of the presence of semen at the time of interview and, thus, the defendant therefore could not reasonably be expected to mention the relevant fact.

Key Principle: **A bare admission of part of the prosecution case does not constitute a fact relied on for the purposes of s.34.**

R. v Betts and Hall 2001
The defendants were convicted of causing grievous bodily harm with intent. The prosecution case was that the motive for the attack was that the victim was having an affair with the wife of the defendants' friend. Hall gave a no comment interview. At trial he testified that he knew that the victim was having an affair with his friend's wife.

Held: (CA) Appeal allowed. An admission of part of the prosecution case without relying on any distinct fact did not constitute a fact relied on because a bare admission cannot be said to be the assertion of a fact.

Commentary
The example given by Lord Justice Kay in *Betts and Hall* is that of a defendant who admits for the first time at trial that a fingerprint is his but offers no explanation for it being found at the crime scene. In such a case the defendant makes a bare admission of part of the prosecution case but does not rely on any fact. If he goes further and puts forward at trial an explanation for the finding of

his fingerprint for the first time, the situation would be different and it would be appropriate for the jury to be invited to draw inferences.

Key Principle: **The fact must be one that the accused could reasonably be expected to mention in the circumstances existing at the time. The phrase "in the circumstances" should not be construed restrictively.**

R. v Argent 1996

The victim was stabbed to death in a fight outside an East London nightclub. An eye witness to the fight recognised and named the defendant as being responsible. Two further eye witnesses picked out the defendant in identification parades. The defendant gave two no comment interviews on the advice of his solicitor. At trial, he testified that he had left the nightclub with his wife before the victim was attacked. The trial judge excluded evidence of the first interview under s.78 of PACE but allowed the prosecution to adduce evidence of the second interview. On appeal, it was argued that the judge should have excluded evidence relating to the second interview or, alternatively, that he should not have directed the jury that it was open to them to draw an adverse inference on the grounds that the defendant was acting on the advice of his solicitor.

Held: (CA) The second interview had been properly conducted and the judge was right to admit it . In relation to the s.34 direction, it was for the jury to decide whether the accused could reasonably be expected to mention the relevant facts in the circumstances existing at the time. The personal characteristics of the accused and external factors, such as legal advice, were all relevant. Here the judge had given a satisfactory direction as to these matters and the appeal was dismissed.

Commentary

The Court of Appeal emphasised that a variety of circumstances might be relevant in determining whether the accused could reasonably be expected to mention a fact when questioned or charged. Furthermore, the test was not what some hypothetical reasonable man of ordinary fortitude would do but what the accused, with his particular characteristics, could reasonably be expected to do. The Court listed examples of matters that might be relevant, including time of day, the defendant's age, experience, mental capacity, state of health, sobriety, tiredness, knowledge, personality and legal advice.

Key Principle: **The fact that an accused has been advised by his lawyer to remain silent must be given appropriate weight.**

Condron v United Kingdom 2000

A husband and wife who were self-confessed drug addicts were arrested on suspicion of offences involving the supply of heroin following the execution of a search warrant at their home address. Although they were pronounced fit for interview by a police surgeon, their solicitor formed the view that both appellants were suffering from heroin withdrawal and advised them not to answer any questions.

Held: (ECHR) Appeal allowed. The judge should have told the jury that they could only draw inferences from the accuseds' failure to answer questions in their police interviews if satisfied that their silence could only sensibly be attributed to their having no answer to give or none that would stand up to scrutiny.

Commentary

The Court held that s.34 was not incompatible with Art.6 of the European Convention on Human Rights per se. The accused were not obliged to answer questions and could not be subject to any penal sanction for failing to do so. However, the effect of the judge's failure to direct the jury that they could only draw inferences if sure that the accused remained silent because they had no answer to give or no answer that would stand up to cross-examination, was that they may have drawn inferences even if satisfied that the reason given for silence, namely reliance on their solicitor's advice, was plausible. The Court of Appeal in *R. v Compton*, with reference to *Condron v United Kingdom*, emphasised the importance of correct directions being given by judges to juries in relation to the operation of ss.34 and 36 of the 1994 Act. This is also true in relation to the operation of s.35 (see *R. v Cowan*, below) and s.37.

Key Principle: **Reliance on a solicitor's advice must be genuine and reasonable.**

R. v Hoare 2004

The defendant owned a glassware manufacturing company. He produced and supplied amphetamine with a street value of £20 million from chemicals bought ostensibly for use in the course of his business. His solicitor advised him to make no comment in interview and he remained silent. At trial, he maintained that he was manufacturing the chemical for others, he did not know what it was and he believed it was for use in cancer research. He indicated that he had relied upon his solicitor's advice and, being someone who had not previously been arrested or interviewed by the police, had given a no comment interview. During cross-examination, he indicated that he had been stunned and surprised and had lacked sleep and that most people would rely upon their lawyer's advice.

Held: Even where a solicitor had in good faith advised his client to remain silent and the defendant had genuinely relied upon that advice in the sense that he had accepted it and had believed he was entitled to follow it, a jury might still draw an adverse inference if it was sure that the true reason for silence was that the accused had no explanation, or no satisfactory explanation, to give.

Commentary

The Court of Appeal in *Hoare* attempted to reconcile the approach of the Court of Appeal in *Betts and Hall* 2001 with that of the Court of Appeal in *Howell* 2003 regarding the significance of legal advice in the context of the drawing of a s.34 inference. The Court of Appeal in *Betts and Hall* had referred to the "genuineness" of the accused's decision to rely on legal advice to be silent whereas the Court of Appeal in *Howell* had indicated that the fact that legal advice to be silent had genuinely been relied upon by the accused did not automatically preclude the drawing of a s.34 inference. The Court of Appeal in *Hoare* held that the decisions in *Betts and Hall* and *Howell* were not inconsistent and indicated that the fact that the accused, in giving a no comment interview genuinely relied upon legal advice that was given to him in good faith by his solicitor did not preclude the jury from drawing a s.34 inference in respect of the accused's failure to mention a fact that he subsequently relied on at his trial. Rather, in such circumstances, if the jury believed that the accused was silent because he had no satisfactory answer to give, the jury were still entitled to draw a s.34 inference, but should not do so if the fact was not one that the accused could reasonably have been expected to mention in the circumstances. Thus, it appears that genuine reliance upon silence for "tactical reasons", where the accused had no innocent explanation or none that would withstand questioning, will not preclude the drawing of a s.34 inference whereas where it is asserted that there was an "operating reason" for silence which is consistent with innocence, such as those identified by the Court of Appeal in *Argent* (e.g. that the accused was tired, drugged, etc.), this may result in a jury concluding that it was reasonable for the accused to remain silent.

Key Principle: **The jury can be invited to draw one of two adverse inferences from a defendant's failure to mention facts when questioned or charged. These are either that the defendant had no answer to give or that he had no answer that would stand up to questioning or investigation.**

R. v Beckles and Montague 1997

Beckles appealed convictions for robbery, false imprisonment and murder. The victim had picked up a prostitute, who took him back to Montague's fourth floor flat. Both defendants robbed the victim at knifepoint, refused to allow him to leave and eventually threw him out of the window. Upon his arrest, Beckles told police that the victim jumped out of the window. He then gave a no comment interview. He was subsequently picked out by the victim on an identification parade. At trial, Beckles admitted being present in the flat but denied being in the room when the victim went out of the window. The trial judge directed the jury that they could infer either that he had fabricated his story after the interview or that he was biding his time and waiting to see whether he would be identified.

Held: (CA) Appeal dismissed. Recent fabrication is not the only inference available from silence.

Commentary

Section 34 provides that the jury may draw such inferences as appear proper from an accused person's failure to mention relevant facts when questioned or charged. There is no guidance in the

Act as to what inferences may be proper. *Obiter* comments in previous cases had suggested that there was only one possible inference to be drawn from silence, namely that the accused had fabricated the story some time after the interview (*R. v Condron* 1996, *R. v Roble*). The Court of Appeal in *Beckles and Montague* confirmed that there was a second possible inference, namely that the accused already had his story ready but did not give it because he was afraid that it would not stand up to police questioning and investigation. The current specimen direction suggests four possible adverse inferences: *"that [the accused] had no answer then/had no answer that he then believed would stand up to scrutiny/has since invented his account / has since tailored his account to fit the prosecution case"* (Specimen Direction 40, para.2).

Beckles subsequently appealed to the European Court of Human Rights and his appeal was eventually allowed on other grounds. The 1997 decision appears to remain good law insofar as it relates to the proper inferences available from a failure to mention facts in interview.

Key Principle: **Where the accused invited the jury not to draw inferences from his silence on the grounds that he was following his solicitor's advice, it will generally be necessary for the accused or his solicitor to give evidence confirming both the advice that was given and the basis or reason for it.**

R. v Roble 1997

It was accepted that the defendant had inflicted a number of knife wounds upon the complainant during a fight outside a nightclub. He gave a no comment interview on the advice of his solicitor. At trial, he raised the issue of self-defence for the first time, claiming that the knife had fallen from the complainant's pocket during the fight and that he had picked it up and used it when he saw another knife in the complainant's hand. The defendant's solicitor gave evidence on a *voir dire* and confirmed that she had advised him to remain silent in interview. She said that the defendant was a Somali refugee and, although conversant in English, was unable to understand difficult legal concepts. She did not give evidence about what, if anything, the defendant had told her about how the knife came into his possession. The judge ruled that adverse inferences were capable of being drawn and directed the jury accordingly. The solicitor was not called to give evidence before the jury.

Held: (CA) The judge was entitled to give a s.34 direction. The only evidence which the jury heard in relation to the defendant's silence in interview came from the defendant, who testified that he had been advised to say nothing. In the absence of any reason for this advice, this was unlikely to be sufficient to prevent the jury from drawing adverse inferences. The appeal was dismissed.

Commentary

Where a defendant asserts that he genuinely and reasonably relied on his solicitor's advice to remain silent and, accordingly, that no adverse inference should be drawn against him, he will need to call evidence in support of this assertion (*R. v Condron* 1996). It appears that it will not usually be sufficient for the accused to testify that his solicitor advised him to say nothing. The Court of Appeal in *Roble* held that the evidence must usually go further and indicate the reasons for the advice as this is relevant when the jury is assessing the reasonableness of the defendant's decision to rely upon it.

Key Principle: **Where a defendant testifies that his solicitor advised him to remain silent, or calls his solicitor to give evidence to this effect, no waiver of privilege is involved. However, where either the defendant or his legal adviser goes further and states the reason for that advice, privilege is waived.**

R. v Bowden 1999

The defendant and two others robbed a local McDonald's restaurant. The defendant was identified from CCTV footage and by an off-duty police officer who was a customer in McDonald's at the time of the robbery. The prosecution also relied on evidence that the defendant, who was in receipt of benefits, booked a holiday to the Canary Islands four days after the robbery. His holiday photographs included a picture of him in a celebratory pose outside a branch of McDonald's. At the start of his police interview, the defendant's solicitor confirmed on tape that he had advised his client to remain silent and stated that the reason for this advice was that he considered the CCTV footage that he had been shown to be of poor quality. At trial the defendant gave evidence and denied the robbery. He claimed that his mother had paid for his holiday and gave an explanation for the photograph. He said that he remained silent on the advice of his solicitor and elicited evidence of the solicitor's statement made at the start of the interview. The prosecution argued that, in adducing evidence of the advice to remain silent and the reasons for that advice, the defendant had waived privilege and they were entitled to question him about what he had said to his solicitor. The judge agreed and prosecuting counsel asked the defendant whether he had told his solicitor about two of the facts relied on at trial, namely that his mother had paid for the holiday and the reasons for the photograph outside McDonald's. The defendant said that he could not remember what he had told his solicitor. The judge directed the jury that they could draw a s.34 inference from the defendant's failure to mention these facts in interview and he was duly convicted.

Held: (CA) Appeal dismissed. Where a defendant explains the basis upon which he has been advised to remain silent, or where his solicitor acting as his legal representative gives such an explanation, a waiver of legal professional privilege is involved. The prosecution were therefore entitled to question the defendant about what he had disclosed to his solicitor prior to that advice being given.

Commentary
As has been seen above, where a defendant maintains that no inference should be drawn because he remained silent in interview on the advice of his solicitor, he will usually be expected to give evidence confirming that advice or call his solicitor to do so. Where he simply states that his solicitor advised him not to answer any questions, no waiver of privilege is involved. This is because the courts have recognised the importance of an accused person being able to receive legal advice without being required to reveal the terms of the advice received (*R. v Beckles 2004*; *R. v Loizou* 2006). Consequently, the defendant cannot be asked in cross-examination questions such as "What did you tell your solicitor?" or even, "Did you tell your solicitor the truth?" as this information will be privileged (*R. v Wilmot* 1989). However, where the defendant goes beyond saying that he declined to answer questions on legal advice and explains the basis on which he has been so advised (or where his solicitor acting in the scope of his authority as the accused's agent gives such an explanation), it appears that privilege will be waived and the defendant (or his solicitor if he

gives evidence) may be questioned about the nature of the advice given and the factual premises upon which it was based. The Court of Appeal in *Bowden* held that such a waiver of privilege can occur at any stage. In *Bowden* itself, the solicitor had waived privilege on behalf of his client when he stated during the police interview the basis for advising his client to make no comment.

Key Principle: **Where the defendant or his solicitor explains the reason for advising silence in interview in response to an allegation by the prosecution of recent fabrication, no waiver of privilege takes place.**

R. v Loizou 2006

The appellant was convicted of transferring criminal property, namely £87,010 in cash. She was jointly charged with three other defendants. The Crown's case was based upon evidence that the four defendants were in one another's company throughout the day on which the money was transferred. There was also evidence of incriminating conversations and mobile telephone messages. The appellant gave a no comment interview. At trial she gave evidence that she was working as a translator for one of the men involved in the offence. She claimed that she believed him to be a legitimate businessman and was not aware that anything dishonest or criminal was taking place.

During her evidence in chief, the appellant stated that she said "no comment" in interview on the advice of her solicitor. She was asked by her own counsel about the reasons for this advice and replied: *"He didn't see a charge. He couldn't understand why I was being charged with money laundering."*

The Crown accepted that the appellant's solicitor had advised her to make no comment but suggested that her account at trial was a recent fabrication. In cross-examination, the appellant was asked whether she had told her solicitor of the facts put forward at trial, in particular the suggestion that she was an innocent interpreter. Following legal argument in the absence of the jury, the trial judge took the view that this was a valid question. The appellant replied that she had not given her solicitor this information. On appeal, it was argued that she should not have been asked about the account given to her solicitor on the grounds that this information was subject to legal professional privilege.

Held: (CA) Where the accused goes beyond saying that she remained silent on legal advice and states the reasons for that advice, a waiver of privilege will not be involved if the evidence is given in response to a suggestion of recent fabrication. However, here the evidence about the reasons for the advice was given before the prosecution had suggested that the appellant fabricated her account and so privilege was waived.

Commentary

Following their earlier decision in *R. v Wishart* 2005, the Court of Appeal noted that the accused does not waive privilege either where he merely gives evidence that he was advised by his solicitor to make no comment or where evidence of what the accused said to his solicitor is given in response to an allegation of recent fabrication. Here the appellant's counsel had elicited evidence about the reasons for her solicitor's advice, namely that he could not understand why she was being charged, during examination in chief. At that stage the prosecution had not yet alleged that her account had been fabricated at some point between interview and trial. She had thus waived privilege during examination in chief and the prosecutor was entitled to cross-examine her to see whether the account that she gave to her solicitor equated with the account being given at trial. It appears that where the accused does not waive privilege and the prosecution allege recent fabrication, she may then give or call evidence that she mentioned the facts earlier to her legal adviser in order to rebut that allegation without waiving privilege at that stage. The rationale for this appears to be that an allegation of recent fabrication is potentially very damaging and, in the interests of fairness, an accused faced with such an allegation should be entitled to defend herself without taking the risk of waiving privilege.

Key Principle: **Adverse inferences can only be drawn from a failure to mention a fact when questioned where the purpose of the questioning is to discover whether or by whom an offence has been committed.**

R. v Pointer 1997

Police officers attended a nightclub and posed as potential purchasers of Ecstasy. A number of officers gave evidence that, on several occasions, the defendant either supplied them with drugs or directed them to another supplier. The defendant, a young man of good character, was arrested and interviewed under caution. He made no reply on the advice of his solicitor. At trial, the interviewing officer conceded that he believed that there was enough evidence for a successful prosecution prior to interview. The trial judge ruled that the fact that the defendant was interviewed and did not answer questions on legal advice was admissible, although the specific questions asked and answers given were not put before the jury. The judge then directed the jury that they might well think it unwise to draw adverse inferences from the defendant's silence in interview, although he did not specifically direct them not to do so.

Held: (CA) Section 34 did not apply because the interviewing officer was not trying to discover whether or by whom an offence had been committed. However, the judge's direction made it clear to the jury that it would not be right for them to draw an adverse inference and so the conviction was safe.

Commentary
Section 34 provides that inferences may only be drawn from a failure to mention a fact in interview where the accused was questioned under caution by a constable trying to discover whether or by whom an offence had been committed. Here the interviewing officer conceded that he believed that there was already a strong prosecution case prior to interview. The Court of Appeal accepted that inferences could not be drawn under s.34 in these circumstances but dismissed the appeal in view of the overwhelming identification evidence. It is submitted, however, that where s.34 does not apply, the jury should be directed that they must not hold the accused's silence in interview against him.

It is perhaps surprising that this point has not been taken more often, given that it will often be the case that the evidence is strong prior to interview and that the true purpose of an interview is not to discover whether or by whom an offence has been committed.

––––––––––

Key Principle: **The trial judge can direct the jury that they may not draw an adverse inference but this discretion should only be exercised in exceptional circumstances.**

R. v Argent 1996
The facts of this case are considered above.

Held:　The ratio of this case is set out above.

Commentary

The Court of Appeal accepted that evidence of a no comment interview might properly be excluded under s.78 of PACE in certain circumstances. The exercise of the court's exclusionary discretion might be appropriate, for example, where an interview followed an unlawful arrest where a breach of the Codes of Practice had occurred. In *Argent* itself, the judge had been entitled to admit evidence of the second interview in which the defendant had made no comment because the interview had been conducted properly in the presence of the defendant's solicitor. The Court of Appeal stressed that where a no comment interview is admitted, the question of whether or not adverse inferences can be drawn from a defendant's failure to mention facts relied on at trial is normally one for the jury. Only rarely would it be appropriate for the judge to direct the jury that they should, or should not, draw appropriate inferences.

Key Principle:　**The accused cannot be convicted solely or mainly on inferences from silence.**

Murray v United Kingdom 1996

The defendant was alleged to be a member of the Provisional IRA. He was convicted of aiding and abetting the unlawful imprisonment of an IRA informer. Along with others, he was arrested at the house where the informer was being imprisoned. He was denied access to a solicitor for 48 hours. He was interviewed 12 times for a total of over 21 hours and made no reply to all questions. The defendant did not give evidence at trial but, through cross-examination of a co-accused, it was suggested that he had arrived at the house shortly before the police did and that his presence there was entirely innocent. In convicting the defendant, the judge made it clear that he had drawn inferences from the defendant's silence in the police station and from his silence at trial.

Held:　(ECHR) The right to silence and the privilege against self-incrimination are generally recognised international standards that lie at the heart of the notion of a fair trial. However, they do not prevent the accused's silence in situations which clearly call for an explanation from being taken into account, although a conviction must not be based solely or mainly on silence.

Commentary
Murray was tried in Northern Ireland in 1991. The right to draw inferences from silence was part of the temporary terrorism legislation in Northern Ireland at the time. That legislation, like the 1994 Act, provided that a conviction must not be based solely on silence. In *Murray*, the European Court of Human Rights stressed that a conviction should not be based solely *or mainly* on an inference from silence. The Court also held that the questioning of a suspect in circumstances where he is denied access to legal advice might give rise to a violation of Art.6. Following this decision, ss.34, 36 and 37 of the Criminal Justice and Public Order Act were amended to prevent the drawing of adverse inferences in circumstances where the accused is denied access to legal advice, even where the denial is lawful.

Section 36—Failure to Give Evidence at Trial

Section 35 of the 1994 Act provides that adverse inferences may be drawn where the accused chooses not to give evidence at trial or where, having been sworn, he fails to answer a question without good cause. Inferences cannot be drawn if the accused's guilt is not in issue or if his physical or mental condition makes it undesirable for him to testify.

Key Principle: **The judge retains a discretion to prevent the drawing of inferences. This discretion should only be exercised in favour of the accused where there is an evidential basis for doing so.**

R. v Friend 1997
The 15-year-old accused was convicted of murder. He did not give evidence at his trial but the defence called a psychologist, who testified that the accused had a mental age of between 9 and 10. It was submitted that adverse inferences under s.35 were not appropriate because the accused's mental condition made it undesirable for him to give evidence. The judge rejected

this submission and directed the jury that they could draw adverse inferences from the accused's failure to give evidence.

Held: (CA) Appeal dismissed. The judge reached his conclusion in a proper and balanced manner after listening to the evidence of the psychologist. The judge's exercise of discretion could only be impugned if it was *Wednesbury* unreasonable (i.e. if no judge could have rationally reached the conclusion that the judge did). The fact that the accused had the mental age of a child did not automatically make it undesirable for him to give evidence.

DPP v Kavanagh 2005
Two police officers attended the accused's home after receiving a 999 call from his younger brother. They entered the house, spoke to the brother and subsequently discovered the accused, who was heavily inebriated, on the landing. The accused became aggressive and violent and head-butted one of the officers. At his trial for assaulting a police constable in the execution of his duty, the accused's mother gave evidence that the accused had been suffering from depression and had spent a year on medication, although he was no longer taking anything. The accused did not give evidence and, on the basis of the mother's evidence, the magistrates declined to draw an adverse inference under s.35.

Held: (QBD) The mother's evidence was wholly inadequate to justify a court concluding that it was undesirable for him to give evidence. The prosecution's appeal was allowed.

Commentary
It appears that it is always open to a judge to advise the jury not to draw inferences. However, as these cases make clear, there will need to be some evidential basis for suggesting that adverse inferences are not appropriate, or some exceptional factor making that a fair course to take. In *Friend* the Court of Appeal found that the circumstances were not exceptional. In *Kavanagh* the Divisional Court held that the fact that the defendant might have some difficulty in giving evidence was insufficient to justify a conclusion that it was undesirable for him to give evidence. Following *R. v A* 1997, it appears that the judge should normally hold a *voir dire* to decide the issue and that the defence will bear the burden of proof.

Key Principle: **A statement or submission by an advocate is not evidence from which the court can properly conclude that it is undesirable for the defendant to give evidence.**

R. v Ricciardi 1996

The appellant paid a stolen cheque for £59,625 into his bank account. The signatures on the cheque were forged and the appellant's fingerprints were found on it. He gave an account in interview but did not give evidence at trial. His barrister said that there was a reason why he did not give evidence but it was so sensitive that it could not be revealed. The judge invited the jury to draw inferences from his silence and he was convicted of theft of the cheque.

Held: (CA) An enigmatic assertion of the kind made here was not a good reason for directing the jury not to draw an adverse inference. The appeal was dismissed.

Commentary

As the decision of the Court of Appeal in *R. v Kavanagh* made clear (see above), there must be an evidential basis for directing the jury not to draw an inference under s.35 of the 1994 Act when the accused fails to testify.

Key Principle: **The court must ensure that the accused is aware that inferences may be drawn if he fails to testify.**

R. v Gough 2001

A house was burgled and the defendant was identified as being the driver of a car that had been seen near the burgled house at the relevant time. In interview and in his defence statement the defendant denied being present in the area. At his trial, the defendant admitted through his counsel that he had been the driver of the car but continued to deny involvement in the burglary. He absconded on the second day of the trial. The judge allowed the trial to continue and directed the jury that they could draw inferences from the defendant's failure to attend his trial and to give evidence.

Held: (CA) A judge should not direct a jury that they may draw adverse inferences from a defendant's silence at trial

unless satisfied that the defendant knew of the potential consequences of failing to testify. The judge could not be satisfied of
this in the defendant's case because he had absconded.
However, the conviction was safe in view of the weight of the
evidence against him.

Commentary
Section 35(2) of the Criminal Justice and Public Order Act 1994
places a mandatory requirement on the court to satisfy itself that
the accused is aware that the stage has been reached at which he
can give evidence and, if he chooses not to do so, the jury may
draw such inferences as appear proper. It appears that a defendant
who fails to give evidence because he absconds may be in a better
position than a defendant who attends his trial but declines to
testify, as adverse inferences will not be available in the former
case but will be available in the latter.

Key Principle: **Failure to give a proper direction on adverse
inferences may lead to the conviction being quashed.**

R. v Cowan 1996
The appellant was convicted of unlawful wounding. The
Crown's case was that he assaulted the victim outside a public
house following a fracas inside the premises. The appellant was
identified by two witnesses. The appellant's case was that he
was part of a group but someone else in the group assaulted the
victim. He did not give evidence. The trial judge did not warn
the jury that they could not convict solely on silence at trial. He
did not warn them that they could only hold the accused's
silence against him if satisfied that the reason for his silence was
that he had no answer to the case against him or none that
would stand up to cross-examination.

Held: (CA) Appeal allowed. When directing the jury, the trial
judge was required to warn them of the following:

1. the burden of proof remains on the prosecution
   throughout and the standard of proof is beyond reasonable doubt;

2. the defendant is entitled to remain silent;

3. an inference cannot on its own prove guilt;

4. they must be satisfied that the prosecution have established a case to answer; and

5. they must only draw an inference against the defendant if they conclude that his silence can only sensibly be attributed to his having no answer or none that would stand up to cross-examination.

Commentary

Following *Murray v UK 1996*, the judge must now also tell the jury that a conviction may not be based solely or mainly on silence. It appears that although the judge has to be satisfied that there is a prima facie case against the defendant before allowing it to go to the jury, the jury must be specifically directed that they cannot draw any inference against the defendant unless they are satisfied that there is a case to answer. Presumably the reason for this direction is that, although the judge may have concluded that the prosecution have established a prima facie case, it is the jury who are the tribunal of fact and they may have a different view.

5. EXAMINATION, CROSS-EXAMINATION AND RE-EXAMINATION OF WITNESSES

Memory Refreshing

Key Principle: **Before a witness testifies, the witness may read through a written statement that the witness made at a time reasonably close to the events that the trial concerns.**

R. v Richardson 1971
The appellant was convicted of burglary. Five prosecution witnesses had refreshed their memory from their police statements shortly before going into the witness box, the prosecution having informed the witnesses that they could do so if they wished.

Held: (CA) Appeal dismissed. Memory refreshing from a written statement in the witness box was only permitted if the written statement was contemporaneous. There was, however, no general rule that witnesses could not see statements that they had made at a time reasonably close to the event that the trial concerned before they went into the witness box.

Commentary
Richardson's case concerns the position where a witness wishes to memory refresh before the witness goes into the witness box.

Key Principle: **At common law, a witness may memory refresh in the witness box from a document that the witness made or verified while the facts were still fresh in the witness's memory.**

Attorney-General's Reference No.3 of 1979
One of the issues that fell to be determined by the Court of Appeal in this case was whether a police officer who had taken brief jottings while interviewing the accused and within a short time thereafter had made a note in his notebook, incorporating the jottings and expanding on them from his recollection, should be permitted to memory refresh from the notebook.

Held: (CA) The rule was that memory refreshing was permissible where the witness had made or verified the statement while the facts were fresh in his memory. Thus, memory refreshing from the notebook was permissible.

Commentary

This case demonstrates that the common law test which determines whether a witness may use a document in the witness box for memory refreshing purposes is whether the witness made or verified the statement when the facts were fresh in the witness's memory. This common law test still governs memory refreshing in civil proceedings, but the test in criminal proceedings is now that laid down by s.139 CJA 2003, under which a witness may memory refresh from a document that the witness made or verified at an earlier time provided that the witness testifies that the document records the witness's recollection of the matter at the earlier time and the witness's recollection of the matter at the earlier time is likely to have been significantly better than it is by the time when the witness testifies.

Key Principle: **A memory refreshing document may become admissible in evidence where the witness who memory refreshes is cross-examined on the document.**

R. v Sekhon 1986

The appellant was convicted of offering to supply a controlled drug. The police had kept a log of observations of the appellant, entries in the log having been verified by being signed by the officers who made the observations. At the trial, while giving evidence, the officers had made use of the log for memory refreshing, and had been cross-examined on the contents of the log, the defence suggesting that the police officers had falsified the records. The jury had asked to see the log, and the judge had permitted the jury to see it.

Held: (CA) Appeal dismissed. Documents could be used for memory refreshing without being put before the jury, but such documents had to be available for inspection by the other party, who could cross-examine on the document where this was relevant. The fact that such cross-examination had taken place would not normally make the document evidence in the proceedings, but where cross-examination involved a suggestion that a witness had subsequently made up his evidence, the document could be admitted to rebut the suggestion and to show whether it was genuine. Equally, where the document and the witness's testimony were inconsistent, the document could be admitted as evidence of the inconsistency. Again, the document could also be put before the jury where it would otherwise be difficult for them to follow the cross-examination. Moreover, there could also be cases where it was convenient to use the document as an aide memoire where the witness's evidence was long and involved.

Commentary

Sekhon demonstrates that a memory refreshing document will not normally be admissible in evidence, but that it may become admissible in certain circumstances where the witnesses is cross-examined on the document. Section 120 CJA 2003 provides that where this occurs, the statement is admissible as evidence of the matters stated. The position in civil proceedings, which is governed by s.6 of the Civil Evidence Act 1995, is effectively the same.

Previous Consistent Statements

Key Principle: **Evidence of a previous consistent statement made by a witness is inadmissible unless either an exception to the rule against previous consistent statements or an exception to the rule against hearsay is applicable.**

R. v Roberts 1942

The appellant was convicted of murder. At his trial the judge had refused to admit evidence of a previous consistent statement made by the appellant to his father following the appellant's arrest.

Held: (CCA) The judge had been entitled to rule that the evidence was inadmissible. Such evidence was inadmissible because it was irrelevant. If the statement had been made to the father at the time of the shooting it would have been admissible as a statement accompanying and explaining the act. Equally, had it been suggested to the accused during cross-examination that he had recently concocted his defence of accident, the statement would have been admissible to show that he had not recently concocted it.

Commentary

The evidence had properly been excluded because it did not fall either within an exception to the rule against previous consistent statements or within an exception to the hearsay rule. Were the facts of this case to arise again today, it is submitted that while the statement would not fall within any of the exceptions to the hearsay rule created by s.120 CJA 2003 (under which evidence of certain types of previous consistent statement is admissible), if the admission of the statement was in the interests of justice it could potentially be admitted under s.114(1)(d) CJA 2003.

Key Principle: **Evidence of a previous consistent statement may be admissible in criminal proceedings under s.120 CJA 2003 where the statement takes the form of a complaint made at the first reasonable opportunity by the victim of an offence with which the accused is charged.**

R. v Xhabri 2005

The facts of this case are considered in Chapter 12.

Held: (CA) The decision in this case is considered in Chapter 12.

Commentary

Section 120 CJA 2003 concerns the admissibility in criminal proceedings of evidence of previous consistent statements made by witnesses who are called to give oral evidence in the proceedings. Where evidence of a consistent statement is admissible under any of the various hearsay exceptions created by s.120 of the 2003 Act, the statement is admissible as evidence of the matters stated, i.e. the statement is admissible under an exception to the rule against hearsay.

In *Xhabri*, the Court of Appeal held that the requirements of s.120(7) of the 2003 Act were satisfied because the complainant claimed that she was the person against whom the offences to which the trial related had been committed, her statements concerned conduct which, if it was proved, would constitute part of the relevant offences, the statements were made as soon as could reasonably be expected after the alleged conduct (i.e. during a continuing course of conduct), the statements were not made in consequence of threats or promises and the complainant was to give evidence before the hearsay evidence was adduced. It should be noted that in order for hearsay evidence to be admissible under s.120(7) of the 2003 Act it is, additionally, necessary to establish that the witness's oral evidence would have been admissible as evidence of the matters stated (it seems that this would have been the case in relation to the complainant's evidence in *Xhabri*) and it is also necessary for the witness (i.e. the complainant in *Xhabri*) to testify that, to the best of her belief, she made the statement and it states the truth.

Key Principle: **Evidence of more than one complaint made by the victim of an offence may be admitted under s.120 CJA 2003.**

R. v Openshaw 2006

The appellant was convicted of a number of sexual offences against his stepdaughter, the offences having been committed between 1987 and 1995. At the trial, the judge admitted evidence of complaints made by the complainant to a friend and to the friend's mother in 1995 and to the complainant's brother four months later, the complaints concerning the sexual abuse of the complainant by her stepfather from childhood.

Held: (CA) Appeal dismissed. The judge had correctly ruled that more than one complaint could be admitted under s.120 CJA 2003. Statements admitted under s.120 were admissible as evidence of the matter stated, not merely as evidence of consistency, and there was a need in fairness to restrict evidence of self-serving multiple complaints, but the judge had correctly ruled that the complaint made to the brother did have a relevance over and above that of the earlier complaint. The judge had correctly applied the criteria laid down by s.120. In particular, the second complaint had, in the context of the case, been made "as soon as could reasonably be expected".

Commentary

The case provides another example of the application of the s.120(7) CJA 2003, which is referred to in the commentary to *R. v Xhabri*, above.

Key Principle: **In civil proceedings a previous consistent statement may be admissible with the leave of the court.**

Morris v Stratford-upon-Avon RDC 1972

The plaintiff, a dustman, employed by the defendants, was injured in an accident at work, when his leg was injured by a lorry, and brought an action in negligence against the defendants. The plaintiff asserted that the accident had been caused by the negligence of one of the council's employees, Mr Pattison, who had been driving the lorry. The defendants claimed that the plaintiff's injuries had been caused by his own negligence in descending from the lorry while it was moving. Following the examination in chief of Mr Pattison, the judge, in the exercise of his discretion under the Civil Evidence Act 1968, admitted a statement that Mr Pattison had made nine months after the accident as evidence for the defence. The judge found for the defendant.

Held: (CA) Appeal dismissed. The judge had exercised his discretion properly. The statement had been taken as a proof of evidence and was not contemporaneous. These factors went to the weight of the evidence but could also be relevant to the exercise of discretion.

Commentary

The provisions of the 1968 Act which this case concerned were repealed by the Civil Evidence Act 1995. Under s.6 of the 1995 Act, the previous consistent statement of a witness who has been called may be admitted either to rebut an allegation of recent fabrication or otherwise with the leave of the court. It is submitted that the facts of *Morris*'s case provide an example of circumstances in which a judge would be entitled to admit evidence of a previous consistent statement under s.6 of the 1995 Act, the statement being admitted under the 1995 Act as evidence of the matters stated. The weight of the statement would be a matter for the court to determine under s.4 of the 1995 Act. In so doing, the court should consider all circumstances from which an inference could be drawn as to the reliability or otherwise of the evidence, including its lack of contemporaneity and the purpose for which it was made.

Hostile Witnesses

R. v Joyce 2005

The facts of this case are considered in Chapter 12.

Held: (CA) The decision in this case is considered in Chapter 12.

Commentary

Where a witness who is called by a party to criminal proceedings does not wish to tell the truth on behalf of that party, the judge may give the party who called the witness leave to treat the witness as a hostile witness and, thus, permit the party to cross-examine the witness by asking the witness leading questions about previous inconsistent statements. Where the witness does not admit making the inconsistent statement, it may be proved under s.3 of the Criminal Procedure Act 1865. Where the witness admits making the statement or it is proved under s.3 of the 1865 Act, the statement is admissible as evidence of matters stated of which the witness's oral evidence would be admissible (i.e. it is admissible under an exception to the rule against hearsay created by s.119 of the Criminal Justice Act 2003). Thus, where a witness's previous inconsistent statement is admitted, the jury will have the options of believing the statement, of believing the witness's testimony or, in the context of the inconsistencies between the statement and the testimony, of deciding that none of the witness's evidence can be relied upon.

Cross-Examination

Key Principle: **As a general rule, where it is intended to suggest that a witness's evidence is untrue, the issue should be raised with the witness via cross-examination.**

R. v Fenlon 1980

The appellant was convicted of rape. At the trial, the appellant was the first of several co-defendants to give evidence. When the appellant finished giving his evidence in chief, the judge told counsel for his co-defendants that they were bound to cross-examine the appellant concerning any differences between the cases of their clients and the appellant's case.

Held: (CA) The House of Lords had held in *Browne v Dunne* 1893 that where it was intended to suggest that a witness was not speaking the truth it was necessary for counsel to direct the witness's attention to this fact by cross-examination in order to give the witness an opportunity to provide an explanation. This rule applied not only to counsel for the prosecution but also applied to defence counsel. Thus, the judge had been correct to point out this duty to defence counsel.

Commentary

This case is authority for the general rule that where a party wishes to suggest that a witness is not speaking the truth it is necessary to put this to the witness in cross-examination rather than merely adducing evidence to contradict the witness's testimony without giving the witness an opportunity to deal with the suggestion. The House of Lords in *Browne v Dunne* indicated that such cross-examination was not required where it was clear that the witness had already had notice of the intention to impeach the credibility of his evidence. The Court of appeal in *Fenlon* indicated that such cross-examination must make clear to the witness the respects in which the witness's evidence is not accepted, but that such cross-examination need not be conducted in minute detail. In *R. v Lovelock* 1997, the Court of Appeal held that it had been sufficient for cross-examining counsel, who had not expressly asserted that the witness was lying, to adopt a "raised eyebrow approach" to the witness's evidence.

Key Principle: **In general, where a question put to a witness during cross-examination merely concerns the credibility of a witness and is, thus, a collateral matter, the cross-examining party is not entitled to adduce evidence in rebuttal of the witness's answers.**

R. v Edwards 1991

The appellant was charged with robbery and with the possession of a firearm at the time when he committed the robbery. At his trial, the evidence against the appellant comprised both the evidence of an accomplice and evidence of police interviews during which the accused had allegedly confessed. The appellant asserted that the confessions had been fabricated by police officers, but he was convicted. Following the trial, the defence became aware of matters concerning the conduct of the investigating officers in the context of other investigations and asserted that had the court that tried the appellant been aware of these matters, the appellant's confessions would have been excluded.

Held: (CA) Appeal allowed. Questions concerning alleged improper conduct could be put to a witness in order to test the witness's credibility. Such questions were proper if the truth of the imputation could seriously affect the court's opinion in relation to the witness's credibility but not if the imputation was so remote in time, or its character was such, that its truth would not, or would only slightly affect, the court's opinion in relation to the witness's credibility, or if there was a great disproportion between the importance of the imputation and the importance of the witness's evidence (*Hobbs v Tinling* 1929). The drawing of the distinction between issues in the proceedings and collateral matters was difficult but it was important because the general rule was that a witness's answers to questions asked during cross-examination concerning collateral matters were final, adducing evidence to contradict the witnesses answers not being permissible (*Harris v Tippitt* 1811), the purpose of the rule being to keep the scope of a trial within proper limits and to prevent the issues from being submerged in detail. Had the evidence concerning the police officers been available at the trial, the police officers could have been cross-examined concerning relevant criminal or disciplinary charges that had been found against them. It would not have been proper, however, to have cross-examined an officer in relation to charges that had not been tried, disciplinary complaints that had not yet been adjudicated upon or in relation to the allegedly discreditable conduct of other officers.

Had cross-examination of the police officers in relation to the abovementioned matters taken place, the cross-examination would solely have related to credit, i.e. to a collateral issue, and would not have fallen within an exception to the general rule if the officers had given answers that did not favour the defence.

Commentary

The classical test to identify a collateral matter is that stated by Pollock C.B. in *Attorney-General v Hitchcock* 1847, i.e., that if the witness's answer is a matter that the cross-examining party would be permitted to prove in evidence, then the cross-examining party may adduce evidence to contradict the witness. Subject to exceptions (see *R. v Mendy* and *R. v Funderburk*, below), the answers that a witness gives in relation to a collateral matter are final, and evidence cannot be adduced in rebuttal by the cross-examining party (*Harris v Tippitt* 1811). Upon the facts of *Edwards*, if the officers had denied the allegations that would have been made against them during cross-examination, the effect of the rule of finality concerning cross-examination in relation to collateral matters would have been that the defence would not have been entitled to adduce evidence in rebuttal of the witness's answers. It should be noted that now that the Criminal Justice Act 2003 is in force, the agreement of the parties or the leave of the court will be required under s.100 of the Act in order for questions to be asked of a witness other than the accused concerning the witness's bad character.

Key Principle: **The rule of finality that prevents a party from adducing evidence in rebuttal of a witness's answers in cross-examination concerning a collateral matter does not apply to evidence which does not merely go to credit but which also relates to an issue in the proceedings.**

R. v Nagrecha 1997

The appellant was convicted of indecent assault. The appellant denied the complainant's allegations. At the trial, the defence wished to cross-examine the complainant concerning allegations of sexual assault that she had made to former work colleagues (that the work colleagues had not believed) and, depending upon the complainants' answers, wished to call a former work colleague to give evidence concerning the allegations that the complainant had made. When the complainant was cross-examined, she denied having made the allegations and the judge did not admit the evidence of the former work colleague in rebuttal of her denials.

Held: (CA) Appeal allowed. The judge should have permitted the defence to adduce the evidence of the former work colleague. The evidence did not merely go to credit, but, rather, it related to the crucial issue of whether an indecent assault had taken place.

Commentary

Nagrecha's case did not concern an exception to the rule of finality that prevents a party from adducing evidence in rebuttal of a witnesses answers in cross-examination concerning a collateral matter (in relation to which see *R. v Edwards* above). Rather, the Court of Appeal in *Nagrecha* held that the evidence that *Nagrecha* concerned did not concern a collateral matter but, rather, concerned an issue in relation to which the only evidence was that of the complainant and the appellant, namely, whether an indecent assault had taken place. Their Lordships indicated that the evidence should have been admitted because it might have resulted in the jury taking a different view of the complainant's evidence. The Court of Appeal distinguished other decisions in which such evidence had been excluded, namely *R. v Snook 1992* and *R. v Todd* 1997, on the basis that in those cases the complainant had admitted making the allegations, and admitting evidence concerning the truth or falsehood of the complaints would have required a lengthy exploration of irrelevant and peripheral issues. In contrast, in *Nagrecha*, the defence had not wished to open up the issue of whether the former complaints had been true or false but, rather, had merely wished to challenge the complainant's denials that she had made complaints in the past, and this would not have required such an exploration.

Key Principle: **The rule of finality that prevents a party from adducing evidence in rebuttal of a witness's answers in cross-examination concerning a collateral matter is subject to exceptions.**

R. v Mendy 1976

The appellant, Mrs Mendy, was convicted of assault occasioning actual bodily harm. The most important defence witness was Mr Mendy, the appellant's husband, who had been kept out of court in the usual way. While a police officer was giving evidence for the prosecution another police officer observed that a member of the public was taking notes. The latter police officer followed the man who had been taking notes and the officer, plus the court officer, both observed him outside talking to Mr Mendy about the case. When Mr Mendy gave evidence he was cross-examined concerning the incident with the man who had taken the notes and denied that it had taken place. The judge permitted the two officers who had observed the incident to give evidence in rebuttal of Mr Mendy's denials.

Held: (CA) Appeal dismissed. The Court of Appeal, having referred to the rule that a witness's answers in relation to questions concerning collateral matters are conclusive and having explained that the practical utility of the rule is that it prevents trials from being indefinitely prolonged by minute examination of the character and credibility of witnesses, recognised that no one seriously suggested that the issue which

Mendy's case concerned was not collateral. Their Lordships also recognised, however, that the rule was not "all-embracing" and that it was permissible to adduce evidence in contradiction of a denial of bias or partiality towards a party and to show that the witness was prejudiced in relation to the case being tried. Upon the facts of *Mendy*'s case, Mr Mendy had been prepared to cheat for the purpose of deceiving the jury and helping the appellant, the jury was entitled to be made aware of this and the evidence had properly been admitted.

Commentary
Mendy's case demonstrates that where, during cross-examination, a witness denies an allegation of bias or partiality, the witness's answers are not final.

Key Principle: **A witness called by another party may be cross-examined in relation to a previous inconsistent statement and the statement may be proved under s.4 of the Criminal Procedure Act 1865 if the requirements of that section are satisfied.**

R. v Funderburk 1989
The appellant was convicted of sexual intercourse with a 13-year-old girl. In the witness box the complainant have given detailed evidence of acts of intercourse between herself and the accused which had taken place on 10 or 11 occasions, her evidence suggesting that on the first occasion she was a virgin. The defence asserted that the complainant's evidence was a complete fabrication for the purpose of supporting her mother who "had it in for the appellant". A problem for the defence was how the complainant could have given the detailed accounts of intercourse that she had given if she had been a virgin. The defence suggested, however, that the complainant was sexually experienced. Thus, during cross-examination, the defence wished to suggest to the complainant that, prior to the first alleged incident with the appellant, she had told a Miss Potts that she had had intercourse with two men, and wished to call Miss Potts to give evidence of the conversation, but the judge did not permit the question to be put to the complainant or the evidence to be called.

Held: (CA) Appeal allowed (on two of three counts). Where questions put in cross-examination solely went to the credibility of witnesses or to collateral facts, the general rule, the purpose of which was to avoid a multiplicity of issues, was that the answers were final and could not be contradicted by rebutting evidence. The authorities showed that contradicting evidence could be adduced where the evidence went to an issue in the case, showed that the witness had made a previous inconsistent statement relating to an issue, showed that the witness was biased, showed that the police were prepared to go to improper lengths to secure a conviction, proved the witness's convictions, showed that the witness had a general reputation for untruthfulness or showed that medical causes would have affected the reliability of the witness's testimony. Apart from the first category, these categories could all be considered exceptions to the general rule of finality.

The general test governing the limits of cross-examination as to credit was that the matters to which the questions related had to relate to the likely standing of the witness with the tribunal which was trying the witness or listening to the witness's evidence (*R. v Sweet-Escott* 1971). Applying this test, the judge had been wrong not to permit the question to be put to the complainant during cross-examination.

In relation to disputed sexual issues between two persons in private the difference between questions that went to credit and those that went to the issue was reduced to vanishing point. If there had been medical evidence that the complainant had not been a virgin at the relevant time the defence would have been allowed to call it and, thus, the conflicting statements had been "relative to the subject matter of the indictment" for the purposes of s.4 of the Criminal Procedure Act 1865. The challenge to the loss of virginity might have affected the jury's view on the central issue of credit and was sufficiently closely related to the subject matter of the indictment that justice required investigation for the basis of the challenge. Thus, the defence should have been permitted to put the question to the complainant and, if she denied having made the statement, they should have been permitted to adduce the evidence of Miss Potts.

Commentary

The test governing the limits of cross-examination from *R. v Sweet-Escott* should be compared to that from *Hobbs v Tinling* (see *R. v Edwards*, above). It is submitted that the two tests are not mutually exclusive but, rather, are complimentary, and that reference to them jointly provides the test that governs the nature of those questions concerning the credibility of a witness which are permissible at common law. It should be noted, however, that where a question concerns the sexual behaviour of a witness, such a question will now only be permissible where leave is given under s.41 of the Youth Justice and Criminal Evidence Act 1999 and that where the question concerns the witness's bad character, leave will be required under s.100 CJA 2003 (or, if the witness is the accused, under s.101 of the 2003 Act).

A party who did not call a witness may cross-examine the witness in relation to a previous inconsistent statement and, where the witness does not admit making the statement, the statement may be proved under s.4 of the Criminal Procedure Act 1865, provided that the statement is "relative to the subject matter of the indictment or proceeding" and that, before the statement is proved, the circumstances of its making, sufficient to designate the occasion on which it was made, are mentioned to the witness, and the witness is asked whether he made it. If the inconsistent statement is in writing and it is intended to prove the statement, s.5 of the 1865 Act requires that before the statement is proved the attention of the witness must be drawn to the parts of the written statement that are to be used to contradict the witness, but that the witness need not be shown the written statement if he is to be cross-examined on it but it is not to be proved. Where a witness admits making a previous inconsistent statement or it is proved under the 1865 Act, it is admissible in criminal proceedings as evidence of matters stated of which the witness' direct oral evidence would be admissible (i.e. under a hearsay exception) under s.119 CJA 2003. Such a statement would also be admissible in civil proceedings as evidence of the matters stated (Civil Evidence Act 1995, s.6).

The Court of Appeal in *Funderburk* identified a number of exceptions to the rule of finality which prevents evidence in rebuttal being adduced to contradict answers given during cross-examination concerning collateral matters. The existence of one of these exceptions (derived from *R. v Busby* 1981), namely, that concerning evidence which showed that the police were prepared to go to improper lengths to secure a conviction, was subsequently doubted by the Court of Appeal in *R. v Edwards*. For examples of two of the others see *Mendy* (above) and *Toohey* (below). The exception which *Funderburk* itself concerned involves evidence that shows that a witness has made a previous inconsistent statement relating to an issue. The Court of Appeal in *Funderburk* itself recognised, however, that evidence that goes to an issue in the proceedings is not admitted under an exception to the rule of finality; this is clearly so as such evidence, by definition does not relate to a collateral matter but, rather, relates to an issue in the proceedings and, thus, does not fall within the rule of finality in the first place (see, for example, *R. v Nagrecha*, above). Thus, while the Court of Appeal in *Funderburk* indicated that evidence that shows that a witness has made a previous inconsistent statement relating to an issue falls within an exception to the rule of finality, it is submitted that since such evidence, being admissible under s.4 of the Criminal Procedure Act 1865 if "relative to the subject matter of the indictment or proceeding", is only admissible if it relates to an issue in the proceedings, such evidence is not admissible under an exception to the rule of finality but, rather, does not fall within that rule in the first place.

Key Principle: **Medical evidence is admissible to show that a witness suffers from a disease or abnormality that affects the reliability of the witness's evidence.**

Toohey v Metropolitan Police Commissioner 1965
The accused was convicted of assault with intent to rob. When the police had found Madden, the alleged victim, with the appellant and his co-defendants, Madden had been in a distressed and hysterical condition. The defendants claimed that they had not assaulted Madden but that they had been trying to take him home when he had bumped into the appellant, banged against a wall, become hysterical and claimed that one of them had hit him and that they were after his money. At the appellant's trial, the defence were not permitted to adduce expert evidence to prove that Madden was normally of an unstable or hysterical disposition.

Held: (HL) Appeal allowed. Medical evidence was admissible to show that a witness suffered from a disease or abnormality of mind that affected the reliability of his evidence.

Commentary
The principle stated by the House of Lords in *Toohey*'s case is not restricted to evidence of mental disease or abnormality. Rather, their Lordships indicated that it encompassed physical disease or abnormality which affected the reliability of a witness' evidence, e.g. where an identification witness was short-sighted.

Sexual Behaviour

Key Principle: **Where the operation of s.41 of the Youth Justice and Criminal Evidence Act 1999, in preventing cross-examination of a sexual offence complainant in relation to her sexual behaviour and/or preventing the defence from adducing evidence of her sexual behaviour, would prevent the accused from having a fair trial for the purposes of Art.6 of the European Convention on Human Rights, it will be necessary to read s.41 down such that the questioning is permitted and/or the evidence is admissible.**

R. v A 2001

The respondent was charged with rape, his defence being consent or, in the alternative, belief in consent. The defendant claimed that the intercourse in question formed part of a continuing three-week consensual sexual relationship between the complainant and the respondent. At a preparatory hearing, defence counsel applied for leave to cross-examine the complainant about the alleged consensual sexual relationship between the complainant and the respondent and to adduce evidence in relation to it. The judge, under s.41 of the Youth Justice and Criminal Evidence Act 1999, held that the complainant could not be cross-examined in relation to the alleged sexual relationship and that the accused could not adduce evidence in relation to it. The judge indicated that the ruling would prima facie violate the respondent's right to a fair trial under Art.6 of the European Convention on Human Rights and gave leave to appeal to the Court of Appeal. Before the Court of Appeal, the prosecution conceded that evidence of the sexual relationship was admissible under s.41(3)(a) in relation to the issue of belief in consent. The Court of Appeal held, however, that, under s.41, the evidence was inadmissible in relation to the issue of consent. The prosecution accepted that the judge would have to direct the jury that the evidence was solely relevant to the issue of belief in consent and was not relevant to the issue of consent. The Court of Appeal indicated, however, that directing the jury in this way might result in an unfair trial because the sexual relationship might be relevant to both issues. The Court of Appeal granted the prosecution leave to appeal, and defence counsel indicated that he would invite the House of Lords to read s.41 down under s.3 of the Human Rights Act 1998 or, alternatively, to make a declaration of incompatibility. The Home Secretary then applied for, and was given, leave to intervene, the House of Lords thus hearing submissions on behalf of the Home Secretary as well as submissions on behalf of the Director of Public Prosecutions and the respondent.

Held: (HL) Appeal dismissed. Applying ordinary methods of statutory construction to s.41 could not cure the problem of the excessive breadth of s.41 so far as it concerned previous sexual experience between the complainant and the defendant. Under s.3 of the Human Rights Act 1998, however, it was possible to read s.41, particularly s.41(3)(c), as being subject to an implied provision that evidence or questioning that was required to ensure that the defendant was given a fair trial under Art.6 of the European Convention on Human Rights was not inadmissible. Thus, logically relevant sexual experience between complainant and defendant could be admitted under s.41(3)(c), though there would be cases where such sexual experience would be irrelevant, it being for trial judges to determine where the line was to be drawn. In the instant case, it was for trial judge to determine the permissibility of the questioning and the admissibility of the evidence, but he was required to do so on the basis of the broader interpretation of s.41(3)(c) that s.3 of the Human Rights Act 1998 required.

Commentary

Under s.41 of the Youth Justice and Criminal Evidence Act 1999, evidence of the sexual behaviour of a sexual offence complainant is only admissible, and cross-examination of the complainant in relation to her sexual behaviour is only permissible, with the leave of the court. The court can only give leave if one or more of a number of narrow gateways created by the section are available, and, even then, only if refusing leave might render a conclusion of the jury, or the court, in relation to a relevant issue, unsafe.

Three narrow gateways relate to the issue of consent, two of these being contained in s.41(3)(c), the House of Lords in *R. v A* held that s.41(3)(c) should be read down, under s.3 of the Human Rights Act 1998, such that evidence of the complainant's sexual behaviour with the accused would be admissible, and cross-examination of the complainant in relation to it would be permissible, in circumstances in which its exclusion would render the accused's trial unfair under Art.6 of the European Convention on Human Rights. Under s.41(3)(c)(i), evidence of the complainant's sexual behaviour may be admissible, or cross-examination in relation to it may be permitted, where the issue is one of consent and the evidence or cross-examination concerns sexual behaviour that is allegedly so similar to the complainant's sexual behaviour which took place as part of the event which is the subject matter of the charge that the similarity cannot reasonably be explained as a coincidence. The s.41(3)(c)(ii) gateway concerns sexual behaviour on the part of the complainant which is allegedly so similar to other sexual behaviour on the part of the complainant which took place at or about the same time as the event charged that the similarity cannot reasonably be explained as a coincidence. Adopting normal methods of statutory interpretation (i.e. without recourse to s.3 of the 1998 Act), the s.41(3)(c) gateways appear to be extremely narrow, because of the requirement that the similarity be such that it cannot reasonably be explained as a coincidence.

Key Principle: **Cross-examination of a sexual offence complainant concerning the making of false complaints in the past or a failure to make a complaint against the accused in the context of investigation of other sexual offence allegations will not be cross-examination concerning the complainant's sexual behaviour, provided that the cross-examination possesses an evidential basis, and, thus, s.41(4) of the Youth Justice and Criminal Evidence Act 1999 will not prevent such cross-examination even though its main purpose is to discredit the complainant.**

R. v T; R. v H 2002
The two appeals that the case concerned both concerned rulings made in preparatory hearings.

The first appellant was charged with the indecent assault and rape of his niece many years earlier. The judge ruled that he could not grant leave (under s.41 of the Youth Justice and Criminal Evidence Act 1999) to the defence to cross-examine the complainant concerning occasions on which she had been asked questions about sexual matters concerning her and had not made allegations concerning the appellant. The basis of the judge's ruling was that the questions concerned the complainant's sexual behaviour did not relate to a relevant issue in the case but, rather, would be asked for the purpose of impugning the complainant's credibility.

The second appellant was charged with the indecent assault of his stepdaughter and the judge ruled that, due to the operation of s.41, the defence could not cross-examine the complainant for the purpose of showing that she had lied about sexual and non-sexual matters in the past (e.g. to show that, prior to alleged commission of the offence with which the accused was charged, she had told her brother that she had been raped). The defence contended that the statements allegedly made by the complainant were lies, i.e. that the events to which they related had not taken place. The basis of the judge's ruling was that the questions concerned the complainant's sexual behaviour and that, since they would be asked for the purpose of impugning the complainant's credibility, they would be inadmissible under s.41(4).

Held: (CA) Appeal allowed. The questions in both appeals were relevant in the normal, non-statutory, sense. If their main purpose was to impugn the complainants' credibility then, due to the operation of s.41(4), they could not relate to a relevant issue in the case for the purposes of s.41. Normally, however, questions or evidence concerning a complainant's false statements in the past about sexual assaults, or about a failure to make a complaint against the accused when complaining about other sexual assaults, did not relate to the complainant's sexual behaviour but, rather, related, respectively, to the complainant's past statements or failure to complain. Thus, the questions which the two appeals concerned were not automatically excluded by s.41 even if they principally went to credibility. The defence was, however, required to have a proper evidential basis for asserting both that the complainant made the statements and that they were untrue, otherwise the questions would relate to sexual behaviour (i.e. this would be the case if the statements were true), though this would not provide a watertight guarantee that evidence of sexual behaviour would be excluded.

Commentary
The effect of s.41(4) of the 1999 Act is that the judge cannot give the defence leave to cross-examine a sexual offence complainant in relation to her sexual behaviour, or to adduce evidence of her sexual behaviour, where the main purpose is that of impugning the complainant's credibility. It should be noted, however, that, as the Court of Appeal recognised in *R. v F* 2005, the s.41(4) restriction does not apply where leave is sought under the gateway created by s.41(5) (which applies where the purpose of the cross-examination or evidence is to rebut or explain evidence of the accused's sexual

behaviour that was adduced by the prosecution). It should also be noted that, as the Court of Appeal indicated in *R. v F* 2005, the mere fact that cross-examination of a sexual offence complainant in relation to her sexual behaviour may impugn the complainant's credibility does not mean that this is the main purpose of cross-examination and, moreover, that, as the Court of Appeal indicated in *R. v T*; *R. v H*, in circumstances in which the operation of s.41(4) would render the trial unfair under Art.6 of the European Convention on Human Rights, it might be necessary, under s.3 of the Human Rights Act 1998 to adopt a narrow definition of "credibility" for the purposes of s.41(4). The instant appeals demonstrate, however, that where evidence or cross-examination does not concern the complainant's sexual behaviour, the s.41 leave requirement will not apply and, consequently, even if the questions or evidence solely or mainly relate to the complainant's credibility, the operation of s.41(4) will not prevent the admission of the evidence or the asking of the questions.

Re-Examination

During re-examination a witness may not be asked questions concerning new matters which are unconnected with the subject-matter of cross-examination (*Queen Caroline's Case 1820*; *Prince v Samo* 1838). Where, exceptionally, the party who called a witness is permitted to raise new matters during re-examination, it appears that additional cross-examination should also be permitted.

Special Measures Directions

Key Principle: **The fact that the accused is not eligible for a special measures direction does not mean that such a direction should not be made in relation to prosecution witnesses.**

R. v Camberwell Green Youth Court 2005
The appeal concerned a number of cases. In the context of prosecutions of child defendants aged 14, 15 and 16 for robbery, magistrates had made special measures directions ordering that child witnesses aged 13 and 14 gave their evidence for the prosecution by live link, the magistrates having been advised by their clerk that under s.21(5) of the Youth Justice and Criminal Evidence Act 1999 they had no discretion in this regard. In the

context of prosecutions of child defendants aged 14, 15 and 16 for robbery and assault, magistrates had declined to make special measures directions (live link and video-recorded interview as evidence in chief) in relation to prosecution witnesses aged 12, 15 and 16 in consequence of inequality of arms between prosecution and defence, the defendants and the witnesses all being children but defendants not being eligible for special measures directions. A Divisional Court dismissed the applications for judicial review made by the former three defendants and allowed the applications for judicial review made by the Director of Public Prosecutions in the latter three cases.

Held: (HL) Appeals dismissed. It was difficult to think of reasons unconnected with the quality of the equipment on the day of the trial, the content and quality of the recording or the unavailability of the witness for cross-examination, which would make live link or the admission of a video recording unjust. Where a witness was not available for cross-examination the court possessed the power to exclude the witness's video recording and where there was a real risk of injustice if the tribunal of fact was not permitted to see a witness in the flesh there was nothing to prevent the judge or magistrates on the day taking whatever steps were necessary in order to secure a fair trial. The starting position was, however, the statutory presumption that there was nothing intrinsically unfair in children giving their evidence by live link or video recording.

The special measures that the case concerned permitted the defendants to challenge the witness directly during the trial, the court had the opportunity to scrutinise the video recording and to exclude some or all of it and, where the interests of justice so required, the court was able to allow the witness to testify in the court room or to expand on the video recording. Nothing in the case law of the European Court of Human Rights that had been cited before their Lordships suggested that the procedure violated the defendants' right to a fair trial under Art.6 of the European Convention on Human Rights.

The answer to the problems of child defendants (e.g. lack of support and guidance, of emotional and social maturity and of basic educational and literacy skills) was not to deprive the court of the best evidence of other witnesses because the special measures scheme did not apply to child defendants. While defendants were excluded from the special measures scheme, the Court of Appeal in *R. v H* 2003 had made clear that the court possesses wide inherent powers to make sure that the accused is given a fair trial. Thus, in order to enable the defendant to give a coherent account, the defendant could be allowed the equivalent of an interpreter to assist with communication, the jury could be read a detailed written statement so that they knew what the defendant wanted to say and the defendant could be asked leading questions based on the written statement. The 1999 Act did not prevent the court from exercising its inherent powers so as to assist the defendant to give his best quality evidence. In *R. (S) v Waltham Forest Youth Court* 2004 the Administrative Court had held, however, that the court did not possess the inherent power to permit a defendant to give evidence by live link; Baroness Hale (with whose decision the rest of their Lordships agreed) reserved her position in relation to the issue of whether the *Waltham Forest* case had been wrongly decided.

If, in an exceptional case, the giving of evidence by video recording or live link by a child witness was disadvantageous for the defendant, the court possessed ample power to discharge the direction under s.20(2) or to allow the witness to give evidence in open court under s.24(3) and the making of a direction that a video recording was admitted as evidence in chief would not be mandatory, where a risk of injustice was perceived, due to the operation of ss.21(4)(b) and 27(2).

Commentary

Under the special measures scheme created by Chapter 1 of Part 2 of the Youth Justice and Criminal Evidence Act 1999, the court can direct that special measures, such as the giving of evidence in chief by video-recorded interview or the examination in chief, cross-examination or re-examination of a witness by live link, apply to the evidence of an eligible witness. The special measures scheme does not apply to the accused. Essentially, witnesses may be eligible for special measures because they are under 17 years of age, because the quality of their evidence is likely to be diminished because of mental disorder, significant impairment of intelligence and social functioning or physical disability or disorder or because of fear or distress in connection with testifying (a sexual offence witness being eligible unless the witness does not wish to be eligible). In general, where, in the context of a special measures application, the court determines that special measure(s) would be likely to improve the quality of the evidence of an eligible witness, the court will direct the application to the witness' evidence of those special measures that would be likely to maximise the quality of the witness' evidence so far as practicable. In relation to child witnesses, however, the "primary rule" is, essentially, that the court will direct that any relevant video recording is admitted as evidence in chief and that evidence that is not given by video recording will be given by live link, though, a special measures direction must not provide for the admission of a video recording where this would not be in the interests of justice (s.21(4)(b) and s.27(3)), and the primary rule does not apply if compliance with it would not be likely to maximise the quality of the witness' evidence so far as practicable. When a child witness is in need of special protection, however, (e.g., because the offence is a sexual offence, kidnapping or involves an assault, injury or threat of injury), the effect of s.21(5) is that the primary rule applies even though compliance with it would not be likely to maximise the quality of the witness' evidence so far as practicable. Where a special measures direction directs that a witness gives evidence by live link, however, the court, in the interests of justice, may direct that the witness gives evidence in some other way (s.24(3)). Moreover, the court possesses the power to discharge or to vary special measures directions (s.20(2)).

6. EVIDENCE OF OPINION

Non-Expert Witnesses

Key Principle: **Non-expert opinion evidence is admissible as a way of conveying to the court facts that the witness personally perceived.**

R. v Davies 1962
The appellant, a sergeant in the Royal Artillery serving in Germany, was convicted at a court martial of driving a vehicle on the road when he was unfit to do so through drink or drugs, contrary to s.6 of the Road Traffic Act 1960 and driving without due care and attention contrary to s.3 of the same Act. A car driven by the appellant was found to have had a collision with a stationary vehicle. Evidence from a witness was given at the court martial as to both the appellant being under the influence of drink and as to him being in no condition to drive. The appellant appealed on the ground that the witness's evidence in relation to his fitness or otherwise to drive was not admissible.

Held: (Courts-Martial Appeal Court) The witness was entitled to give his impression as to whether the accused had taken drink, though he was required to describe the facts on which he relied. However, the further evidence as to the accused's fitness or otherwise to drive should not have been admitted. The fact that the witness was himself a driver did not give him the status of an expert witness as to this issue. This was the very issue that the court was required to determine. There had been, however, sufficient evidence to allow the court martial to reach the conclusion that it did even if the evidence as to fitness to drive had not been admitted. Appeal dismissed.

Commentary
The admissibility of non-expert opinion evidence in criminal proceedings is governed by the common law. The position at common law is, essentially, that the non-expert witness may give evidence of opinion as a way of conveying to the court facts that the expert witness had personally perceived, but the non-expert may not give expert opinion evidence and, strictly should not give opinion evidence in relation to an "ultimate issue" (i.e. should not give opinion evidence in relation to the very issue that the court has to decide). Thus, in *Davies*, the Courts-Martial Appeal Court

recognised that the witness had properly been permitted to give evidence of his opinion that the appellant had been drinking, provided that he was able to give evidence of the primary facts that he had perceived which had formed the basis of this opinion. Their Lordships indicated, however, that the witness should not have been permitted to give evidence of his opinion that the appellant had been in no condition to drive, both because the witness was not an expert witness (the issue of fitness to drive being, it appears, one requiring an expert opinion) and, it seems, because the issue was an "ultimate issue".

The admissibility of non-expert opinion evidence in civil proceedings is governed by s.3(2), (3) of the Civil Evidence Act 1972. Essentially, the position in civil proceedings, under s.3(2), (3) of the 1972 Act, equates with the common law position described above except in that s.3(2), (3) abolished the ultimate issue rule in the civil context. In practice, it may well be that the ultimate issue rule is no longer strictly enforced in criminal proceedings either, but if this is the case it is submitted that the jury should be directed to the effect that it is the opinion of the jury, and, not those of the witnesses, which determines the issues before the court.

Expert Witnesses

Key principle: **A witness may be competent to give expert evidence even though the witness has no formal qualifications and has not been trained; an expert witness may be permitted to give evidence in relation to an ultimate issue in criminal proceedings.**

R. v Stockwell 1993

The appellant was convicted of robbery and attempted robbery in June 1991. There was security camera footage of both incidents. In the first incident the appellant was disguised with glasses and a wig and was clean shaven. In the second incident the appellant was also clean shaven. He had grown a beard shortly before being arrested. At the original trial, the prosecution sought leave to call a facial mapping expert to assist the jury in deciding whether the man shown on both of the videos was the appellant. The appellant appealed against his conviction. It was argued that the evidence of the facial mapping expert should not have been admitted because the jury were capable of deciding for themselves whether the appellant was the man in the photographs taken by the video cameras.

Held: (CA) Appeal dismissed. Although there might be cases where a jury could reach a conclusion about identity without help, where, as in this case, the appellant had changed his appearance, that identification might not be so straightforward. In such a situation there was no reason why expert evidence might not be given if it could help the jury with this identification process. While facial mapping was a new technique, the Court of Appeal agreed with the trial judge that the courts should not set themselves against new developments which have a proper foundation. While the expert had no scientific qualifications, training, professional body or database, the judge had properly concluded, on the basis of his experience (as an artist working in the field of medicine and life science) and the assistance that he could provide (by comparing facial mapping proportions, etc.), that his evidence was admissible. Although the expert could give an opinion as to the ultimate issue of whether the appellant and the robber in the video photograph were the same man, the judge was required to make clear to the jury that they were not bound to follow the expert's view and that the issue was for them to decide.

Commentary

The *Stockwell* case demonstrates a number of principles relating to the admissibility of expert evidence in criminal proceedings. First, that a witness may be competent to give expert evidence even though he has no formal qualifications and has not been trained, provided that the witness possesses the expertise that the court requires in order to resolve the issue before it. Second, that, as was recognised by the Court of Appeal in *Stockwell* and as is demonstrated by a number of the cases that are considered in the present chapter, expert evidence may be admissible in criminal proceedings if it provides the jury with relevant information and assistance that it would otherwise not possess. Third, that the criminal courts are not opposed to admitting expert evidence which is based upon new techniques, provided that the expert evidence does provide the jury with relevant information and assistance that the it would otherwise not possess and that the expert does possess the expertise necessary to make his opinion of value to the jury. Finally, that while statute has not abolished the ultimate issue rule (i.e. the rule that an expert witness should not give his opinion in relation to the very issue that the court is required to determine) in the context of criminal proceedings, in practice a criminal court may well be prepared to admit expert evidence in relation to an ultimate issue, though the judge will be required to make clear to the jury that it is the opinion of the jury, and not that of the expert witness, that determines the relevant issue.

Key principle: **an expert witness is only competent to give expert evidence in his own field of expertise.**

R. v Barnes 2005

This case arose out of a conviction for robbery and grievous bodily harm. The appellant had obtained access to the home of Mr and Mrs Pickles, under the pretence of being a police officer. Once inside, he became violent and assaulted Mr Pickles. He remained in their home for some time before leaving. Shortly thereafter, a taxi was called to collect a man from a pub a short distance from the Pickles home. This man asked the taxi driver to take him to his destination via Cheetham Hill, where he got out of the cab, threw a drinks bottle into the car park of a derelict pub, and then proceeded on his journey. Scenes of crime officers took fingerprints from inside the Pickles home and from shards of the bottle thrown into the car park. One of the fingerprints, obtained from a bedroom door inside the Pickles home, was compared with fingerprints taken from Barnes in a previous incident and in an incident subsequent to what occurred at the Pickles home. The fingerprints matched. The defendant appealed against his conviction on the grounds that fresh expert evidence was available which, had it been given at the original trial, might reasonably have affected the jury's verdict. This evidence was from a wood grain expert, Mr Murat, and sought to show that the fingerprint supposed to have been found in the Pickles home could not have come from the bedroom door.

Held: (CA) Appeal dismissed. The comparison between the print and the bedroom door from where it was supposed to have been taken was a matter to be undertaken by an appropriately qualified and skilled expert. Although Mr Murat had expertise in identifying wood-grain in wood, he had no expertise in the interpretation of fingerprint lifts or the identification of wood-grain on lifts. In these circumstances, any expert evidence that Mr Murat could give could not afford any ground for regarding the verdict of the jury as unsafe.

Commentary
The Court of Appeal in *Barnes* recognised that Mr Murat did possess expertise in his own field (wood grain) but that he did not possess expertise in the field in relation to which his evidence was relied upon by the appellant (identifying whether the wood grain on the lift was from the bedroom door). Thus, their Lordships recognised that he was not "qualified" (i.e. competent) to give expert evidence in the relevant field and, thus, it seems, that his evidence was not admissible in relation to the relevant issue. Upon the assumption that his evidence was admissible in relation to this issue, however, their Lordships held that the weight of his evidence was so limited that it could not throw doubt on the safety of the conviction.

Key principle: **Expert evidence is not admissible if the judge or jury can form their own conclusions without the assistance of an expert witness.**

R. v Turner 1975
The appellant, Terence Turner, was convicted of the murder of his girlfriend, Wendy Basterfield. Turner had hit Basterfield several times over the head with a hammer, killing her. His defence at the original trial was provocation. Immediately before the incident Basterfield, who was pregnant, had apparently told him that she had been sleeping with other men and that the child was not his. Turner, who thought the child was his, had been very upset at what he heard. His hand had chanced upon a hammer kept in the vehicle in which Turner and Basterfield were sitting and he had hit her with it a number of times. Turner claimed that he had been very upset, he had not intended to cause the victim any harm, he had not realised that what he had picked up was a hammer and had stopped hitting her once he had realised that it was a hammer. Counsel for Turner wanted to call a psychiatrist to give evidence as to Turner's personality and his mental and emotional state, as evidence of provocation and credibility. The judge asked to see the evidence which the psychiatrist proposed to give and was handed a report prepared by a Dr Smith. Essentially, the report indicated that the appellant was a quiet, non-aggressive person who was not mentally ill and that his behaviour was explainable, because his relationship with the victim was such that he

would be vulnerable to being overwhelmed by anger if the victim confirmed that she had been sleeping with other men and that the baby was not his. Having read the report, the judge ruled that it was irrelevant and inadmissible. Turner appealed against his conviction on the ground of the judge's refusal to admit psychiatric evidence that supported his defence of provocation.

Held: (CA) Appeal dismissed. An expert's opinion was admissible to give the court scientific information which was likely to be outside the knowledge and experience of the judge or jury. If, on the facts, the judge or jury could draw their own conclusions without additional help then an expert opinion was not needed. The provocation claimed by the appellant was something that came within ordinary human experience and the jury had been capable of deciding what reliance to place on the appellant's evidence without the help of expert opinion.

Commentary
In *Stockwell* (above), the expert evidence was admissible because, the accused, having changed his appearance, the facial mapping expert could help the jury to determine whether the accused was the man whose image had been captured by the camera footage. In contrast, in *Turner*, the evidence that the accused was not mentally ill was expert evidence but was not relevant to an issue in the proceedings and the jury did not need the assistance of a psychiatrist to explain to them how an ordinary man who was not mentally ill was likely to react in such circumstances.

Key principle: **Expert evidence is admissible where it relates to relevant matters that fall outside the experience of the jury.**

R. v Smith 1979
In July 1978, Stanley Smith was convicted of the murder of Bob Montgomery and sentenced to life imprisonment. Smith and Mr and Mrs Montgomery occupied rooms in the same house. Smith murdered Montgomery after apparently quarrelling with Montgomery's wife earlier on in the day that the murder took place. Montgomery returned from an evening drinking, was told about the argument and went to Smith's room where he was sleeping. A quarrel was heard by the other occupants of the

house and Smith was found in the room with a knife in his hand. Montgomery was also in the room, lying on his back and covered with stab wounds. He died shortly thereafter.

Smith originally told the police, both orally and in a written statement, that he was asleep in bed, someone, who he thought was Montgomery, had burst into his room, he had grabbed his knife and stabbed him. Smith was examined by two psychiatrists, who both came to the view that Smith's responsibility for his actions was substantially impaired. However, at his trial Smith chose not to use the defence of diminished responsibility and instead suggested the defence of automatism (i.e. he claimed that he had been sleepwalking when he killed the victim). In response, the prosecution sought leave to cross-examine Smith on remarks he had made to the psychiatrists who examined him, in order to demonstrate that Smith's defence of automatism was a recent idea. Leave was granted. The prosecution were also allowed to call the psychiatrists to give evidence in rebuttal of the plea of automatism. Smith appealed on the grounds that the cross-examination should not have been allowed and that the psychiatrists should not have been called to give their opinions in rebuttal of the automatism defence.

Held: (CA) Appeal dismissed. The type of automatism alleged by Smith was not something that the ordinary member of the jury would have experience of. Therefore, the jury were entitled to have the benefit of expert medical evidence on this issue.

Commentary
Expert evidence is admissible where it relates to relevant matters that fall outside the experience of the jury. This, of course will be subject to the witness whose expert evidence is tendered being competent to give such evidence. *Smith* may be contrasted with *Turner* on the basis that a jury will presumably be well aware that an ordinary man who has just been informed that his girlfriend has been unfaithful may become extremely angry whereas the possibility that a man may commit a murder while sleepwalking will presumably fall outside the jury's experience.

Key principle: **The fact that the reliability of expert evidence is questionable does not mean that the evidence will neces-**

sarily be inadmissible, though if it is admitted it may be necessary to give the jury an appropriate warning.

R. v Luttrell and Others 2004

The appeal of Luttrell was against a conviction for conspiracy to handle stolen goods. The goods concerned were high value computer and electrical items. A number of undercover police officers were involved in infiltrating the activities of Luttrell and a number of other men and keeping them under surveillance. At the original trial, evidence was given by a lip-reading expert as to a conversation recorded by CCTV involving Luttrell. This evidence was ruled admissible in principle despite the submission of the defence that there was no sufficiently well established field of lip-reading expertise for it to be accepted as a reliable body of knowledge or experience. Luttrell appealed on the grounds that lip-reading evidence is novel and unreliable and should therefore not be admitted. Alternatively, if such evidence is admissible, it should be treated carefully by the judge, who should direct the jury as to the potential weaknesses in the evidence.

Held: (CA) Appeal dismissed. Expert evidence was admissible if two conditions were satisfied, namely, if (a) study or experience would give the opinion of a witness an authority that the opinion of a witness who was not so qualified would not possess and (b) the witness whose evidence was tendered as expert evidence was qualified to give such evidence. Where such evidence was admissible, however, its weight was a question of fact for the jury. It was not a requirement of admissibility that expert evidence was only admissible where the evidence could be seen to be reliable. Rather, while unreliability could result in inadmissibility (e.g. where the evidence was so unreliable that it had too little probative value to influence a decision, the conditions of admissibility thus not being satisfied, or where it resulted in the court excluding expert evidence in the exercise of its discretion under s.78 of PACE) reliability in itself went to the weight of expert evidence rather than to the admissibility of such evidence. Lip-reading evidence as to the content of a conversation recorded on video was capable of passing the ordinary tests of relevance and reliability and was therefore potentially admissible in evidence. A special warning was required from judge to jury where there was a difficulty with a particular type of evidence that the jury might be unaware of or might not understand. Lip-reading evidence did require a warning from the judge to the jury as to its limitations. The precise terms of this warning would depend upon the facts of each case, but generally would cover the risk of mistakes as to the words that the lip-reader believed were spoken and the particular strengths and weaknesses of the material. There should be a reminder that the quality of the evidence would be affected by matters such as lighting, angle of view, distance involved, familiarity with the language spoken, awareness of the context of the speech and whether the probative value of the evidence depended upon isolated words and phrases or the general impact of long passages of conversation.

Commentary
Luttrell makes clear that where expert evidence is capable of assisting the jury in relation to a matter that falls outside its experience, the fact that the reliability of the evidence is questionable does not render it inadmissible as a matter of law. Rather, the weight of expert evidence is a matter for the jury to determine in the context of matters such as conflicting expert opinion, cross-examination of the expert witnesses, the reliability of the techniques applied by the experts, etc. Where, however, evidence which is tendered as expert evidence is so unreliable that it has little or no probative value (perhaps because the technique used by the expert is so unreliable that evidence based upon it does not possess an authority which an unqualified witness would lack or perhaps because, due to the expert's lack of skill he is not competent, i.e. "qualified") to give expert evidence based on the technique, its lack of reliability may affect its admissibility. Moreover, a criminal court would be able to exclude unreliable expert evidence tendered by the prosecution in the exercise of its exclusionary discretion, either under s.78 of PACE or at common law.

Key principle: **Expert evidence is only admissible in civil proceedings where the matter to which it relates falls outside the knowledge and experience of a layman.**

Liddell v Middleton 1995
This case concerned an appeal from a judgment given in a road traffic accident. The accident involved a vehicle driven by Mr Middleton and a pedestrian, who was hit by the vehicle while

standing in the middle of the road, waiting to cross to the other side. The accident happened at night and the evidence suggested that Mr Liddell may have been drunk at the time. There was also evidence to indicate that the vehicle driven by Mr Middleton was travelling in excess of the 30 mph speed limit. At the original trial, the judge found the issue of liability as to 75 per cent against the defendant and 25 per cent against the plaintiff by way of contributory negligence. The judge placed reliance on the evidence of an expert witness called on behalf of the plaintiff, who had concluded that Middleton was grossly negligent in failing to see Liddell.

Held: (CA) Both parties were equally to blame for the accident that had occurred. In this case, the expert's evidence, which was based entirely on eyewitness accounts, was entirely irrelevant and inadmissible. Expert evidence was only admissible under s.3 of the Civil Evidence Act 1972 where it related to a matter which was outside the knowledge of a layman. Expert evidence could be necessary in road traffic cases where, for example, there were no witnesses and deductions as to the speed or relative positions of the vehicles had to be made from evidence such as marks on the road or damage to vehicles. What the expert was not entitled to do was conclude from eyewitness statements and/or the evidence of the eyewitnesses that the defendant was travelling at a certain speed or could have seen the plaintiff at a certain point. These facts were for the trial judge to find for himself upon the basis of the evidence that he accepted.

Commentary
The admissibility of expert evidence in civil proceedings is governed by s.3(1), (3) of the Civil Evidence Act 1972. Essentially, the test laid down by s.3(1) is that expert opinion is admissible in civil proceedings if the relevant matter to which it relates is one in relation to which the witness is qualified to give expert evidence. Thus, the s.3(1) test of admissibility essentially equates with that encountered at common law in the context of civil proceedings, i.e. the witness must be "qualified" (i.e. competent) to give expert evidence and, as the Court of Appeal recognised in *Re M and R Minors* 1996, the evidence must relate to a matter in relation to which a layman would require the assistance of an expert in order "to make a properly informed decision". The Court of Appeal in *Re M and R Minors* also recognised, however, that the effect of s.3(3) of the 1972 Act, in providing that, for the purposes of s.3, a

"relevant matter" includes an issue in the proceedings, was to abolish the common law ultimate issue rule in the context of civil proceedings. The ultimate issue was, however, to be determined by the opinion of the judge, not by that of the expert. Moreover, a criminal court was not obliged to admit expert evidence in relation to an ultimate issue if a layman would not require expert evidence in relation to that issue in order to make a properly informed decision. The Court of Appeal in *Re M and R Minors* 1996 recognised that the expert evidence in *Liddell v Middleton* was not inadmissible because it related to an ultimate issue (because s.3(3) of the 1972 Act had abolished the ultimate issue rule in civil proceedings) but, rather, was inadmissible because it did not relate to a matter in relation to which a layman would require expert assistance in order to make a properly informed decision. This was so because the judge did not require expert assistance where his task was merely that of evaluating the accounts of eye-witnesses.

It should be noted that the admissibility of expert evidence is now subject to Part 35 of the Civil Procedure Rules 1998, which were not in force when *Re M and R* was decided. Thus, even where expert evidence is admissible under the test laid down by s.3(1), (3) of the 1972 Act, the judge may still refuse to admit it, in the exercise of its powers under CPR Part 35 (the permission of the court under CPR Part 35 being required if expert evidence is to be adduced), the judge may limit expert evidence in relation to the relevant issue to that of a single joint expert or he may refuse permission to call the expert witnesses to give oral evidence, limiting the expert evidence to the experts' written reports.

Key principle: **Expert witnesses may rely upon the research of others when forming their expert opinions.**

R. v Abadom 1982

Steven Abadom was convicted of robbery at Newcastle upon Tyne Crown Court in March 1980. Abadom and three other men, all masked and gloved, broke into office premises and demanded to know where money was kept. During the robbery, an internal window was broken by one of the robbers. Having arrested Abadom, the police found a pair of shoes at his home which had glass fragments both adhering to and embedded in them. It was alleged at the trial that the fragments came from the window that had been broken during the robbery. Two expert witnesses were called by the prosecution. Both were scientific officers at Home Office forensic laboratories with extensive experience in analysing fragments of glass. One of these experts relied on statistics collated by the Home Office Central Research Establishment in his evidence that the glass found in the shoe and in the window had identical refractive indices and that this refractive index occurred in only 4 per cent of samples analysed by the research establishment. Abadom appealed against his conviction on the ground that the evidence concerning statistics from the Home Office Central Research Establishment was inadmissible because it was hearsay evidence.

Held: (CA) Appeal dismissed. The statistical evidence relied on by the expert witness to reach a conclusion about the relationship between the glass on the shoe and the glass in the window was an essential part of his role as an expert witness in this case. Once the facts on which an expert's opinion is based have been proved by admissible evidence, they are entitled to draw on the work of others, whether published or not, as part of the process of reaching a conclusion. Any materials used in this way should be referred to by the expert in their evidence.

Commentary
The common law hearsay exception under which expert witnesses may draw on the body of expertise that is relevant to their fields was preserved, in the context of criminal proceedings, by s.18 of the Criminal Justice Act 2003. Hearsay evidence is generally admissible in civil proceedings (unless excluded by some other rule of evidence) under s.1 of the Civil Evidence Act 1995. Both the Criminal Procedure Rules 2005 and the Civil Procedure Rules 1998 require that an expert's report must provide details of the literature on which the expert relied.

Key principle: **It is the opinion of the court, and not that of the expert witness, which determines the issues before the court.**

Armstrong v First York 2005
In this case, Mr Armstrong and Miss Connor were travelling together in a car to a hotel in York for a weekend break. In York

city centre their vehicle was hit by a glancing blow from a bus while stationary at traffic lights. The vehicle suffered minor damage. Both Mr Armstrong and Miss Connor felt back pain during the weekend and called into a hospital on their way home to Liverpool. The hospital was very busy at the time and they were advised to see their GPs the following day. Both did so and, having instructed solicitors, both were referred to separate medical experts. Both described the collision as causing their vehicle to move. Both the claimants and the defendant bus company instructed a single joint expert, a Mr Childs, a forensic motor vehicle engineer. He concluded that the damage to the vehicle was not consistent with it moving, even only on its springs, and this being the case there could have been no movement of the vehicle's occupants. At the original trial the judge found for the claimants and awarded them damages of £1,023 and £2,156 respectively. The defendants appealed.

Held: (CA) Appeal dismissed. The judge had been entitled, having weighed up the evidence of both sides, to conclude that there must have been something inaccurate in Mr Childs' report. There was no principle that an expert's evidence was dispositive of liability in such circumstances, rather, the judge was not required to find that two clearly honest witnesses had come to court to deceive him. Thus, it had been for the judge to determine the matter upon the basis of all the evidence received, and the Court of Appeal could find no flaw in the judge's reasoning.

Commentary

In *Amstrong v First York*, the judge was totally satisfied that the claimants were telling the truth and, consequently, even though he could not find an error in the expert's evidence, since the expert's evidence could not be reconciled with that of the claimants, he found that there must have been an error in the expert's evidence that he could not identify. Thus the case clearly demonstrates that it is the opinion of the judge in a civil case (or the jury or magistrates in a criminal case) which determines the issues before the court, and not that of the expert witnesses and that the court is not bound to accept even the evidence of a single joint expert but, rather, may prefer the evidence of the witnesses of fact. The Court of Appeal recognised, however (with reference to the decision of the Court of Appeal in *Cooper Payen Ltd v Southampton Container Terminal Ltd* 2003), that the position may be different in circumstances in which there is no evidence to rebut the evidence of a single joint expert. Similarly, in the context of criminal proceedings, there may be circumstances in which a trial judge would be required to direct the jury to accept expert evidence (e.g. where, as was the case in *R. v Pearce* 2000, the accused is charged with murder, all of the medical evidence supports the defence of diminished responsibility and there is no evidence to contradict the expert evidence).

Key principle: **An expert witness must comply with the requirements laid down by rules of court concerning matters such as his duty to the court and the contents of his report.**

Stevens v Gullis 1999

This case arose out of a dispute as to payment and quality of work in a building contract. The claimant claimed the sum of £8,674.89 plus VAT for work done and materials supplied to the defendant, which were certified by the defendant's architect. The defendant counterclaimed for a sum in excess of £127,000 covering defective, incomplete or delayed work. A Mr Isaac was instructed on behalf of the defendant and prepared schedules to support the counterclaim. Both claimant and defendant were given leave to produce evidence from two expert witnesses. The experts were directed to meet and to prepare a joint memorandum of matters agreed or disagreed between the parties. The experts instructed by claimant and defendant did eventually meet but, despite numerous reminders, the defendant's expert, Mr Isaac, did not respond satisfactorily to the drawing up of the memorandum of agreement. Eventually, an order was made requiring Mr Isaac to comply with requirements laid down by Part 35 of the Civil Procedure Rules 1998 concerning the contents of expert's reports. Failure to do so by a date specified in the order would result in the defendant being debarred from calling Mr Isaac as an expert witness in third party proceedings against the defendant's architect. The order was not complied with (Mr Isaac not having stated in his report that he understood his duty to the court and had complied with it and not having set out the substance of his instructions in his report) and the judge ordered that the defendant was debarred from calling Mr Isaac as an expert witness in both the third part proceedings and in the proceedings between the claimant and the defendant. The third party proceedings were also dismissed. The defendant appealed.

Held: (CA) Appeal dismissed. The judge had been entitled to make the orders that he had made. Mr Isaac had shown by his conduct that he had had no conception of the requirements placed on an expert by the Civil Procedure Rules. The requirements of the practice direction to CPR Part 35, that an expert understands his responsibilities and gives details of his qualifications and other matters, were intended to focus the expert's mind on his responsibilities. Mr Isaac clearly had had no conception of these requirements.

Commentary

Part 35 of the Civil Procedure Rules 1995 and the Practice Direction—Experts and Assessors, which supplements CPR Part 35, lay down requirements concerning, among other matters, the contents of expert reports and the duties of expert witnesses. Part 33 of the Criminal Procedure Rules 2005, which came into force in November 2006, imposes similar requirements in the context of criminal proceedings.

Key principle: **Where a party to civil proceedings disagrees with the report of a single joint expert it may be appropriate for the court to permit the party to adduce the evidence of the party's own expert.**

Daniels v Walker 2000

The claimant was hit by a car at a young age. The injuries sustained in the accident by the claimant were severe and resulted in the claimant requiring care in some form for the rest of his life. It was important to both parties to determine the nature and extent of the care required. To this end, the parties agreed that a report should be prepared by a jointly instructed occupational therapist. On receiving the report, the defendant's solicitors were concerned at the extent of care recommended in it. They expressed a wish to obtain a report from their own occupational therapist. The claimant's solicitors refused this request and the defendant's solicitors applied to the court for leave to do so. The judge decided that no further expert evidence should be called on the issue of care but that the defendant was allowed or invited to put written questions to the jointly instructed expert. The defendant appealed.

Held: (CA) Appeal allowed. The judge should have ordered that there should be an opportunity for the claimant to be examined by the defendant's own expert. Where a substantial sum of money was involved, the correct approach was to view the joint instruction of an expert as a first step in obtaining expert evidence on a particular issue. If, having done so, a party wished to obtain further information for valid reasons before deciding whether or not there were parts of the report that it wished to challenge, then they should be permitted to do so, subject to the court's discretion. If the sum involved was modest, it might be disproportionate to permit a party to obtain a second report and might be sufficient merely to permit the party to put a question to the single joint expert. Where the sum involved was substantial, the starting point, if possible, was that a joint report was obtained. If, in such circumstances, there was disagreement re the joint report which the putting of questions to the single joint expert did not resolve and one or both parties obtained their own reports, the question would be what expert evidence should be called at the trial. Before the court permitted the giving of oral expert evidence at the hearing, however, a meeting between the experts should have taken place in order to determine whether an agreement could be reached.

Commentary
Under Part 35 of the Civil Procedure Rules 1998, the permission of the court is required to adduce admissible expert evidence, the court is empowered to direct that expert evidence in relation to an issue be given by a single joint expert, oral expert evidence, as opposed to an expert's report, is only admissible with the Court's permission and the court is empowered to direct that a meeting between experts takes place. Moreover, under CPR Part 35, a party is entitled to put written questions to the other party's expert within 28 days of service of the expert's report, the expert's answers to such questions being treated as part of the report.

In relation to the exercise of the court's powers under the civil procedure rules, the starting point, as the Court of Appeal in *Daniels* recognised, is the overriding objective of the Civil Procedure Rules 1998, namely, that of dealing with cases justly. This includes, to the extent to which it is practicable, ensuring that the parties are on an equal footing, saving expense, dealing with cases proportionately to their financial value, their importance, their complexity and the financial position of the parties, ensuring that they are dealt with expeditiously and fairly and allotting an appropriate share of the court's resources to them. The Court of

Appeal in *Daniels* indicated, however, that in making case management decisions in civil proceedings such as those which *Daniels* concerned, the court was not required to consider arguments based on Art.6 of the European Convention on Human Rights, as Art.6 arguments would add unnecessary complexity to case management issues and would discredit the Human Rights Act 1998.

Key principle: **Where medical evidence is required to resolve an issue in the context of a substantial claim and the parties assert than in order to resolve the issue they should each be permitted to adduce their own expert evidence, it may not be appropriate for the judge to direct that expert evidence in relation to the issue be given by a single joint expert.**

Oxley v Penwarden 2000

This case concerned an action in negligence against a Dr Penwarden for failing to diagnose and treat a vascular condition in the leg of Mr Oxley, resulting in the leg having to be amputated above the knee. Dr Penwarden denied negligence. It was clear that the medical issues to be resolved would require expert evidence. The parties were originally allowed by directions to each instruct their own experts, limited to one General Practitioner expert per side and one vascular surgery expert per side. However, at a case management conference, the judge expressed his view that this was a case where it would be appropriate for the parties to agree to instruct a single joint expert vascular surgeon, although allowing a general practitioner expert to be called by each side. Reference was made to rule 35.7 of the Civil Procedure Rules 1998, which deals with the power of the court to direct that evidence is given by a single joint expert. Neither party agreed with this view and appealed on this point.

Held: (CA) Appeal allowed. The note attached to CPR 35.7 made clear that there was no presumption in favour of the appointment of a single joint expert. The object was to prevent the appointment of multiple experts where this was not justified, given the nature of the issues involved. In this case, it was necessary for the parties to each appoint their own expert and have the opportunity of calling that expert evidence before the court.

Commentary

While the Court of Appeal in Oxley's case indicated that there is no presumption in favour of the appointment of a single joint expert, it should be noted that the Practice Direction—Experts and Assessors, which supplements Part 35 of the Civil Procedure Rules 1998 indicates that, where possible, matters which require expert evidence should be dealt with by a single joint expert. Similarly, in *Peet v Mid-Kent Healthcare NHS Trust* 2001, which is considered below, Lord Woolf indicated that unless there is a reason for not having a single joint expert, it is a single joint expert that should be instructed. Fundamentally, it must be remembered that, as was recognised by the Court of Appeal in *Daniels v Walker*, above, the court, in determining whether to direct that evidence in relation to an issue be given by a single joint expert, must seek to give effect to the overriding objective of the Civil Procedure Rules 1998, i.e. that of dealing with cases justly. A substantial clinical negligence claim, such as that which the *Oxley* case concerned, in which both parties assert that resolution of the issue of causation requires them to instruct their own experts, appears to provide an example of the sort of case in which justice does require that the parties be permitted to adduce their own expert evidence. In contrast, as the Court of Appeal recognised in the *Daniels* case, where the value of the case is modest, it may merely be appropriate to permit the parties to instruct, and put questions, to a single joint expert, and may be disproportionate to permit them to instruct their own experts.

Key principle: **In the absence of agreement between the parties (or a direction by the court), a single joint expert should not have a conference with one party in the absence of the other.**

Peet v Mid-Kent Healthcare NHS Trust 2002

This case concerned a claim for medical negligence against Mid-Kent Healthcare NHS Trust. The defendant made an offer to the claimant to pay 95 per cent of the full liability quantum of damages which were to be assessed. The claimant accepted this offer and the settlement was approved. In due course, an order was made that there should be seven jointly instructed non-medical experts to provide evidence dealing with quantum of damages. The claimant's parents wished to have a conference with the jointly instructed experts without a representative of the defendants being present. The defendants would not agree to this proposal. The master was asked to give a ruling on this matter and took the view that such a conference was not appropriate. The claimant appealed.

Held: (CA) Appeal dismissed. The idea of having a conference with a jointly instructed expert where one side was not present was inconsistent with the whole concept of the jointly instructed single expert. The framework was designed to ensure an open process so that both parties know what information was given to the expert and the expert owed an equal duty of openness and confidence to both parties. It was not appropriate for one party to have a conference with a jointly instructed expert to in effect test the evidence of that expert. Thus, as indicated in the Code of Guidance for Experts and Those Instructing Them, the position was that a single joint expert should not attend a meeting or conference, other than a joint meeting or conference, unless all the parties agreed in writing. This did not mean, however, that experts could not communicate with each other in order to obtain information required for their reports. Equally, the nursing expert had interviewed the claimant's parents for the purposes of preparing her report in the absence of the defendants, and this was unobjectionable.

Commentary
The Protocol for the Instruction of Experts to Give Evidence in Civil Claims, which has replaced the Code of Guidance on Expert Evidence, provides that a single joint expert should not attend a meeting or conference, other than a joint meeting or conference, unless either all the parties agreed in writing *or the court so directs*.

In *Peet*, Lord Woolf indicated that: there should only be a single joint expert unless there is a reason for not having a single joint expert; where a single joint expert is instructed the expert's report should normally stand as the expert's evidence; the court possesses discretion to permit a single joint expert to be called to amplify the report or for cross-examination if the report requires amplification or testing, but the court should restrict such amplification or cross-examination so far as is possible; and where a report is produced by a single joint expert the court still possesses discretion to permit a party to adduce his own expert evidence where there is a good reason for so permitting.

Key principle: where material supplied to an expert witness as part of his instructions is referred to in the statement of instructions which forms part of the expert's report, the civil court will not order the instructing party to disclose the material unless the statement of instructions is inaccurate or incomplete.

Lucas v Barking, Havering and Redbridge Hospitals NHS Trust 2003

In this case, Mr Lucas was making a claim for personal injury suffered, he alleged, as a result of the defendant's negligence. Two experts' reports were produced with his particulars of claim. In both cases, a witness statement made by the claimant and provided to the experts was referred to. One of the expert reports also referred to a previous report of an expert. The defendant sought an order for inspection of the documents referred to in the experts' reports, pursuant to r.31.14(2) of the Civil Procedure Rules. This rule provides that a party may apply for an order for inspection of a document mentioned in an expert's report which has not already been disclosed. The claimant resisted the application for an order on the grounds that the documents were part of the instructions to the experts and therefore fell within the exception in r.31.14(2), found in r.35.10(4). The defendant was successful in obtaining an order for inspection under r.31.14(2). The claimant appealed.

Held: (CA) Appeal allowed. Material supplied by the instructing party to the expert as the basis upon which the expert is being asked to advise should be considered as part of the instruction and therefore be subject to r.35.10(4).

Commentary

Under Part 35 of the Civil Procedure Rules 1998, one of the matters that an expert is required to include in his report is a statement of the substance of the material instructions on the basis of which the report was written. CPR 35.10(4) provides, however, that, while the instructions are not privileged, the court will not either order disclosure of documents or permit questioning in court by other parties in relation to the instructions unless there are reasonable grounds for regarding the statement as inaccurate or incomplete. Thus, upon the facts of *Lucas*, since there was no reason for suggesting that the material instructions in the expert's reports were inaccurate, the order for disclosure was refused, and the appeal was allowed. The Court of Appeal recognised, however,

that the position could change if in the course of the trial it
subsequently appeared that the statements of instructions in the
experts' reports were inaccurate or incomplete.

7. PRIVILEGE AND PUBLIC INTEREST IMMUNITY

Without Prejudice Communications

Key Principle: **Without prejudice communications remain privileged after a settlement has been reached, are inadmissible in subsequent proceedings connected with the same subject matter even though the proceedings involve a third party and are protected from discovery by third parties.**

Rush and Tompkins Ltd v Greater London Council 1989
The appellants entered into a contract with the Greater London Council to build a number of dwellings on an estate in Ealing. The appellants engaged the respondents as sub-contractors. In consequence of delay, the respondents put in claims for loss and expenses to the appellants and the appellants asserted that they were entitled to be reimbursed by the council in respect of the respondents' claims, but the council would not agree the respondents' claim so the appellants would not pay the respondents. Eventually, the appellants commenced proceedings against the council and the respondents, claiming an inquiry into the losses and expenses to which the respondents were entitled and a declaration that they were entitled to be reimbursed by the council. Prior to the trial, however, the appellants entered into a compromise with the council, as part of which the appellants accepted responsibility for the respondents' claims. The appellants thus discontinued their proceedings against the council, but the respondents counterclaimed to recover the loss and expenses. The respondents took out a summons for the specific discovery of without prejudice correspondence between the appellants and the council showing the basis upon which the respondents' claim had been valued for the purposes of the settlement between the appellant and the council. The official referee refused discovery, but the Court of Appeal reversed his order on the basis that the without prejudice rule ceased to operate once a settlement had been reached.

Held: (HL) The without prejudice rule rendered admissions made in a genuine attempt to reach a settlement inadmissible in subsequent litigation connected with the same subject matter, and admissions made to reach a settlement with a different party within the same litigation were also inadmissible whether or not settlement was reached. Thus contents of the without prejudice correspondence between the appellants and the council would not have been admissible to establish any admission relating to the respondents' claim. The right to discovery and production of documents did not depend upon their admissibility in evidence, but the public policy that applied to protect genuine negotiations from being admissible was extended to protect them from being discoverable to third parties. Thus, the respondents' appeal was allowed and the official referee's decision was restored.

Commentary

The House of Lords in *Rush & Tompkins* recognised that the public policy basis of the without prejudice rule is that of encouraging litigants to reach a settlement. Their Lordships recognised that the rule applies to oral and written negotiations that are genuinely aimed at settlement and that while good practice is to head such correspondence "without prejudice", the rule will still apply to correspondence that is not so headed provided that it is clear that the negotiating parties were seeking to settle the action. Their Lordships believed that if the privilege came to an end once a settlement had been reached, this would run counter to the purpose of the without prejudice rule because it would discourage a party from negotiating a settlement with another party if he knew that a third party could then use admissions made in the course of the negotiations against him.

The without prejudice rule is partly based on public policy and partly based on express or implied agreement between the parties that communications in the course of negotiations would not be admissions as, while its main effect is to protect admissions, if the remainder of the communications made during the negotiations were not protected, this would discourage parties from speaking freely during negotiations (i.e. if they had to carefully monitor each sentence to see if it contained an admission) (*Unilever PLC v The Proctor and Gamble Company* 1999). It is submitted that the speeches of the majority of their Lordships in the recent decision of the House of Lords in *Bradford & Bingley plc v Rashid* 2006 do not cast any doubt upon the proposition that the protection without prejudice rule extends beyond that of admissions made in the course of negotiations. Rather, it appears that the basis of their Lordship's decision that the letters which Rashid's case concerned were not protected by the without prejudice rule was that this was so because the letters were neither written in the context of a dispute nor in the course of an attempt to settle a dispute.

There are a variety of exceptions to the without prejudice privilege, including, for example, the use of without prejudice communications where the issue is whether a compromise agreement was concluded and, where an offer was made without prejudice except as to costs, in relation to the issue of costs.

Key Principle: **A letter that is not written as part of genuine negotiations to settle a dispute may be admissible in evidence whether or not it is headed "open letter".**

Dixons Stores Group Ltd v Thames Television plc 1993

In the context of defamation proceedings, without prejudice correspondence took place between the plaintiffs and the defendants (the correspondence being clearly marked "without prejudice"), but the negotiations did not result in a settlement of the dispute. The defendants' solicitors then wrote a letter to the plaintiffs' solicitors, which was intended to be an open letter but was not marked "open letter", indicating that they wished to negotiate a settlement and suggesting the making of an apology and a statement in open court. Because a query arose as to whether the letter was a without prejudice communication, the defendants' solicitors then sent a nearly identical letter which was headed "open letter". At the trial, the defendants wanted to put the terms of the letter to witnesses called by the plaintiffs, but the plaintiffs asserted that the letter was privileged as a without prejudice communication.

Held: (QBD) A letter which was a reply to a without prejudice letter or which was part of a continuing sequence of negotiations was privileged and could only be given in evidence if both parties waived the privilege but a letter which contained an offer to settle an action could be written as an open letter and used in the proceedings if it was not part of continuing negotiations and was relevant to an issue in the proceedings. Here, the letter had been written after the without prejudice negotiations had finished and was relevant to an issue in the proceedings (i.e. to the assessment of damages). Even though the first letter had not been headed "open letter", both letters had been in exactly the same position as neither had been part of the negotiations and the fact that the first letter had lacked the heading "open letter" while the second letter had possessed it did not mean that the first letter was privileged while the second one was not, it being the substance and context of the letters that governed their admissibility. Thus it was open to the defendants to put the terms of the letters to the plaintiffs' witnesses.

Commentary

Where negotiations begin on a without prejudice basis and one of the negotiating parties wishes to change them to an open basis, that party must make clear to the other party that the negotiations are being changed to an open basis (*Cheddar Valley Engineering Ltd v Chaddlewood Homes Ltd* 1992).

Self-Incrimination

Key Principle: **At common law, a person may rely upon the privilege against self-incrimination so as to prevent exposure to a criminal charge, a penalty or a forfeiture.**

Blunt v Park Lane Hotel Ltd 1942

In the context of proceedings for slander, the defendant applied for leave to administer interrogatories to the plaintiff, one of which was directed to establishing that she (the defendant) had been guilty of unchaste conduct with a number of men on a number of occasions both at the Park Lane Hotel and elsewhere. Master Horridge gave leave to administer the interrogatories and Hallett J. dismissed the plaintiff's appeal.

Held: (CA) A person was not bound to answer a question the answer to which would tend to expose the person to a criminal charge, penalty or forfeiture which was reasonably likely to be preferred or sued for. The plaintiff would not be exposed to the risk of ecclesiastical penalties, however, because the jurisdiction of the ecclesiastical courts to punish for adultery was obsolete. It was only in divorce proceedings that discovery tending to establish adultery was not permitted. The mere fact that answering a question might prejudice the good fame of the party who was required to answer was no ground of protection, the fact that an admission of adultery might have resulted in the plaintiff's minister refusing the sacraments to her not being a penalty within the meaning of the rule. Thus the plaintiff's appeal was dismissed.

Commentary

Where answering a question would not tend to expose a person to a criminal charge, penalty or forfeiture, then the person will not be entitled to rely upon the privilege against self-incrimination. While in the context of criminal proceedings the privilege against self-incrimination may still be claimed in the context of exposure to a criminal charge, a penalty or a forfeiture, in the civil context the privilege can now only be claimed in relation to exposure to a criminal charge or penalty, and not in relation to exposure to a forfeiture (Civil Evidence Act 1968, s.16).

Key Principle: **A witness is only entitled to rely upon the privilege against self-incrimination if there are reasonable grounds to apprehend danger to the witness if he is compelled to answer the incriminating question.**

R. v Boyes 1861

The accused was charged with bribing voters at a Parliamentary election and a witness (who was called to give evidence of having received a bribe from the accused) objected to giving evidence on the ground that he would incriminate himself. The witness was then given a pardon, which he accepted, but still objected to giving evidence, because while the Crown could not prosecute him, the House of Commons could still impeach him. The judge instructed the witness to answer the question and the witness then testified that the accused had bribed him. The accused was convicted.

Held: (QB) To entitle a witness to the privilege there had to be reasonable grounds to apprehend danger to the witness if the witness was compelled to answer. Where this was the case, the witness was to be given great latitude in judging the effect of a question as a question that appears innocent could form part of a link in a chain of evidence. The danger, however, had to be real and appreciable, and a remote possibility that would not affect a reasonable man was not to be permitted to obstruct the administration of justice. The accused did not run the slightest risk of impeachment by the House of Commons, which had never occurred in a bribery case, thus the witness was not in the slightest real danger and it had been the judge's duty to compel the witness to answer.

Commentary

Where there is only a remote possibility that proceedings might be brought against a witness if he answers an incriminating question, the witness will not be entitled to rely upon the privilege against self-incrimination.

Key Principle: **The privilege against self-incrimination may be claimed where answering a question or producing a document would tend to expose a person to proceedings for the recovery of a penalty imposed under the EEC treaty that is recoverable via proceedings in the English Courts.**

Rio Tinto Zinc Corporation v Westinghouse Electric Corporation 1978

Two companies claimed privilege, under s.14 of the Civil Evidence Act 1968, against the production of documents.

Held: (HL) The companies were entitled to claim privilege under s.14 because the production of the documents would have tended to expose them to proceedings for the recovery of a penalty (for breach of an Article of the EEC Treaty prohibiting certain cartels) that was recoverable in English Law (i.e. via proceedings in the English Courts) under the European Communities Act 1972. Section 14 of the 1968 Act encompassed not only penalties imposed as the result of legal proceedings but also penalties imposed by administrative action and recoverable by legal proceedings. Even though the Commission of the European Communities, having known of the existence of the cartel for some time, had taken no action, if the companies had been compelled to produce the documents it was not fanciful to assume that this would have tended to increase the risk, to which the companies had already been exposed, of proceedings for the recovery of a penalty.

Commentary

Section 14 of the Civil Evidence Act 1968 is a statutory formulation of the privilege against self-incrimination which makes clear that, in the context of civil proceedings, the privilege may only be claimed in respect of criminal offences under United Kingdom law and penalties provided for by United Kingdom law, and also makes clear that, again in the civil context, the privilege includes the right to refuse to answer a question or produce a document that would tend to expose a person's spouse to proceedings for a criminal offence or recovery of a penalty. Indeed, the Civil Partnership Act 2004 has recently amended s.14 such that it now also includes the right to a refuse to answer a question or produce a document that would tend to expose a person's civil partner to such proceedings.

Under the common law regime that still applies in the context of criminal proceedings, the better view appears to be that the privilege does not extend to encompass incrimination of a person's spouse or civil partner (Lord Diplock in the *Rio Tinto* case having asserted that the common law privilege is restricted to the incrimination of the person claiming it and not to anyone else). It appears, however, that, as in the context of civil proceedings under s.14 of the 1968 Act, the common law privilege does not encompass exposure to a criminal charge, penalty or forfeiture other than under United Kingdom law (see *Brannigan v Davidson* 1997).

The *Rio Tinto* case demonstrates that the privilege may be claimed where a person is already exposed to the risk that proceedings will be brought if answering the question or producing the document will increase the risk that proceedings will be brought. It appears, however, that the privilege will not protect a person who is already exposed to the risk that proceedings will be brought if answering the question or producing the document will add nothing of substance to that risk (*Khan v Khan* 1982).

Key Principle: **The Courts are entitled to substitute an alternative protection in place of the privilege against self-incrimination.**

A. T. & T. Istel Ltd v Tully 1993

A health authority engaged the second plaintiff company to provide computer services. The plaintiff company agreed to buy the share capital of the second plaintiff company. The first defendant and others had controlled the second plaintiff company and after the sale the first defendant remained a director of the second plaintiff company and still played a prominent part in the management of the second plaintiff company. The health authority then suspected that they were being swindled out of millions of pounds by the second plaintiff company, i.e. by the first defendant and others. The police arrested the first defendant and others, but no one was charged. The first plaintiff then brought civil proceedings against the defendants alleging a large commercial fraud. Buckley J. ordered the defendants to disclose various documents, the order including a paragraph to the effect that disclosure made in compliance with it was not to be used in prosecuting the person required to make disclosure. Wright J. set aside part of the order on the basis that it infringed the defendants' privilege against self-incrimination and the Court of Appeal upheld Wright J.'s decision.

Held: (HL) The Crown Prosecution Service could not be bound against their wishes by the part of Buckley J.'s order that said that disclosure made in compliance with it could not be used in prosecuting the person who was required to disclose but the Crown Prosecution Service had been informed of the order and asked whether they wished to intervene before the Court of Appeal and had indicated by letter that since they had already obtained a large amount of material from the defendants independent of the civil proceedings which they could use in prosecuting them, they did not wish to be heard in the civil proceedings. Thus, since the Crown Prosecution Service could only rely on evidence obtained independent of the civil proceedings, the privilege against self-incrimination was not necessary as compliance with Buckley J.'s order would not create a real danger that the defendants would be prejudiced in criminal proceedings. Thus, the plaintiffs' appeal was allowed and Buckley J.'s order was restored.

Commentary
While *Istel and Tully* demonstrates that the courts are entitled to substitute an alternative protection in place of the privilege against self-incrimination, the case also makes clear that the alternative protection must provide adequate protection. Their Lordships made clear that for an order such as Buckley J.'s to provide an adequate alternative protection in substitution for the privilege against self-incrimination, it is necessary that the prosecuting authorities are notified of the proposed order and unequivocally agree not to use material divulged in accordance with the order either directly or indirectly.

Key Principle: **Where answers that the accused was com-**

pelled to give are adduced in evidence in criminal proceedings, this may result in a violation of Art.6 of the European Convention on Human Rights.

Saunders v United Kingdom 1998

The applicant was chief executive of a company which successfully competed to take over another company. A critical factor in the successful take-over bid was the price of the former company's shares, part of the former company's offer to shareholders in the latter company having been a share exchange. During the takeover bid, the price of shares in the former company rose dramatically but afterwards the share price fell dramatically. The rise had been achieved via an unlawful share support operation which had been funded by the former company. The Secretary of State for Trade appointed inspectors under provisions of the Companies Act 1985 to investigate the former company's affairs. In the course of the investigation, the applicant, among other witnesses, was interviewed by the inspectors. When a criminal investigation subsequently began, the transcripts of the interviews together with other documents obtained by the inspectors were given to the police. The applicant was charged with various criminal offences. The trial judge held that under the 1985 Act, inspectors were entitled to ask witnesses incriminating questions which the witnesses were bound to answer, the answers to such questions being admissible in evidence. At the accused's trial, the transcripts were read to the jury in order to both establish the state of the applicant's knowledge and to refute evidence given by him to the jury. The applicant was convicted.

Held: (ECHR) The Court was solely concerned with the use during the applicant's criminal trial of the statements that he had made to the inspectors, as to require that a preparatory investigation such as that carried out by the inspectors should be subject to the Art.6(1) guarantees would unduly hamper the effective regulation of complex commercial and financial activities, such effective regulation being in the public interest. While the right of silence and the right not to incriminate oneself were not specifically mentioned in Art.6, they both lay at the heart of a fair procedure under Art.6. The latter right presupposed that, in criminal proceedings, the prosecution would not resort to evidence obtained via coercion or oppression in defiance of the accused's will. It was primarily concerned with respecting the will of the accused to remain silent and did not extend to material which the accused could be compelled to provide but which had an existence independent of the suspect's will, i.e. pre-existing documents, breath, blood or urine samples, etc. The right not to incriminate oneself was not confined to admissions of wrongdoing or directly incriminating remarks, because testimony that was obtained under compulsion which appeared to be non-incriminating could later be used by the prosecution, for example, to contradict other statements made by the accused or to undermine the accused's credibility. Thus, what was crucial was the way in which evidence obtained under compulsion was used in criminal proceedings. The applicant had been compelled to answer the questions put to him by the inspectors as a refusal could have led to a finding of contempt of court and a fine or imprisonment. Some of the applicant's statements had been of an incriminating nature because they had contained admissions of knowledge of information which tended to incriminate the applicant. The transcripts had been used in the trial in a way which sought to incriminate the applicant. The public interest could not be relied upon so as to justify the use in criminal proceedings, for the purpose of incriminating the accused, of answers compulsorily obtained in a non-judicial investigation. Thus, there had been an infringement of the applicant's right not to incriminate himself, and he had been deprived of a fair hearing in violation of Art.6(1) of the European Convention on Human Rights.

Commentary

The *Saunders* case makes clear that the admission of evidence in criminal proceedings which has been obtained from the accused by compulsion in circumstances in which statute has abrogated the privilege against self-incrimination is capable of violating Art.6 of the European Convention on Human Rights. Thus, prior to the Human Rights Act 1998 coming into force, the Youth Justice and Criminal Evidence Act 1999 modified a number of statutory provisions (including those with which the ECHR was concerned in *Saunders*) so as to prevent the prosecution in criminal proceedings from relying upon answers that the accused had been compelled to provide. It should be noted that the protection so provided is not as great as the common law privilege against self-incrimination provides where it has not been modified by statute. This is so because the common law privilege does not merely entitle a witness to refuse to answer incriminating questions but also entitles a witness to refuse to produce pre-existing incriminating documents. The amendments brought in under the 1999 Act do not provide such protection because the ECHR in *Saunders* recognised that the Art.6 right not to incriminate oneself does not extend to material which has an existence regardless of the witness's will. Thus, in *AG's Ref (No.7 of 2000)* 2001, admitting documents in criminal proceedings was held not to give rise to a violation of Art.6 even though the accused had been compelled to produce them.

Key Principle: **Compelling a person to answer incriminating questions does not, in itself, inherently give rise to a violation of Art.6 of the European Convention on Human Rights.**

R. v Hertfordshire County Council, ex parte Green Environmental Industries 2000

A council inspector found large quantities of clinical waste stored at two sites. The sites seemed to have been leased or licensed to the appellant and there was no licence authorising the depositing or keeping of waste on the sites. After the council had employed contractors to remove the waste they served a request for information on the appellant under s.71(2) of the Environmental Protection Act 1990, asking for particulars of, for example, those persons or organisations who had supplied the appellant with clinical waste, those persons who had carried clinical waste on its behalf, etc. The appellant replied, asking for confirmation that the answers would not be used in prosecuting the appellant company. The council refused to provide such an undertaking, and subsequently issued a summons alleging that the appellant had contravened s.71(2) by failing to provide the information, which was a criminal offence. The appellant then challenged the s.71(2) request but the appellant's application for judicial review and appeal therefrom to the Court of Appeal were both dismissed.

Held: (HL) The appellant had been right to concede before the House of Lords that s.71(2) impliedly excluded the privilege against self-incrimination. The purpose of s.71(2) was not merely to obtain evidence against offenders but also to protect public health and the environment and the statutory policy would have been undermined if the privilege against self-incrimination could have been claimed. It was more likely that Parliament had intended the admissibility of incriminating answers at a criminal trial to be a matter for the exercise of the trial judge's exclusionary discretion under s.78 of PACE. Further, a s.71(2) request did not form a part of criminal proceedings, and thus did not infringe the principle prohibiting the interrogation of a person who had been charged or accused, s.71(2) did not make provision for oral interrogation, the recipient of the request could answer at his leisure and the fairness of a subsequent criminal trial had not been prejudiced since the judge could exclude the accused's answers under s.78 of PACE.

The European Court of Human Rights in *Saunders v United Kingdom* had indicated that the public interest could not be invoked to justify the admission in criminal proceedings of answers obtained via a non-judicial investigation so as to incriminate the accused, but the ECHR had also indicated that it was not casting any doubts on the propriety of using compulsory powers at the stage when the inspectors had examined the applicant in *Saunders*. Upon the facts of the case before the House of Lords, answers obtained under s.71(2) had not been tendered against the appellant in criminal proceedings and while the council had possessed the power to prosecute, the request for information could not have been described as an adjudication. Thus, *Saunders* did not provide authority for allowing the appellant not to answer the s.71(2) request for information. For these and other reasons, their Lordships held that the appellant had been obliged to answer the s.71(2) questions.

Commentary

This case demonstrates that the abrogation or modification of the privilege against self-incrimination so as to require a person to answer incriminating questions does not in itself violate Art.6 of the Convention, the issue being whether the answers are subsequently relied upon by the prosecution in criminal proceedings. The House of Lords indicated that if a judge in criminal proceedings is faced with prosecution evidence obtained under s.71(2), the matter will be one for the exercise of the judge's exclusionary discretion under s.78 of the Police and Criminal Evidence Act 1984, the judge being required to consider whether, under Art.6(1), he is required to exercise that discretion so as to exclude evidence of the s.71(2) answers.

Key Principle: **Limited qualification of the right not to incriminate oneself will not violate Art.6 of the European Convention on Human Rights provided that it is directed towards a legitimate aim and is proportionate to that aim.**

Brown v Stott 2001
The defendant, who had been drinking, was taken to the police station in relation to the theft of a bottle of gin from a supermarket. At the police station, the defendant, being the keeper of a vehicle the driver of which had allegedly committed an offence to which s.172 of the Road Traffic Act 1988 applied (i.e. driving after consuming excessive alcohol), was required, under s.172, to say who had been driving her car at the time when she would have travelled to the supermarket car park. Had she not answered the question, the defendant would potentially have been guilty of a criminal offence under s.172. The defendant admitted that she had been the driver and was charged with driving a car after consuming excessive alcohol. The defendant subsequently raised the issue of whether it would be compatible with her right to a fair trial under Art.6 of the European Convention on Human Rights for the prosecution to adduce evidence of the admission that had been obtained from her under s.172 at her trial.

Held: (PC) The case law of the European Court of Human Rights made clear that the overall fairness of a criminal trial could not be compromised but also made clear that the constituent rights specifically mentioned by or implicit within Art.6 were not absolute and that limited qualification of those rights was acceptable if directed towards a legitimate aim and proportionate to that aim. There was a clear public interest in enforcing road traffic legislation in the context of the high incidence of death and injury on the roads resulting from the misuse of motor vehicles, s.172 did not represent a disproportionate approach to the serious social problem of maintaining road safety and relying on the defendant's admission would not undermine her right to a fair trial. The section merely required the answering of a single question, the answer to which was not directly incriminating, the penalty for failing to answer the question was moderate and non-custodial and where there was evidence of improper coercion or oppression the court possessed ample power to exclude an admission obtained under s.172. It was not easy to see why a requirement to answer a question was objectionable when a requirement to undergo a breath test was not. Moreover, car owners and drivers knew that they subjected themselves to a regulatory regime that was imposed because they could cause grave injury. Thus, at the accused's trial, the prosecution were entitled to adduce evidence of the answer that she had given under s.172.

Commentary
While *Saunders v United Kingdom* demonstrated that the use in criminal proceedings of answers that the accused was compelled to provide against his will is capable of violating Art.6 of the Convention, *Brown v Stott* demonstrates that the statutory abrogation of the privilege against self-incrimination will not necessarily have this effect even though answers that the accused was compelled to provide are adduced in evidence against him. Rather, the case demonstrates that the admission in evidence in criminal proceedings of answers that the accused was compelled to give may be compatible with Art.6 in circumstances in which the statutory provision under which those answer were provided has a legitimate aim and is not a disproportionate response to that aim.

Legal Professional Privilege

Key Principle: **Legal advice privilege attaches to confidential communications between legal adviser and client that were made for the purposes of legal advice.**

Balabel v Air India 1988
In the context of their action for specific performance of an underlease, the plaintiffs sought discovery from the defendant of: communications between the defendant and the defendant's solicitors other than communications seeking or giving legal advice; of the defendant's solicitors' drafts, working papers, attendance notes and memoranda relating to the underlease; and of the defendant company's internal communications, other than those seeking advice from its Indian legal advisers. Master Munrow upheld the defendant's claim of legal professional privilege but Judge Paul Baker Q.C. allowed the plaintiff's appeal in relation to certain of the documents, namely, documents which did not seek or convey legal advice but which merely recorded information or transactions (whether or not containing instructions to carry the transactions out) and documents which merely recorded meetings at which the plaintiffs were present. The defendant appealed to the Court of Appeal.

Held: (CA) The purpose of the privilege was to enable the seeking and giving of legal advice in confidence and the test was whether the communication was made confidentially for the purposes of legal advice. In applying the test, the purposes of legal advice were to be construed broadly. Thus, while solicitor–client communications conveying or requesting legal advice were obviously privileged, this did not mean that all other communications between solicitor and client were not privileged. Rather, where information passed between solicitor and client as part of a continuum of communications concerning a transaction, such as negotiations for a lease, for the purpose of keeping them both informed, in order that advice could be sought and given, as and when this was required, legal professional privilege would attach to the communications. Thus, the documents that the appeal concerned were privileged, and the defendant's appeal was allowed.

Commentary
The *Balabel* case concerns the form of legal professional privilege that is now commonly referred to as legal advice privilege. Essentially, this form of legal professional privilege attaches to confidential communications between legal adviser and client for the purpose of requesting or giving legal advice. Unlike the other form of legal professional privilege, known as litigation privilege, which is considered below, legal advice privilege may arise whether or not the communications in respect of which privilege is claimed concern litigation. Thus, for example, legal advice privilege arose in *Balabel* even though the communications related to a non-litigious matter (negotiations for an underlease). The significance of the *Balabel* case is in making clear that legal advice privilege does not merely attach to communications which request or give legal advice, but, rather, that it may also attach to other communications between legal adviser and client, provided that, construing the test broadly, the communications were made confidentially for the purposes of legal advice.

Key Principle: **Legal advice privilege does not attach to communications with third parties.**

Three Rivers District Council and Others v Governor and Company of the Bank of England (No.5) 2003
In the context of civil proceedings against the Bank of England for misfeasance in a public office concerning the performance of

the Bank's supervisory duties in relation to BCCI (a bank that collapsed in 1991), the Bank claimed that legal advice privilege attached to certain documents that had come into existence between the time when BCCI collapsed and the making of the Bank's final submissions to the Bingham Inquiry (an independent inquiry that had been set up to enquire into the supervision of BCCI). After the Bingham Inquiry was established the Bank had set up the BIU, composed of three Bank officials, to deal with communications between the Bank and the Inquiry. The BIU's communications with the Inquiry were subject to extensive legal advice from the Bank's solicitors. The claimants did not seek disclosure either of communications between the BIU and the Bank's solicitors or of the solicitor's internal memoranda or drafts, because they accepted that the BIU was the client of the Bank's solicitors and that legal advice privilege thus attached to such communications. Rather, the claimants sought disclosure of documents prepared by employees or ex-employees of the bank, even if those documents had been prepared for submission to the Bank's solicitors. The Bank agreed that legal advice privilege did not attach to documents emanating from independent third parties that were passed on to the Bank's solicitors for the purpose of giving the Bank legal advice. Moreover, the Bank did not claim litigation privilege in relation to the communications because the Bingham Inquiry was not adversarial and as the House of Lords had decided in *Re L (a minor) (police investigation: privilege)* 1996 (a case which is considered below) litigation privilege only arises in the context of adversarial proceedings. The bank did, however, claim that legal advice privilege attached to the documents prepared by the employees and ex-employees. This assertion of legal advice privilege in the documents prepared by the employees and ex-employees had succeeded before Tomlinson J., who held that internal confidential documents which were not communications with third parties and which were brought into existence with the dominant purpose of use in obtaining legal advice are privileged. The claimants thus appealed to the Court of Appeal.

Held: (CA) Legal advice privilege could only be claimed in respect of communications between client and legal adviser. The client was the BIU and, consequently, legal advice privilege did not attach to the documents prepared by the employees and ex-employees, who were not the client. Thus, the Court of Appeal allowed the claimant's appeal.

Commentary

Legal advice privilege attaches to confidential communications between legal adviser and client but, unlike litigation privilege (the other form of legal professional privilege), does not attach to communications between legal adviser or client and third parties. Thus, the crucial issue in *Three Rivers (No.5)* was who or what exactly was the client for the purposes of legal advice privilege. The Court of Appeal treated the BIU as the client, and equated information provided to the Bank's solicitors by its employees and ex-employees with information provided by independent third parties. It should be noted that in *Three Rivers District Council and Others v Governor and Company of the Bank of England (No.6)* 2004 (considered below), which was not an appeal from *Three Rivers (No.5)*, the House of Lords declined to express any views in relation to the correctness of the decision of the Court of Appeal in *Three Rivers (No.5)*.

Key Principle: **Legal advice privilege attaches where the seeking or giving of advice from legal adviser to client takes place in a relevant legal context.**

Three Rivers District Council and Others v Governor and Company of the Bank of England (No.6) 2004

Subsequent to the decision of the Court of Appeal in *Three Rivers District Council and Others v Governor and Company of the Bank of England (No.5)* 2003, the facts of which were considered above, the Bank of England disclosed documents to the claimants, as required by the Court of Appeal's order, but did not disclose communications between the BIU and the Bank's solicitors. The claimants subsequently sought disclosure of further documents from the Bank of England. Tomlinson J. held that legal advice privilege only attached to communications between the BIU and the Bank's solicitors for the purpose of seeking or obtaining advice concerning the Bank's legal rights and obligations and did not attach to communications between the BIU and the Bank's solicitors for the purpose of seeking or giving advice concerning the presentation of the Bank's evidence and submissions to the Bingham Inquiry. The Court of Appeal dismissed the Bank's appeal, on the basis that legal advice privilege did not attach to advice from the Bank's solicitors concerning the presentation of the Bank's case to the inquiry because the advice was not advice as to the Bank's legal rights and liabilities. The bank then appealed to the House of Lords.

Held: (HL) Appeal allowed. The rationale underlying the existence of legal advice privilege was that seeking and giving of legal advice by and to clients so that they could arrange their affairs was in the public interest, that this could only be achieved if the client put the full facts before the legal adviser and that the client might not be prepared to do so unless the client was sure that what he told the lawyer would not be disclosed in the absence of the client's consent. Legal advice privilege did not attach to all advice given by a legal adviser to his client but attached where the seeking or giving of such advice took place in a relevant legal context. Where the position was not clear, the judge was required to consider whether the advice relates to the client's private or public law rights, liabilities, obligations or remedies. If it did not, then legal advice privilege would not apply. If it did, the judge was required to consider whether the communication fell within the policy underlying the existence of the privilege. The purpose of preparing the Bank's evidence and submissions to the Inquiry had been that of enhancing the prospect of the Bank persuading the Inquiry that the Bank had properly discharged its public law supervisory duties in relation to BCCI. The presentational advice given to the Bank by its solicitors concerned what should prudently and sensibly have been done by the Bank in the relevant legal context of the Bingham Inquiry and fell within the policy reasons that underlay legal advice privilege. Thus, legal advice privilege attached to the communications that the Bank's appeal concerned.

Commentary

In *Balabel* (see above), Taylor L.J. indicated that, for the purposes of what is now referred to as legal advice privilege, legal advice is not restricted to telling the client the law but also includes advice as to what the client should sensibly do in the relevant legal context. In *Three Rivers (No.6)* the House of Lords accepted that legal advice privilege will only arise where communications between legal adviser and client take place in a relevant legal context, but held that the presentational advice that the appeal concerned had been sought and given in such a context. It appears, however, that in circumstances in which advice given by a solicitor to his client, such as advice on investments or finance, lacks a relevant legal context, legal advice privilege will not attach to it.

While this is so, it also seems that advice in relation to matters such as conveyancing, tax planning and the drafting of wills, and the information provided by the client to the legal adviser in order to obtain such advice, clearly falls within the ambit of legal advice privilege.

Key Principle: **Litigation privilege will only arise where at least the dominant purpose for which the communication between legal adviser or client and third party was made was that of submission to the legal adviser in anticipation of litigation.**

Waugh v British Railways Board 1980

The plaintff's husband was employed by the British Railways Board. His death resulted from injuries received during a collision involving a locomotive which he was driving. In the context of an action for damages against the Board, the Board, claiming legal professional privilege, resisted an application for discovery of a report made by two of the Board's officers two days after the accident. The report had been made equally for railway operation and safety purposes and for the purpose of obtaining legal advice in anticipation of litigation. Master Bickford Smith ordered disclosure of the report, but Donaldson J. allowed the Board's appeal from the Master's order and the Court of Appeal dismissed the plaintiff's appeal. The plaintiff appealed to the House of Lords.

Held: (HL) Appeal allowed. In order for the privilege to arise, submission to the legal adviser in view of litigation had to be at least the dominant purpose for which the document was prepared (though it did not have to be the sole purpose). Thus, disclosure of the report was ordered.

Commentary

What is now known as litigation privilege (the term was not in use at the time when the *Waugh* case was decided), is one of the two forms of legal professional privilege, the other form being legal advice privilege. As was seen above, legal advice privilege applies in the context of legal adviser–client communications and may arise regardless of whether the communication in respect of which privilege was claimed was made for the purposes of litigation. In contrast, litigation privilege can arise in the context of communications between legal adviser or client and a third party but can only arise if at least the dominant purpose for which the communication was made was that of submission to the legal adviser in view of litigation. It should be noted that for litigation privilege to arise, litigation must at least have been reasonably in prospect at the time when the communication was made (*USA v Philip Morris Inc* (CA) 2004).

Key Principle: **Litigation privilege does not arise in the context of non-adversarial proceedings.**

Re L (a minor) (police investigation: privilege) 1996

In the context of care proceedings concerning the daughter of drug addicts who became ill after ingesting methadone, the girl's mother claimed that the girl had taken the methadone accidentally. A district judge gave the parents leave to disclose the court papers to a medical expert in order to obtain a report concerning the frequency of the child's methadone consumption, the expert's identity to be disclosed to the parties and the report to be filed, the report thus being available for the parties to inspect and copy. The girl's mother obtained a report from an expert witness. The expert's report cast doubt upon the mother's account of the accidental ingestion of methadone by her daughter. The report was filed by the mother's solicitors. Subsequently, Bracewell J. ordered disclosure of the report to the police. The mother appealed to the Court of Appeal, which dismissed her appeal, and then appealed to the House of Lords.

Held: (HL) Appeal dismissed. Litigation privilege did not arise in relation to the report, because litigation privilege was a component of adversarial proceedings whereas care proceedings were essentially non-adversarial proceedings.

Commentary

As Lord Scott recognised in the House of Lords in *Three Rivers District Council and Others v Governor and Company of the Bank of England (No.6)* 2004 (which was considered above), the decision of the House of Lords in *Re L* established that litigation privilege does not arise in the context of non-adversarial proceedings, such as the inquisitorial proceedings with which the House of

Lords was concerned in *Three Rivers (No.6)*. In contrast, as Lord Scott also recognised in *Three Rivers (No.6)*, legal advice privilege may arise in relation to legal adviser–client communications whether or not litigation was in prospect at the time when the relevant communication was made. Thus, legal advice privilege, unlike litigation privilege, may arise in the context of non-adversarial proceedings.

Key Principle: **Where an existing unprivileged document passes through the hands of a legal adviser this does not give rise to legal professional privilege.**

R. v King 1983

The appellant was charged with conspiracy to defraud. The defence requested the prosecution to send certain documents in their possession to a handwriting expert instructed by the defence. The prosecution sought the production of documents that the defence had sent to the handwriting expert for comparison with those sent to the expert by the prosecution. The judge ruled that these documents were not privileged and, thus, the expert was called, produced a document and gave evidence of his findings in relation to it, though the prosecution did not attempt to adduce evidence concerning the instructions that the expert had been given by the defence. The appellant was convicted.

Held: (CA) While legal professional privilege attached to confidential communications between solicitor and expert witness, the privilege neither attached to chattels or documents upon which an expert based his opinion nor to the expert's independent opinion. It was conceded that the document would not have been privileged in the hands of the appellant and no greater privilege could attach to it because it had passed through the hands of the appellant's solicitor. The judge had thus properly permitted the expert to be called to produce the document, and the appellant's appeal against conviction was dismissed.

Commentary

In relation to the ability of the prosecution to call a witness who had been instructed by the defence, it is often said that "there is no property in a witness"; that is, the fact that communications between a party or the party's legal adviser and a witness are privileged does not prevent another party from calling the witness to give evidence of facts perceived by the witness and, in the case of an expert witness, of opinions formed by the witness upon the basis of those facts.

The *King* case is also authority for the proposition that where a document would not have been privileged in the hands of the client, the fact that the document has passed through the hand of the client's legal adviser does not give rise to legal professional privilege. It should be noted that the definition of "items subject to legal privilege" provided by s.10 of the Police and Criminal Evidence Act 1984 for the purposes of the 1984 Act does not include items which were neither made in connection with the giving of legal advice nor for the purposes of legal proceedings.

It should be noted that where a legal adviser makes a copy of a document for the purposes of legal proceedings the copy may be privileged even though the original document is not privileged (*Watson v Cammell Laird & Co* 1959). Equally, where a legal adviser makes copies of or obtains unprivileged documents and ordering the production of the documents might reveal the nature of the legal advice to the client, legal professional privilege will attach to the documents (*Lyell v Kennedy* 1884). Legal professional privilege will not attach in either of these situations, however, if the original unprivileged document has ever been in the control of the client (*Sumitomo Corporation v Credit Lyonnais Rouse Ltd* 2002).

Key Principle: **Once legal professional privilege is established there is no exception to its absolute nature.**

R. v Derby Magistrates Court, ex parte B [1996]

The appellant was arrested on suspicion of the murder of a girl, who had been killed by strangulation but had also been stabbed many times. Having originally admitted that he was solely responsible for the girl's murder, he was charged with her murder. Prior to his trial, however, the appellant made a statement to the effect that his stepfather had murdered the girl, the appellant having been present and taken some part under duress. The appellant was tried for and acquitted of the girl's murder. Shortly after the trial, the appellant was again inter-

viewed by the police and admitted that he alone had killed the
girl, but the appellant retracted this confession when his solicitor arrived. A few months later, the appellant made a statement
to the police re-affirming that his stepfather had killed the girl.
Several years later, the girl's mother brought civil proceedings
for assault and battery against the appellant and the stepfather,
during which the appellant gave evidence that implicated the
stepfather. Rougier J. held that the cause of death had been
strangulation by the stepfather but that the appellant and the
stepfather were jointly responsible for the stab wounds. Nearly
a year after the giving of judgment in the civil proceedings, the
stepfather was charged with the girl's murder. During committal proceedings, the appellant was called by the prosecution
and, during cross-examination, was asked about the instructions
he had given to his solicitors between originally admitting to the
police that he was solely responsible for the murder and making
the statement implicating his stepfather prior to his trial. The
appellant refused to waive privilege, so the stipendiary magistrate granted witness summonses requiring the appellant and
his solicitors to produce all attendance notes and proofs of
evidence disclosing the instructions. Leave was obtained to
apply for judicial review of the stipendiary magistrate's decision
to issue the witness summonses, but the Divisional Court
refused the applications. The House of Lords then gave leave to
appeal.

Held: (HL) Once legal professional privilege had been established, there was no exception to its absolute nature. Thus, the
appeal was allowed and the High Court was directed to quash
the stipendiary magistrate's decisions.

Commentary

In deciding to grant the witness summonses, the stipendiary
magistrate had followed the decision of the Court of Appeal in *R.
v Ataou* 1998. In *Ataou*, the Court of Appeal had held that where
a client claimed privilege against the defendant in the context of
criminal proceedings, the court could order production of the
privileged documents in circumstances in which the interests of the
defendant, who was seeking to breach the privilege, outweighed
those of the client, who was seeking to maintain the privilege. In
the *Derby Magistrates* case, the House of Lords, recognising that
the principle stated by the Court of Appeal in *Ataou* seemed to
conflict with the rule that once privilege has arisen, the protection
given by the privilege continues unless and until it is waived by the

client, and indicating that it was necessary to uphold the privilege in the interests of persons who might otherwise be deterred from telling their solicitors the truth in the future, overruled both the decision of the Court of Appeal in *Ataou* and, also, the earlier decision of Caulfield J. in *R. v Barton* 1972, to which the Court of Appeal in *Ataou* had referred.

Subsequent to their decision in the *Derby Magistrates* case, in *Re L (a minor) (police investigation: privilege)* 1996 (see above), the House of Lords indicated that the decision in the *Derby Magistrates* case concerned the form of legal professional privilege that is now commonly referred to as legal advice privilege. It should be noted, however, that in *Re L*, the House of Lords did not suggest that the court had the power to override litigation privilege but, rather, held that, upon the facts of *Re L*, the privilege had not arisen in the first place.

Key Principle: **Where a party waives legal professional privilege in a document, privilege will be waived in the entire document unless the document concerns several distinct subject matters.**

Great Atlantic Insurance Co v Home Insurance Co 1981
In his opening speech at a trial, the plaintiffs' counsel read out the first two paragraphs of a memorandum from the plaintiffs' American attorneys to the plaintiffs. The first two paragraphs provided an account of an unprivileged conversation. Counsel was not aware that the memorandum contained additional material and did not intend to waive privilege in a privileged document.

Held: (CA) The whole memorandum was privileged because it was a communication from the attorneys to the plaintiffs which related to a matter on which the attorneys were instructed to act as the plaintiffs' legal advisers and the fact that it contained an account of an unprivileged conversation did not alter the confidentiality that attached to it as a whole by virtue of the legal adviser–client relationship. Had the memorandum dealt with two entirely distinct subject matters, severance would have been possible and the plaintiffs could have waived privilege in the first two paragraphs while claiming it in the rest of the memorandum, but this was not the case because the first two paragraphs and the rest of the memorandum dealt with the same subject matter. Even though neither the plaintiffs nor their legal advisers had intended to waive privilege, the deliberate introduction by the plaintiffs of the part of the memorandum into the trial record in consequence of a mistake made by the plaintiffs waived privilege in the whole document. While the plaintiffs had not wished to waive the privilege, it had been waived on their behalf by counsel while acting as their agent.

Commentary

A party who is entitled to claim legal professional privilege, i.e. to claim the right not to disclose a privileged communication to the other parties, may choose to waive the privilege, i.e. to disclose the relevant communications. A party might choose to do so where the party wishes to adduce the relevant communication (e.g. an expert witness's report) in evidence. The privilege belongs to the client, and thus the legal adviser is not entitled to waive privilege on the legal adviser's behalf in the context of proceedings involving the legal adviser to which the client is not a party (*Procter v Smiles* 1886). The legal adviser may, however, waive privilege on the client's behalf while acting within the scope of his authority as the client's agent.

Key Principle: **Where a party acquires secondary evidence of a privileged communication, the party who is entitled to claim privilege may be able to obtain injunctive relief to prevent the other party from making use of the privileged material.**

Guinness Peat Properties Ltd and others v Fitzroy Robinson Partnership (a firm) 1987

In the course of civil proceedings, the defendants' solicitors permitted the plaintiffs' solicitors to inspect a copy of a privileged letter in the mistaken belief that the file in which the letter was contained was a file of unprivileged documents and failed to claim privilege in the letter in their list of documents. The defendants' solicitors eventually discovered their mistake when there was an exchange of experts' reports which both referred to the letter. The defendants' solicitors, claiming that the letter was privileged and had been inadvertently included in the file, wrote to the plaintiffs' solicitors requiring them to deliver up all copies of the letter, to delete all references to it in the experts' reports and to give an assurance that they would not use the letter or its contents at the trial. The plaintiffs issued a summons seeking a further and better list of the memoranda referred to in the letter. The defendants then issued a summons seeking an order restraining the plaintiffs from making any use of the letter. The judge held that privilege had not been lost. He granted an injunction restraining the plaintiffs from using or relying on the copy of the letter and ordering them to deliver up the copy and any further copies and an injunction restraining the plaintiffs from making any use of information derived from the letter. He also gave the defendants leave to amend their lists of documents.

Held: (CA) The defendants had not lost their right to claim privilege because the mistakes that their solicitors had made were obvious ones of which the plaintiffs were aware. The court should have granted an injunction to protect the defendants who had moved promptly once they became aware of the mistake and it had not been too late to put the clock back. Thus, the judge's decision had been correct and the appeal was dismissed.

Commentary
Essentially, at common law, a party who obtains a copy of a privileged document is entitled to adduce it in evidence regardless of how the copy was obtained, (*Calcraft v Guest* 1898), but this is subject to the possibility of obtaining an injunction, in the exercise of the court's equitable jurisdiction, so as to prevent the party from relying upon the secondary evidence (*Ashburton v Pape* 1913). Where the party in possession of the secondary evidence was not enabled to inspect the privileged documents in consequence of the inadvertence of the party who was entitled to claim privilege, the right of the latter party to obtain an injunction will not be dependant on the conduct of the former party (*Goddard v Nationwide Building Society* 1986). Where, however, the former party was permitted to inspect the privileged documents due to the inadvertence of the latter party, the Court of Appeal in *Guinness* indicated that it is normally too late for the party entitled to claim privilege to obtain an injunction, but that injunctive relief may be available either where the other party either procured inspection by fraud or where the other party realised that he was only permitted to see the document via an obvious mistake. Even in these circumstances, however, the Court of Appeal in *Guinness* recognised that the court may refuse injunctive relief on general

equitable principles (e.g. delay in applying for the injunction) and that an injunction cannot be granted where the secondary evidence has already been adduced by the other party at the trial. Subsequent authorities have made clear that even where the solicitor who inspected the privileged document did not realise that there had been a mistake, the court is still likely to regard the mistake as obvious and to grant an injunction if the mistake would have been obvious to the reasonable solicitor (see *Al Fayed and others v Commissioner of Police of the Metropolis* 2001). While CPR 31.20 provides that a party who is permitted to inspect a privileged document by inadvertence may only make use of the document or its contents with the court's permission, the courts seem to adopt the same approach in relation to the exercise of the CPR 31.20 discretion as they do in relation to the granting of injunctive relief (*Al Fayed and others v Commissioner of Police of the Metropolis* 2001).

Key Principle: **Communications made for the purpose of facilitating crime or fraud are not subject to legal professional privilege.**

R. v Central Criminal Court, ex parte Francis & Francis 1989

The police were investigating the affairs of a suspected drugs trafficker and believed that he used the proceeds of his activities to fund the purchase of properties by members of his family. A judge ordered the solicitors of G, a member of the suspect's family, to produce all files relating to G's financial transactions and dealings. A second judge subsequently narrowed the order so as to only relate to the purchase of a particular property by G. The jurisdiction of the court to make a production order under s.27 of the Drug Trafficking Offences Act 1986 did not extend to material which consisted of or included "items subject to legal privilege". Section 10 of the Police and Criminal Evidence Act 1984, which provided a definition of "items subject to legal privilege", provided, in s.10(2), that "Items held with the intention of furthering a criminal purpose are not items subject to legal privilege." The solicitors applied for judicial review to have the production order quashed. The Divisional Court held that for the purposes of s.10(2), the relevant intention includes the client's intention but may also include the intention of a third party, e.g. where the client is the innocent instrument or beneficiary of the criminal purpose of a third party. Thus, even if G has benefited unknowingly from the proceeds of drugs trafficking, the criminal purpose of the suspect was sufficient to bring the case within s.10(2) and the production order had properly been made.

Held: (HL) Appeal dismissed. Items were excluded from the definition of items subject to legal privilege if the items were held with the intention of the solicitor, the client or a third party of furthering a criminal purpose.

Commentary
Section 10(2) of the 1984 Act reflects the common law principle (established in *R. v Cox and Railton* 1884) that communications for the purpose of facilitating crime or fraud are not privileged. This is so even where neither the solicitor nor the client were aware of the criminal or fraudulent purpose.

Public Interest Immunity

Key Principle: **A public interest immunity claim may take the form of a contents claim or a class claim and may relate both to the production of documents or to the exclusion of oral evidence.**

Duncan v Cammell Laird 1942
A submarine built by the defendants sank while undergoing Admiralty tests shortly before the Second World War, most of those on board being killed. In the context of civil proceedings brought by representatives or dependants of some of the deceased which took place during the Second World War, the respondents objected to producing a number of documents because the Treasury Solicitor, acting upon the instructions of the First Lord of the Admiralty, had directed the respondents to so object, the First Lord claiming Crown Privilege in the documents. The First Lord of the Admiralty swore an affidavit stating that he had considered the documents with the help of his technical advisers and had formed the opinion that their disclosure would be injurious to the public interest. The documents included letters concerning the submarine's trim before it sank, reports concerning the condition of the submarine when it was raised, plans and specifications of the submarine, etc. A Master refused to order inspection of the documents, Hilbery J.

confirmed the Master's decision and the Court of Appeal confirmed the judge's order.

Held: (HL) Appeal dismissed. Documents that were relevant and were otherwise liable to be produced were not to be produced where the public interest required that they be withheld, and this test could be satisfied either via consideration of the contents of a specific document or where the document belonged to a class of communications which were to be withheld from production on public interest grounds. The decision to object was one for the minister, who, having seen and considered the documents, had formed the view that they should not be produced on public interest grounds, though where this was not convenient or practicable, the decision could be taken by the permanent head of the department. Before the trial the objection could be taken by affidavit or during the trial it could be conveyed via the production of a certificate signed by the minister, though the court could require the personal attendance of the minister. Where the objection was validly taken it was conclusive and the judge was not to look at the documents before ruling that they were not to be produced, though it was for the judge to rule whether the objection was sufficient to justify the minister in objecting to production of the documents (e.g. that production could result in the government being criticised was not a good ground but that production would be injurious to national defence or diplomatic relations was a good ground). While the appeal concerned the production of documents, the same principle was applicable to the exclusion of oral evidence. The appeal was dismissed.

Commentary

While *Cammell Laird* concerned the production of documents, the House of Lords recognised that the same principle was applicable to the exclusion of oral evidence. Their Lordships also indicated that the expression "Crown Privilege" was unsatisfactory. This was so because what is now known as public interest immunity is not a branch of privilege at all since, unlike privilege, which could be waived by the party who was entitled to claim it, it did not exist for the benefit of the litigant and could be insisted on by the judge even though no objection was taken by a party.

Class claims and contents claims may both still be made though, as is indicated in the commentary to *R. v Chief Constable of West Midlands Police, Ex parte Wiley* 1995 below, the policy of central government is no longer to make class claims.

As the decision of the House of Lords in *Conway v Rimmer* 1968 (considered below) demonstrates, it is no longer the case that the courts will never go behind a ministerial certificate or affidavit in order to determine whether production should be withheld on public interest grounds, though it should be noted that the House of Lords in the *Conway* case did not doubt the decision in *Duncan v Cammell Laird* on its facts.

Key Principle: **The statement of a Minister claiming public interest immunity is not conclusive, the court being entitled to balance the public interest against disclosure against the public interest in favour of disclosure and to inspect the relevant documents prior to deciding whether their production should be ordered or withheld.**

Conway v Rimmer 1968

The appellant, a probationer police officer, was charged with stealing a torch from another probationer, found not guilty but then, following the production of a probationary report, was dismissed from the police force. The appellant sued the respondent, a superintendent, for malicious prosecution. Production of five reports on the appellant which had been prepared while he was a probationer was withheld on the ground of Crown Privilege even though both the appellant and the respondent required their production. Crown Privilege had been claimed via an affidavit sworn by the Home Secretary on the ground that four of the documents fell into one class, and the fifth into another, the production of which would be injurious to the public interest.

Held: (HL) Appeal allowed. The documents were potentially of crucial importance in relation to the issues of malice and want of probable cause. The courts were entitled to balance the public interest in withholding documents or evidence, as expressed by a Minister, against the public interest in ensuring the proper administration of justice (i.e. in ensuring that all relevant material was before the court). Full weight was to be given to the minister's view and there were certain classes of document (e.g. Cabinet minutes) that were never to be disclosed regardless of their content, but there was a wide difference between documents of that type and routine reports. The proper test to be applied in relation to such documents was whether withholding their production was really necessary for the proper functioning of the public service. Where the Minister's reasons could properly be weighed by a judge, the judge was required to consider the probable importance of the documents or evidence on the facts of the case before him. If the judge decided that the documents probably ought to be produced it was best that the judge saw them before he ordered their production and if the Minister had not expressed his reasons clearly the judge would need to see the documents before ordering their production. It was essential that the police were able to claim Crown Privilege in order to prevent the disclosure of information that was potentially useful to criminals, but it seemed improbable that harm would be done by disclosing probationary reports, etc. Thus, the House of Lords ordered the production of the documents for inspection and, following examination of the documents, restored the order requiring their production, there being nothing in them that was detrimental either to the proper administration of the Cheshire force or to the public interest.

Commentary
The House of Lords in *Conway v Rimmer* held that a statement by a Minister claiming public interest immunity does not conclusively prevent the court from ordering production of the relevant documents. Rather, the court is entitled to balance the public interest in favour of disclosure against the public interest against disclosure and to inspect the relevant documents prior to reaching its decision. Lord Reid indicated, however, that there were certain classes of document the production of which should never be ordered. Lord Reid also indicated that the facts of the *Conway* case concerned class claims and that it was unlikely that serious difficulties would arise where a minister stated that the disclosure of the contents of a specific document would be against the public interest.

In *Air Canada v Secretary of State for Trade* 1983, the House of Lords, in the context of RSC Ord 24 r.13(1), which concerned the making of orders for the production of documents for inspection, held that in order to persuade the civil court to inspect the documents in relation to which public interest immunity is claimed it was necessary for the party seeking disclosure to satisfy the court as to the likelihood that they contained material supportive of the case of the party seeking disclosure. Now that disclosure in civil proceedings is governed by Part 31 of the Civil Procedure Rules 1998, it is submitted that where public interest immunity is claimed in civil proceedings the court should inspect the documents in relation to which public interest immunity is claimed if the criteria for disclosure laid down by CPR Part 31 are satisfied (e.g. where a party applies for disclosure by a person who is not a party under CPR 31.17, where the documents are likely to support the case of the party seeking disclosure or to adversely affect the case of another party and disclosure is necessary to dispose fairly of the claim or to save costs).

Key Principle: **Public interest immunity is not restricted to central government and the categories of public interest are not closed.**

D v National Society for the Prevention of Cruelty to Children 1978

An informer told the NSPCC that the respondent's daughter had been ill treated, an NSPCC inspector visited the respondent and found that the allegation was untrue. The respondent, whose health was affected, brought proceedings in negligence against the NSPCC and sought disclosure of documents from the NSPCC relating to the informer's identity. Master Jacob ordered discovery and inspection and while Croom-Johnson J. allowed an appeal from the Master's order, the Court of Appeal reinstated the order.

Held: (HL) The public interest that the NSPCC relied upon in objecting to disclosure was analogous to that which protected the identity of police informers (i.e. if the NSPCC could not guarantee the anonymity of its informers, informers would not come forward and its ability to learn of child abuse cases would be drastically reduced). The three categories of persons authorised by statute to bring care proceedings were local authorities, the police and the NSPCC. There was no general rule that whenever a party claimed that there was a public interest in withholding information from disclosure the court was under a duty to weigh it against the public interest in the administration of justice. The immunity relating to police informers was, however, extended to those who give information either to the NCPCC or to a local authority concerning the neglect or ill-treatment of children. There was no reason for confining the public interest ground of non-disclosure to central government, the effective functioning of an organisation authorised under statute to bring proceedings for the welfare of children being (like that of a police force or a local authority concerning the welfare of children who had been boarded out) a public interest that the court was entitled to take into consideration. The balance of the public interest fell on the side of non-disclosure and, consequently, the NSPCC's appeal was allowed.

Commentary
In the *NSPCC* case the House of Lords recognised that public interest immunity claims are not restricted to central government but, rather, indicated that such claims may also be made by bodies such as police forces, local authorities and the NSPCC. Their Lordships were not prepared to accept that as a general rule the court is required to balance the public interest against disclosure against the public interest in favour of disclosure whenever a party asserts that a public interest against disclosure exists, but, rather, were prepared to extend by analogy the category of public interest that applies to police informers to so as to encompass those who informed to the NSPCC. Lord Hailsham indicated that the categories of public interest are not closed and will alter, by restriction or extension, with changing social conditions and social legislation.

Key Principle: **There are no classes of document that are totally immune from production.**

Burmah Oil Co Ltd v Governor and Company of the Bank of England 1979
In the context of civil proceedings brought by Burmah Oil against the Bank of England, the Crown instructed the Bank to object to producing certain of the documents on its list of documents on the ground of public interest immunity, the Bank itself not having had any objection to producing them. The relevant documents included communications between ministers, communications between senior officials of government departments and of the Bank of England, memoranda of meetings, etc. The certificate signed by the Chief Secretary to the Treasury essentially indicated that the documents related to the formulation of government policy, that their production would be injurious to the public interest and that production should be withheld for the proper functioning of the public service, the claim being a class claim rather than a contents claim.

Held: (HL). There were no classes of documents (even Cabinet minutes) that were totally immune from production. The House of Lords inspected the documents in order to perform the balancing exercise between the public interest in the proper functioning of the public service on the one hand and the public interest in the administration of justice on the other. Having inspected the documents, their Lordships upheld the Government's objection to production, the documents not containing material of such evidential value that an order for their disclosure was, in the circumstances, necessary for the fair disposal of the case.

Commentary
The House of Lords in *Conway v Rimmer* had suggested that there were some classes of documents, such as cabinet minutes, that should never be disclosed. In *Burmah*, however, the House of Lords indicated that this was not the case and that the court would be entitled to order the production of such documents in circumstances in which the public interest in the proper functioning of the public service was outweighed by the public interest in the administration of justice.

Key Principle: **When determining in the context of criminal proceedings whether to order disclosure of material concerning the identity of a police informer the court, having examined the material, must balance the public interest in favour of disclosure against the public interest against disclosure; if the material may prove that the accused is innocent or prevent a miscarriage of justice the court should order disclosure.**

R. v Keane 1994
The appellant was charged with offences concerning the counterfeiting of notes. The defence case was, essentially, that the appellant had just been the driver of a car in which the incriminating objects had been found and that he might have been "set up". The judge refused to order the disclosure of documents relating to the sources of information that had led to the appellant's arrest and permitted police witnesses to decide for themselves which questions they would answer during cross-examination concerning the sources of information and which they would not answer. In reaching this decision, the

judge had known that the prosecution wished to protect sources of information for public policy reasons but had not been invited to view the material in relation to which public interest immunity was claimed and had not known the precise scope of the information that the prosecution sought to protect.

Held: (CA) Appeal dismissed. When the prosecution relied upon public interest immunity, the court was required to perform a balancing exercise, the balance coming down resoundingly in favour of disclosure if the material in relation to which public interest immunity is claimed might either prove that the accused was innocent or might avoid a miscarriage of justice. The prosecution were required to put before the court the material that they wished to withhold if the documents: were or might have been relevant to an issue in the proceeding, if they raised or might have raised a new issue the existence of which was not apparent from the prosecution evidence, or if they held out a real prospect of providing a lead on evidence that was or may have been so relevant or which did or might have raised such an issue. The judge was required to balance the public interest in non-disclosure against the importance of the material to the present and potential issues that were of interest to the defence. The more full and specific the indication provided by the defence as to the issues they were likely to raise, was, the more accurately the judge would be able to assess the value of the material to the accused. On the facts of the appeal, defence counsel had been very forthcoming in relation to the issues that he hoped the prosecution disclosure would have addressed. The Court of Appeal, having examined the prosecution material, was satisfied that there was a public interest in not disclosing it and that had it been disclosed it would not have assisted the defence and, indeed, would have assisted the prosecution. Thus, if the judge had been shown the material he would have decided that the balance clearly favoured non-disclosure. The appellant had not suffered any injustice in consequence of his non-access to the documents and the stance that the police officers had been allowed to take when cross-examined had not resulted in any unfairness to the accused. It would not have been possible for the judge to have permitted defence counsel to have had significantly greater scope when cross-examining the police officers without putting the information that needed to be protected at risk. The appellant's conviction was not unsafe.

Commentary
Where public interest immunity is claimed in relation to the identity of a police informer, as Lord Diplock recognised in *D v National Society for the Prevention of Cruelty to Children* 1978, the balance that the court is required to draw is that between the public interest in favour of disclosure (i.e. ensuring that evidence that might help to show that the accused is innocent is disclosed) and the public interest against disclosure (i.e. if the identity of informers was liable to be disclosed in court, people would not be willing to be informers and the police would be hindered in preventing and detecting crime).

The procedure to be followed by the prosecution in relation to the disclosure of unused material and the making of public interest immunity applications in criminal proceedings (see the commentary to *Rowe and Davis v The United Kingdom*, below) is now governed by statute and rules of court but the statutory provisions have not modified the balancing exercise that the court is required to perform when determining whether to order the disclosure of material in the context of a public interest immunity application. Thus (subject to the of the decision of the House of Lords in *R. v H*, considered below), *Keane* remains good authority concerning the nature of the balancing exercise that the judge is required to perform when the prosecution claim public interest immunity in relation to the identity of an informer.

Key Principle: **In order for a new public interest class to be recognised by the courts, there must be compelling evidence that the new class is necessary.**

R. v Chief Constable of West Midlands Police, Ex parte Wiley 1995

The issue before the House of Lords was whether public interest immunity attached to documents created for the purpose of an investigation into the police under Part IX of the Police and Criminal Evidence Act 1984. The appellants (two Chief Constables) and the respondents (who were bringing or intended to bring civil proceedings against the two Chief Constables) both contended that public interest immunity did not attach to the documents.

Held: (HL) In order for a new class-based public interest immunity to be recognised, clear and compelling evidence that the new class is necessary was required. The class relating to police investigations into complaints tended to defeat the objective it was designed to achieve (i.e. by discouraging rather than encouraging complainants to co-operate with police investigations). No sufficient case had been made out to justify the existence of the class, the cases in which the new class had been recognised having, thus, been wrongly decided. This did not mean, however, that public interest immunity could never be claimed in relation to documents that came into existence in consequence of such an investigation, as there could be reasons why it was appropriate to extend immunity to a particular document in consequence of its contents.

Commentary
The public interest immunity class relating to the investigation of police complaints had discouraged the respondents from co-operating in the investigations because they had regarded it as unfair that the police should be able to make use of the material in the context of the subsequent civil proceedings between the respondents and the Chief Constables while the respondents would not be able to.

Lord Woolf in *Wiley* indicated that where a Secretary of State or the Attorney-General concludes that the public interest in favour of disclosure outweighs the public interest against disclosure, it is unlikely that the court will come to a different conclusion. His Lordship also indicated, however, that where documents in relation to which a class claim could be made are in the possession of parties other than government departments (e.g. in the possession of a Chief Constable), the court might have to intervene to protect the public interest rather than permitting the individual to decide that the documents should be disclosed. This was so as permitting an individual to decide that such documents should be disclosed might undermine the class claim (e.g. if the basis of the class claim was to reassure persons making statements that the statements they had made would not be disclosed). Where the Crown does conclude that the public interest in favour of disclosure outweighs the public interest against disclosure, it is, according to Lord Woolf's analysis, misleading to speak of "waiver" of public interest immunity. Rather, in such circumstances, the position is that the public interest requires disclosure. Similarly, Lord Woolf accepted that where the maker of a statement consents to it being disclosed, this is not a question of waiver but, rather, the public interest may cease to attach to the communication.

It should be noted that since 1996 the stated policy of Central Government has been not to make class claims but, rather, only to claim public interest immunity where the disclosure of material could cause real damage to the public interest. This does not, however, prevent other bodies, such as police forces, from continuing to make class claims.

Key Principle: **Permitting the prosecution to withhold material from the defence on the ground of public interest immunity will not necessarily violate Art.6(1) of the European Convention on Human Rights, but the decision must be made by a judge, not by the prosecution.**

Rowe and Davis v United Kingdom 2000

The applicants were convicted of murder and various other offences. The prosecution had withheld material on public interest grounds without informing the accused. The Court of Appeal, having heard defence submissions concerning the factors in favour of disclosure and the nature of the balancing exercise, reviewed the undisclosed evidence in ex parte hearings in the absence of the defence, ruled in favour of non-disclosure and upheld the applicants' convictions.

Held: (ECHR) It was a fundamental aspect of a fair trial that criminal proceedings were adversarial and that there was equality of arms between prosecution and defence. Moreover, Art.6(1) of the Convention required the prosecution to disclose all material in their possession for or against the accused to the defence, but this was not an absolute right and it could be necessary to weigh competing interests such as national security or the need to protect witnesses against the accused's rights. Only such measures which were strictly necessary were permissible under Art.6(1), however, and any difficulties caused to the defence had to be sufficiently counterbalanced by the procedures followed. During the accuseds' trial, the prosecution had withheld material on public interest ground without informing the judge, which could not comply with the requirements of Art.6. The procedure before the Court of Appeal had not been sufficient to remedy the unfairness at the trial, the judge having seen the witnesses give their testimony and having been fully versed in the issues and evidence whereas the Court of Appeal had depended upon transcripts and accounts given to them by counsel for the prosecution. Moreover, the judge could have monitored the need for disclosure throughout the trial, assessing the importance of the undisclosed evidence as new issues emerged. Thus, the failure of the prosecution to lay the undisclosed evidence before the trial judge in order that he could rule on the disclosure issue had deprived the accused of a fair trial. Consequently, there had been a violation of Article 6(1) of the European Convention on Human Rights.

Commentary
It should be noted that subsequent to the trial that eventually lead to the case of *Rowe and Davis* going before the ECHR but prior to the decision of the ECHR in *Rowe and Davis*, the Court of Appeal in *R. v Ward* 1993 (a decision of which the ECHR in *Rowe and Davis* was aware) made clear that in English Law it was for the court, and not for the prosecuting authorities, to determine whether the prosecution were entitled to withhold disclosure on public interest grounds and that where the prosecution were not prepared to put the matter before a court the result would be that the prosecution would have to be abandoned. It should also be noted that while the ECHR held that the appeal proceedings in *Rowe and Davis* were not adequate, for the purposes of Art.6(1), to remedy the defects that had taken place at the trial, it is necessary to judge the fairness of criminal proceedings (i.e. trial and appeal) as a whole and, in appropriate circumstances, it is possible for an appeal to remedy disclosure defects for Art.6(1) purposes (*Edwards v United Kingdom* 1993).

Key Principle: **In criminal proceedings, if the accused could not have a fair trial in the absence of disclosure then disclosure must be ordered even if this results in the discontinuance of the proceedings, though the appointment of special counsel to safeguard the interests of the defence at a public interest immunity hearing will be exceptional.**

R. v H 2004
The appellants were charged with conspiracy to supply heroin. The prosecution case was based on observations of the appellants. The appellants sought disclosure of documents including, in the case of one of the appellants, material relating to covert intelligence sources. The appellant in question wanted to challenge the legality of the police operation and the integrity

of the surveillance evidence. The appellants argued that the judge was required to appoint special counsel to safeguard their interests at hearings held in the absence of the defence. The judge, having only given the documents that he had received from the prosecution a "very perfunctory perusal", ruled in favour of the appointment of special counsel, but the Court of Appeal held that the judge's decision had been premature, because he had not yet looked at the material in detail.

Held: (HL) Appeal dismissed. The prosecution were not required to disclose material which neither weakened their case nor strengthened the defence case, and thus public interest immunity hearings were only be required in borderline cases. Where the court was required to determine a public interest application, the court was required to consider the nature of the material to which the application related in detail. If the material would not weaken the prosecution case or strengthen the defence case, the judge was not to order disclosure. Where, however, the material might weaken the prosecution case or strengthen the defence case, then the judge was required to order disclosure unless there was a real risk of serious prejudice to an important public interest, in which case the judge was required to consider whether the interests of the accused could be protected without disclosure or whether disclosure could take place in a way in which the interests of the accused and the public interest against disclosure could both be adequately protected (e.g. by the editing or anonymising of documents or by the appointment of special counsel). The measures taken were to be the minimum necessary to protect the public interest against disclosure and if the effect of limited disclosure was potentially to render the trial unfair to the accused then full disclosure was to be ordered even if this resulted in the prosecution discontinuing the proceedings. The judge was required to review the position throughout the trial to ensure that the effect of limited disclosure was not to render the trial unfair, to involve the defence as much as possible and to take full account of the defence relied upon by the accused. In general, some measure of disclosure would be possible, and in cases in which the defence could not even be told that an ex parte hearing was taking place, it was questionable whether a prosecution should proceed, as even if special counsel was appointed, no instructions could be received from the defence. On the facts of *R. v H*, the judge had not considered the nature of the material to which the public interest immunity application related and, consequently, his decision to seek the appointment of special counsel had been premature.

Commentary
Prosecution disclosure duties in criminal proceedings are now imposed by provisions of the Criminal Procedure and Public Order Act 1996, as amended, the relevant procedures being governed by Part 25 of the Criminal Procedure Rules 2005 and further guidance in relation to disclosure being provided by the Attorney General's Guidelines on Disclosure. The House of Lords in *R. v H* recognised that, under the 1996 Act, the prosecution are not required to disclose material that is neutral, which damages the defence case or which strengthens that of the prosecution, and that a public interest immunity hearing will, thus, only be required in the case of borderline material. Essentially, depending upon the circumstances, the public interest immunity hearing may take the form of an *inter partes* hearing, an ex parte hearing with notice or even an ex parte hearing without notice. If the judge orders non-disclosure the court must keep the issue of whether non-disclosure remains in the public interest under review throughout the trial.

The decision of the House of Lords in *R. v H* makes clear that where the effect of withholding disclosure would be to make the accused's trial unfair, the judge must order disclosure even if the result would be that the prosecution does not go ahead. The measures taken to protect the material in relation to which public interest immunity is claimed must be as limited as possible, and the defence must be involved in the process to as great an extent as is possible. Finally, so far as the appointment of special counsel to take part in public interest immunity hearings is concerned, the House of Lords in *R. v H* indicated that this would be exceptional and that special counsel should not be appointed unless there was no other way to give the accused a fair trial.

8. ESTOPPEL BY RECORD AND THE USE OF PREVIOUS CONVICTIONS AND JUDICIAL FINDINGS AS EVIDENCE OF THE FACTS UPON WHICH THEY WERE BASED

Key Principle: **A cause of action estoppel will not arise where the earlier proceedings and the later proceedings concern different causes of action.**

Brunsden v Humphrey 1884

While the plaintiff was driving his cab, a van driven by the defendant's employee collided with the cab. The plaintiff successfully sued the defendant in the county court, recovering damages in respect of the damage to his cab. The plaintiff then commenced proceedings in the High Court to recover damages in respect of the personal injuries he had suffered in the collision, and was awarded damages in respect of his personal injuries. The Divisional Court held that the county court proceedings were a bar to the High Court action, so the plaintiff appealed to the Court of Appeal.

Held: (CA) Appeal allowed. The law was that a person could not in different actions recover successive damages for the same cause of action but, rather, was required to recover all damages to which he was entitled in respect of the cause of action when he first brought the action. The plaintiff was entitled to maintain the High Court action, however, because the two actions concerned distinct causes of action. This was so because in the first action the cause of action was the negligent driving and the injury to the cab whereas in the second action the cause of action was the negligent driving and the injury to the plaintiff's person.

Commentary

This case demonstrates that what is now referred to as a "cause of action estoppel" will not arise where the earlier proceedings and the later proceedings concern distinct causes of action, and that this will be so even where both causes of action arise out of the same incident.

The basis of estoppel by record (or *res judicata*) is, essentially, that it is in the public interest that there should be an end to litigation and that a party should not be harassed twice in relation to the same cause of action or issue. In order for a cause of action estoppel or an issue estoppel to arise, it is necessary that the judgment in the earlier proceedings was a final judgment of a court of competent jurisdiction on the merits (*The European Gateway* 1986), the parties in the earlier and later actions were the same (or their privies) and the cause of action or issue in the later action was the cause of action or issue that was decided in the earlier action. It should be noted, however, that in order for a judgment to be conclusive evidence against a party, the estoppel must be "pleaded" by the other party (*Vooght v Winch* 1819). It should also be noted that that a cause of action estoppel or an issue estoppel does not prevent a party from proving that a judgment was obtained by fraud or collusion (*The Duchess of Kingston's Case* 1776).

Key Principle: **A cause of action estoppel may prevent the re-litigation of a cause of action which had already been determined by a court of competent jurisdiction.**

Conquer v Boot 1928

In 1924, the defendant, a builder, contracted to build a bungalow for the plaintiff, agreeing to complete the bungalow "in a good and workmanlike manner". In 1926, the plaintiff successfully sued the defendant in the county court for damages for breach of contract, the particulars of claim indicating that the claim was for breach of contract to complete the bungalow in a good and workmanlike manner, particulars being given of a number of defects. In 1927 the plaintiff brought a second county court action against the defendant, the particulars of claim indicating that the claim was for breach of contract to complete the bungalow in a good and workmanlike manner and with proper materials and for damage to linoleum ruined by dampness as a result of this negligence. When asked to give further and better particulars, the plaintiff gave a list of particulars that were different to those that he had set out in the first action. The defendant relied upon the defence of *res judicata* and the county court judge allowed the plea of *res judicata* so far as a claim for a manhole and airbricks was concerned as this had been obvious at the time of the first action between the same parties but disallowed the plea so far as the bulk of the claim was concerned because the state of dampness and rottenness of the premise had not been apparent at the time of the earlier action.

Held: (CA) Appeal allowed. The particulars were identical in both actions, the only difference being that in the second action the words "and proper materials" had been added to them, the claim in both cases being for a breach of contract to complete the bungalow in a good and workmanlike manner. In *Brunsden v Humphrey* there had been one wrongful act but two distinct causes of action. The plaintiff in *Brunsden v Humphrey* could not, however, have brought several actions in relation to the damage to the cab, e.g. one for a broken wheel, one for a broken window, etc. Equally, the plaintiff in the instant case could not have brought one action for failure to complete the dining room in a proper and workmanlike manner, one for failure to complete the drawing room in a good and workmanlike manner, etc. The instant case fell within the rule of law, stated by Bowen L.J. in *Brunsden v Humphrey*, that damages resulting from a single cause of action had to be assessed and recovered once and for all. The cause of action in the instant case was breach of the contract to complete the bungalow in a good and workmanlike manner and every breach of it, i.e. every brick or every room, did not give rise to a separate cause of action. Thus, the plaintiff could not, by adding further particulars of damage, recover in another action on the same particulars of claim but, rather, having recovered judgment in the first action, was debarred from bringing the second action.

Commentary

This case demonstrates that where a court of competent jurisdiction determines a cause of action between two parties, what is now known as a cause of action estoppel will, if pleaded by one of the parties, prevent the re-litigation of the cause of action in subsequent proceedings between the same parties. In fact, this is so whether the original action was successful or unsuccessful (*Thoday v Thoday* 1964) and whether the parties to the latter proceedings are the same as the parties to the former proceedings or are in privity with the parties to the former proceedings (*House of Spring Gardens Ltd v Waite* 1991).

Key Principle: **An estoppel by record does not arise where a party litigates in a different capacity to that in which the party litigated in the earlier proceedings.**

Marginson v Blackburn Borough Council 1939

Mr Marginson was suing the Council both on his own behalf and as the administrator of his deceased wife. The action concerned a road traffic accident in which Mr Marginson was injured and his wife was killed due, Mr Marginson alleged, to the negligence of a bus driver employed by the Council. The Council claimed that Mr Marginson was estopped from making a claim or recovering damages in consequence of county court proceedings in 1937, but Lewis J. held that the Council's plea of estoppel failed. In the 1937 proceedings, the owners of premises into which the bus had crashed following the collision with the car which Mrs Marginson had been driving had brought proceedings against both the Council and Mr Marginson (his wife having driven the car as his "servant"). In the course of these proceedings the Council and Mr Marginson had brought claims for indemnity and contribution against each other by third party notice and the Council had also claimed damages against Mr Marginson in its third party notice. The county court judge had held that both defendants were to blame, and bore the loss in equal proportions, and had also held that he was entitled to award no damages to the Council because the defendants had been equally to blame for the damage to the Council's bus. [*Note: at the time when the Marginson case was decided, if contributory negligence was established no damages were recovered.*]

Held: (CA) The county court judge in 1937 had made a direct decision between Mr Marginson and the Council that they were both to blame for the accident. This was a clear decision on the same issue between the same persons and conclusively established that both were equally to blame and, consequently, Mr Marginson was estopped from bringing his personal claim for damages. As regards the claim in respect of which Mr Marginson was suing as the personal representative of his deceased wife's estate, however, no estoppel arose from the county court decision. This was so because since the claim in the county court had been brought against Mr Marginson in his personal capacity, the county court decision was not conclusive against Mr Marginson in his representative capacity, Mr Marginson, in law, being, in the two capacities, two separate and distinct persons.

Commentary

In the *Marginson* case an estoppel by record arose to prevent Mr Marginson from re-litigating the same issue against the council in his personal capacity but did not prevent him from re-litigating the same issue against the council in his representative capacity. The case appears to provide an example of what is now known as issue estoppel.

Key Principle: **An estoppel by record does not arise where the parties to the later proceedings are not the parties to the earlier proceedings or their privies.**

Townsend v Bishop 1939

The case, which came before Lewis J. in 1939, concerned an alleged collision, in 1937, between a car, driven by the plaintiff, Leslie Townsend (who was the son of the man who owned the car, Walter Townsend) and a lorry, driven by an employee of the defendant. Leslie Townsend, asserting negligence on the part of the defendant, his servant or agent, claimed damages in respect of his personal injuries and special damages in respect of doctor's and hospital fees and his loss of the share of the profits of his father's business while he was incapacitated. The defendant denied negligence and claimed that the accident was either caused or contributed to by Leslie Townsend. In 1937, Walter Townsend, asserting negligence on the part of the defendant, his servant or agent, had brought a claim against the defendant, claiming damages for the damage to his car and the loss of the services of his son (who was his employee) while he was injured. The defendant had denied negligence and had claimed that the accident was either caused or contributed to by Walter Townsend, his servant or agent. The county court judge had found for the defendant, the judge having found that the defendant had not been negligent but that Walter Townsend, having done "a dangerous thing", had been negligent (in reality, of course, it was Leslie Townsend who, as Walter's servant or agent, had done the "dangerous thing").

Held: (KBD) The doctrine of *res judicata* did not apply, i.e. an estoppel did not arise, because the 1939 litigation was not between the same parties as the 1937 litigation.

Commentary

While Leslie Townsend had been the agent of a party to the 1937 proceedings in which he had been found guilty of negligence he had not been a party to the 1937 proceedings. Consequently, an estoppel by record did not arise in the context of the 1939 proceedings.

Key Principle: **Where a cause of action estoppel does not arise, an issue estoppel may prevent the re-litigation of an issue between parties to earlier proceedings.**

Wall v Radford 1991

The plaintiff, Miss Wall, claiming damages in respect of her personal injuries, alleged that she had to swerve to avoid a car that had overturned while being driven by the defendant, Mr Radford, and had thus collided with another vehicle. The plaintiff's passenger, Mrs Vernon, who was also injured in the accident, had previously brought a successful action against Miss Wall and Mr Radford, the county court judge finding Miss Wall and Mr Radford each 50 per cent liable.

Held: (QBD) The case was one of issue estoppel. While a driver owed a separate duty to another driver to that owed to a passenger, that did not mean that these duties differed in any way on the facts of the instant case. In the instant case, the facts that gave rise to the breach of duty and liability for the breach were both identical, the duty not being a different duty but, rather, being the same duty owed to a different person. Thus, the issue was decided in favour of the defendant, the plaintiff was not permitted to re-litigate the issue of her 50 per cent liability for the collision, and judgment was given for the plaintiff for 50 per cent of the damages.

Commentary

Upon the facts of *Wall v Radford* no cause of action estoppel arose, the cause of action that the case concerned not having been litigated between the parties in the earlier proceedings, but an issue estoppel prevented the plaintiff, Miss Wall, from recovering more than 50 per cent of the damages, the court in the earlier proceedings having found the parties each 50 per cent liable.

Key Principle: **The existence of special circumstances may provide an exception to issue estoppel but not to cause of action estoppel.**

Arnold v National Westminster Bank 1991

The appellants were landlords of premises let to the defendants. The lease provided for rent reviews on five specified periods and provided that, in default of agreement, a fair market rent was to be fixed by arbitration. When the first rent review date came up the arbitrator decided that under the definition of "fair market rent", the hypothetical lease that he was required to consider contained the same provision for rent reviews as the actual lease. On appeal, Walton J. held that the hypothetical lease should have been treated as not containing any provision for rent review. Subsequent case law suggested, however, that Walton J. had made an error of law. Thus, when the second rent review date came up, the plaintiffs brought an action claiming that the rent review clause should be taken into account and the defendants claimed that the plaintiffs were barred by an issue estoppel from re-litigating the point that Walton J. had decided. The Vice-Chancellor held that the plaintiffs were not barred from re-litigating the point because special circumstances could prevent an issue estoppel from arising and these included both the discovery of new facts that were not available at the time of the first decision and a subsequent change in the law. The Court of Appeal affirmed the Vice-Chancellor's judgment.

Held: (HL) Appeal dismissed. The appeal raised an important question concerning the availability of, and the extent of the exceptions to, issue estoppel. Cause of action estoppel arose when the cause of action in the later proceedings was identical to that in earlier proceedings between the same parties or their privies which involved the same subject matter. Where a cause of action estoppel arose, the bar was absolute in the absence of an allegation of fraud or collusion and the discovery of new facts did not permit the earlier judgment to be reopened. Issue estoppel arose where an issue that formed a necessary ingredient in a cause of action had been litigated and in subsequent proceedings between the same parties which involved a different cause of action to which the same issue was relevant one of the parties sought to reopen the issue. There was an exception to issue estoppel in the special circumstances in which further material which could not have been adduced in the earlier proceedings by reasonable diligence and which was relevant to the correct determination of a point that was involved in the earlier proceedings had become available to a party. The Vice-Chancellor had correctly held that such special circumstances were not confined to matters of fact but could also take the form of a change in the law. The decision of Walton J. had been plainly wrong and the case presented special circumstances which required the plaintiffs to be permitted to reopen the question of construction that Walton J. had decided against them.

Commentary
A cause of action estoppel provides an absolute bar to re-litigation in the absence of fraud. In the case of an issue estoppel, however, apart from fraud, an exception exists where special circumstances (i.e. the discovery of new facts or a change in the law) justify the re-opening of an issue.

Key Principle: **It may be an abuse of process for a party to raise a matter in later proceedings that the party could have raised in earlier proceedings.**

Talbot v Berkshire County Council 1994
The plaintiff, Stephen Talbot, was driving his car when he drove into a pool of water on the road, lost control and hit a tree, both the plaintiff and his passenger, Miss Bishop, being injured. Miss Bishop brought an action against Stephen Talbot. Stephen Talbot's insurers' solicitors issued a third party notice against the County Council, alleging nuisance and negligence and claiming contribution but not claiming damages in respect of Stephen Talbot's personal injuries. Miss Bishop joined the County Council as second defendant. Miss Bishop's action was successful, the court apportioning the blame two-thirds against Stephen Talbot and one-third against the council. Stephen Talbot then issued a claim against the County Council and Otton J. held that while Stephen Talbot was prima facie estopped from bringing the action, special circumstances enabled the court to permit him to pursue the action.

Held: (CA) In *Henderson v Henderson* 1843, the court had held that parties to litigation are required to bring their whole case forward and that the plea of *res judicata* applied, other than in special circumstances, not just to the points that the court was required to determine but also to points that properly belonged to the subject of the litigation that the parties, had they exercised reasonable diligence, might have brought forward. This part of the rule in *Henderson v Henderson* was not a true case of *res judicata* but, rather, under the rule, the court would stay or strike out an action as an abuse of process in order to prevent a multiplicity of actions, it being in the public interest that there should be an end to litigation. Had *Henderson v Henderson* been cited in *Brunsden v Humphrey* (considered above) the decision might have been different and had it been relied upon in *Wall v Radford* (considered above) it might have afforded a complete answer to the claim. Upon the facts of the instant case, the plaintiff's claim could and should have been brought at the time of Miss Bishop's action and there were no special circumstances that required that the rule should not apply.

Commentary
The rule in the *Henderson* case is not a form of cause of action estoppel or issue estoppel, though it is based upon the same public policy considerations (see *Johnson v Gore Wood*, below). Rather, the effect of the "rule" is that where a party fails to raise an issue that he could raise in the context of civil proceedings, it may be an abuse of process for the party to raise the issue in subsequent proceedings. The rule, as it was applied by the Court of Appeal in the *Talbot* case, applied unless special circumstances required that it did not apply. Subsequently, however, in *Johnson v Gore Wood* (see below) the House of Lords indicated that in determining whether it was an abuse of process to raise a matter in later proceedings that could have been raised in earlier proceedings the court should make a "broad merits-based judgment" rather than adopting "too dogmatic an approach".

Key Principle: **In determining whether seeking to litigate a matter that could have been litigated in earlier proceedings amounts to an abuse of process under the rule in *Henderson v Henderson*, the court should make a broad merits-based judgment rather than adopting too dogmatic an approach.**

Johnson v Gore Wood & Co (a firm) 2002
Mr Johnson, the plaintiff, appealed against a decision of the Court of Appeal dismissing his action as an abuse of process.

Acting on behalf of Westway Homes Ltd, a company which, for all practical purposes, was a "corporate embodiment" of Mr Johnson, Mr Johnson had instructed Gore Wood & Co, a firm of solicitors, to act for Westway Homes Ltd in relation to a purchase of land from Mr Moores. Gore Wood & Co also acted, from time for time, both for Mr Johnson personally and for some of his other companies. Problems arose in relation to the purchase, resulting in a considerable financial loss to Westway Homes Ltd, who subsequently commenced professional negligence proceedings against Gore Wood & Co. The action was eventually compromised when Gore Wood & Co paid to Westway Homes Ltd a substantial amount of the sum the latter had paid plus costs. Mr Johnson subsequently commenced proceedings against Gore Wood & Co in his personal capacity, claiming that Gore Wood & Co had also owed him a duty of care and that he had suffered substantial loss in consequence of their breach of duty. His reasons for not initiating these proceedings at the time when Westway Homes Ltd began its action were that he had needed full legal aid in order to bring the action, bringing his personal claim would have delayed the action which would have resulted in Westway Homes Ltd going into liquidation before its action was tried, his financial resources and those of Westway Homes Ltd had been exhausted by the litigation, which had resulted from the negligence of Gore Wood & Co, joining the claims would have resulted in an adjournment of the trial date, the more complicated nature of the personal claim would have had an adverse effect of the expensive and time-consuming work of preparing Westway Homes Ltd's case and Mr Johnson had only had limited time to devote to the litigation because he needed to find new employment. The Court of Appeal held that Mr Johnson was the alter ego of Westway Homes Ltd, that he could and should have brought his claim when Westway Homes Ltd brought its claim, that his reasons for not doing so did not excuse him from not doing so and that that there had been an abuse of process under the rule in *Henderson v Henderson*.

Held: (HL) Appeal allowed. *Henderson v Henderson* abuse of process was separate and distinct from cause of action estoppel and issue estoppel but the underlying public interest was the same (i.e. finality in litigation and not vexing a party twice in the same matter). Where the court was satisfied that a claim or defence should have been raised in earlier proceedings (the onus of so satisfying the court being on the party who alleged abuse) this could amount to an abuse without the necessity of identifying an additional element such as a collateral attack or dishonesty, though such additional elements would make the later proceedings more obviously abusive and a finding of abuse would rarely be made unless the later proceedings involved unjust harassment of a party. The fact that a matter could have been raised in earlier proceedings did not necessarily mean, however, that it should have been raised in those proceedings, so as to render its raising in later proceedings necessarily abusive. Rather, the court, instead of adopting an approach that was too dogmatic, was required to make a broad merits-based judgment, taking into account both the public and private interests and the facts of the case and focusing on the question whether, in the circumstances, a party was abusing the process of the court by seeking to raise an issue that could have been raised on an earlier occasion. There was no hard and fast rule to identify abuse, thus, while lack of funds would not normally excuse a failure to raise an issue in earlier proceedings, it was not necessarily irrelevant, particularly if caused by the party against whom it was now sought to bring a claim. It was preferable to ask whether a party's conduct was an abuse in the circumstances rather than asking whether it was an abuse and then asking whether it was justified by special circumstances.

The rule in *Henderson v Henderson* could apply to Mr Johnson even though he had not been the plaintiff in the first action because Westway Homes Ltd was his corporate embodiment, the test of privity of interest, stated by Sir Robert Megarry V.C. (*Gleeson v J Wippell & Co Ltd* 1977), clearly being satisfied. Moreover, the rule in *Henderson v Henderson* could apply even though the first action had ended in a compromise, a second action being no less harassing because the defendant settled the first action. The bringing of the action was not, however, an abuse of process. If the urgency of obtaining an early favourable judgment was a result of Gore Wood & Co's breach of duty, it was wrong to stigmatise that which was in practice unavoidable as abusive. The approach of the Court of Appeal had been too mechanical and the Court of Appeal had given little or no weight to the considerations that had led Mr Johnson to act as he had done.

Commentary
Following the decision of the House of Lords in *Johnson v Gore Wood & Co (a firm)*, the court should only find that the bringing of a claim or the raising of a defence is an abuse of process under

the rule in *Henderson v Henderson* where the party who asserts that this is so satisfies the court that, in all the circumstances, the claim should have been brought or the defence should have been raised in earlier proceedings, the court being required to make a broad merits-based judgment rather than to adopt an approach that is too dogmatic.

Essentially, privity of interest exists between a party to the earlier proceedings and a party to the later proceedings where there is a sufficient degree of identification between the two parties to make it just to hold that the decision in the earlier proceedings should be binding in the later proceedings (*Gleeson v J Wippell & Co Ltd* 1977).

Key Principle: **The use of a civil action to initiate a collateral attack on a final decision made by a court of competent jurisdiction may be an abuse of process.**

Hunter v Chief Constable of West Midlands 1982

The accused had previously been convicted of murder following a criminal trial during which he had asserted that his confession had been forced out of him by threats and by assaults inflicted on him by police officers while he was in police custody. The trial judge in the criminal proceedings, having heard evidence on the *voir dire*, had found that the assaults had not taken place, and had admitted the appellant's confession. The judge had directed the jury to the effect that if they thought that the accused's account concerning the way in which his confession had been obtained might be true they should acquit him, as the other evidence against the accused had been insufficient to discharge the legal burden of proof to the standard required by law. The jury convicted the appellant and the Court of Appeal dismissed his appeal, at which he did not contend that the trial judge's decision to admit the confession had been erroneous. The appellant subsequently sought damages for the assaults that he alleged had been inflicted on him by the police officers while he was in police custody. The Court of Appeal held that the civil action should be struck out as an abuse of process.

Held: (HL) Appeal dismissed. The proper method via which the appellant could have attacked the decision of the trial judge in the criminal proceedings that the accused's confession was admissible would have been to have done so as a ground of his appeal against conviction. The dominant purpose of the civil action for damages was not to recover damages but was to establish that his confession had been obtained by police violence in order to put pressure on the Home Secretary to release him from his life sentence. The general rule of public policy was that the use of a civil action to initiate a collateral attack on a final decision made by a court of competent jurisdiction (including a decision made by a criminal court) against the plaintiff in earlier proceedings during which the plaintiff had had a full opportunity of contesting the decision was an abuse of process, though where fresh evidence that entirely changed the aspect of the case and which could not have been obtained by due diligence at the time of the earlier trial had been obtained subsequent to the earlier trial, this gave rise to an exception to the general rule of public policy. In the instant case the fresh evidence on which the appellant sought to rely was available at the time of the criminal trial or could have been obtained with due diligence and, in any event, would not have entirely changed this aspect of the case.

Commentary
While it appears that the general rule of public policy is that the use of civil proceedings to initiate a collateral attack on the final decision of a criminal court against the plaintiff is an abuse of process, it also appears that this general rule does not apply where a defendant to a negligence action seeks to challenge a previous conviction upon which the claimant relies under s.11 of the Civil Evidence Act 1968 (see *McCauley v Hope* 1998, below).

Key Principle: **The doctrine of issue estoppel does not apply in criminal proceedings.**

Director of Public Prosecution v Humphrys 1977
The respondent was tried and acquitted of driving while disqualified in 1972. At the trial the respondent had not disputed that he was disqualified from driving but had testified that he had not driven any vehicles on public roads in 1972. The respondent was subsequently charged with and convicted of perjury, relating to his evidence at the earlier trial that he had not driven a vehicle during 1972. At the second trial, a police

officer who had given evidence at the first trial was again permitted to testify that the respondent was the rider of the motorcycle that he had stopped in 1972. The Court of Appeal allowed the respondent's appeal upon the ground that an issue estoppel arose preventing the police officer from testifying at the second trial that the respondent had been the rider of the motorcycle that he had stopped in 1972.

Held: (HL) Appeal allowed. The doctrine of issue estoppel did not apply in criminal proceedings.

Commentary
The doctrine of issue estoppel does not apply in criminal proceedings. Where an accused has previously been acquitted or convicted of an offence, the accused may rely upon the pleas in bar of *autrefois acquit* or *autrefois convict* (though under Part 10 of the Criminal Justice Act 2003 there are now circumstances in which the Court of Appeal may quash convictions for certain offences and order a retrial). Moreover, it may be an abuse of the court's process to prosecute an accused for an offence the facts of which are substantially the same as those which formed the basis of an earlier prosecution.

Key Principle: **Relevant evidence is not rendered inadmissible because it shows or tends to show that the accused was guilty of an offence of which he has been acquitted.**

R. v Z 2000
The accused was charged with rape and relied on the defences of consent and belief in consent. He had three previous rape acquittals and a previous conviction for rape. The prosecution wished to call the complainants from the previous trials to give evidence for the purpose of negating the defences of consent and belief in consent in relation to the offence with which the accused was now charged. The judge ruled that the evidence of the three complainants whose complaints had resulted in acquittals was not admissible because, as the Privy Council had held in *Sambasivam v Public Prosecutor, Federation of Malaya* 1950, an acquittal was binding and conclusive in subsequent proceedings between the parties. The Court of Appeal held with regret that it was bound by the principles upon which the judge's decision had been based and dismissed the prosecution's appeal.

Held: (HL) Appeal allowed. Provided that the accused was not placed in double jeopardy, relevant evidence was not rendered inadmissible because it showed or tended to show that the accused was guilty of an offence of which he had been acquitted. The decision of the Privy Council in *Sambasivam* could be explained on different grounds.

Commentary

While there is no common law rule which prevents the prosecution, in attempting to prove that the accused committed offence B, from relying upon relevant evidence which tends to show that the accused was guilty of offence A of which he was acquitted, the admissibility of such evidence was formerly subject to the operation of the common law rules which governed the admissibility of evidence of bad character as "similar fact evidence" and will now be subject to the evidence being admissible under one of the bad character "gateways" created by s.101 of the Criminal Justice Act 2003 (see Chapter 13, below). As the House of Lords recognised in *R. v Z*, the admissibility of such evidence will also be subject to the exercise of the trial judge's exclusionary discretion either at common law or under s.78 PACE 1984.

Key Principle: **Where a previous conviction is admissible in civil proceedings under s.11 of the Civil Evidence Act 1968, the party against whom the conviction is admitted bears the legal burden of rebutting the presumption on the balance of probabilities but there is no general rule that it will be an abuse of process for the party to attempt to do so.**

McCauley v Hope 1998

The plaintiff was injured in a road traffic accident while a passenger in her friend's car, her friend having swerved to avoid a car driven by the defendant and crashed into a tree. The defendant was convicted of driving without due care and attention and did not appeal against conviction. The plaintiff then commenced civil proceedings in negligence against the defendant, the plaintiff's statement of claim indicating that the plaintiff was relying upon the defendant's conviction as evidence of the defendant's negligence. In her defence, the defendant admitted the conviction but alleged that the conviction was erroneous. The defence obtained a report from a consultant engineer and traffic accident investigator, which concluded that the defendant had not caused the accident. A master then gave summary judgment for the plaintiff and a Deputy High Court Judge dismissed the defendant's appeal, the plaintiff having asserted that it was an abuse of process for the defendant to attempt to go behind the conviction and re-litigate the matter that the criminal court had tried.

Held: (CA) Appeal allowed. *Hunter v Chief Constable of the West Midlands Police* (see above) had concerned an attempt by a plaintiff to go behind his conviction as a collateral attack on a conviction recorded in a court of competent jurisdiction. The closing words of s.11(2)(a) of the Civil Evidence Act 1968 ("unless the contrary is proved") gave the defendant a clear mandate to attack his conviction if he had good cause to do so and could discharge the burden of proof imposed by s.11 to the civil standard of proof. Lord Diplock in *Hunter* had recognised that s.11 was not concerned with using civil proceedings to initiate collateral attacks upon final decisions made against plaintiffs by criminal courts and, consequently, that the public policy under which the use of civil proceedings for this purpose is treated as an abuse of process was not applicable. Thus the defendant was at liberty to attempt to prove that her conviction was erroneous.

Commentary
Section 11(1) of the Civil Evidence Act 1968 comprises one of a number of (civil and criminal) statutory exceptions to the common law rule in *Hollington v Hewthorn* 1943 in which the Court of Appeal held that a careless driving conviction was not admissible in subsequent civil proceedings in negligence, which were based upon the same facts as the previous criminal trial, as evidence of the defendant's negligence. Under s.11 of the 1968 Act, a previous conviction is admissible in subsequent civil proceedings if it is a subsisting conviction (i.e. if it has not been quashed) and it is relevant to an issue in the proceedings, the section giving rise to the rebuttable presumption that the person convicted committed the offence of which he was convicted. As Lord Diplock recognised in *Hunter v Chief Constable of the West Midlands Police* 1982, the party against whom this presumption operates bears the legal burden of rebutting this presumption on a balance of probabilities, his Lordship recognising that rebutting the presumption was "likely to be an uphill task". Whether the effect of s.11 goes beyond merely shifting the legal burden of proof on to the

defendant in circumstances such as those encountered in the *McCaulay* case and the conviction itself amounts to cogent evidence in the proceedings has never been conclusively determined (in *Stupple v Stupple* 1971 Lord Denning believed that the conviction amounts to cogent evidence but Buckley L.J. indicated that in determining whether a party has discharged the burden of rebutting the presumption the conviction does not provide any evidential weight).

While the rule in *Hollington v Hewthorn* no longer operates in the various contexts in which it has been abrogated by statute, the broad common law principle that the *Hollington* case established (essentially, that findings made by a court are not admissible in subsequent proceedings between parties other than the parties to the original proceedings or their privies as evidence of the facts found by the earlier court) continues to operate in civil contexts in which such statutory abrogation has not taken place. Thus, for example, in *Secretary of State for Trade and Industry v Bairstow* 2003, the Court of Appeal held that findings made by a High Court judge who had dismissed a wrongful dismissal claim brought by a company director were not admissible in subsequent director's disqualification proceedings as evidence of the facts found by the judge who determined the wrongful dismissal claim.

Key Principle: **Where evidence of the previous convictions of persons other than the accused is admissible under s.74(1) of PACE it may be that the judge should exclude the evidence in the exercise of his exclusionary discretion under s.78 of the 1984 Act.**

R. v O'Connor 1986

The appellant was convicted of conspiracy to obtain property by deception. The prosecution case was that the appellant and Beck, his co-defendant, had agreed to make a false insurance claim in relation to a van which they falsely claimed had been stolen. The insurance claim had been made but was unsuccessful for reasons that were not connected with the alleged conspiracy. Beck had pleaded guilty and evidence of his conviction was admitted at the trial under s.74(1) of PACE.

Held: (CA) The judge should have excluded the evidence under s.78 of PACE 1984 because the admission of the evidence would have had such an adverse effect on the fairness of the proceedings that it should not have been admitted. This was so because as the details of the indictment, which were admitted under s.75 of PACE and to which the jury were informed that Beck had pleaded guilty, alleged that Beck and the appellant had conspired together, it would have been difficult to contend that the jury would not be entitled to infer from Beck's admission not only that Beck had conspired with the appellant but also that the appellant had conspired with Beck, and Beck was not before the court for cross-examination so Beck's admission could not be challenged or tested by the appellant.

Commentary

Section 74(1) of PACE created a statutory exception to the rule in *Hollington v Hewthorn* 1943 which operates in the context of criminal proceedings. As originally drafted, s.74(1) rendered previous convictions of persons other than the accused admissible in criminal proceedings to prove that the person convicted committed the offence of which he was convicted, provided that this was "relevant to any issue in those proceedings". Section 74 has, however, subsequently been amended by the Criminal Justice Act 2003 (see the commentary to *R. v Kempster*, below).

Where a previous conviction is admissible under s.74(1), this gives rise to the rebuttable presumption that the person convicted committed the offence of which he was convicted (s.74(2)). Section 74 does not render admissible previous convictions which are not subsisting (s.75(4)).

Key Principle: **Where evidence of previous convictions of a person other than the accused is tendered under s.74(1) of the Police and Criminal Evidence Act 1984 (PACE) it is important that the judge ascertains the purpose for which the evidence is tendered both in relation to the exercise of his discretion under s.78 of PACE and in relation to his directions to the jury, should the judge admit the evidence.**

R. v Kempster 1989

The appellant was convicted of several counts of robbery and burglary. At the appellant's trial, the prosecution had adduced evidence to prove that the appellant had been seen with his co-defendants immediately before or after the times when the offences had been committed and evidence of co-defendants' guilty pleas was admitted at the trial under s.74(1) of PACE.

Held: (CA) Appeal allowed. In *R. v Robertson*, *R. v Golder* 1987 the Court of Appeal had held that an "issue" for the purposes of s.74(1) did not merely include an essential ingredient of the offence with which the accused was charged but also included other issues, such as evidential issues that arose in the course of the proceedings. The evidence in the instant case had been relevant to the issue of whether the appellant had taken part in the robberies and the burglary. It was important for a judge to determine the purpose for which the evidence was to be adduced before deciding whether the evidence should be excluded under s.78 of PACE and, if the judge admitted the evidence, it was important that the judge directed the jury in relation to the purpose for which the evidence was admitted and ensured that the prosecution did not seek to use it for a different purpose. Upon the facts of the instant case, if it had been made clear to the judge that the prosecution intended to rely on the guilty pleas under s.74 as evidence of the appellant's guilt and if the defence had referred the judge to s.78, the judge might have excluded the evidence. The jury had been encouraged to rely on the evidence as evidence of the appellant's guilt without the judge having made a clearly informed decision concerning the adverse effect of the evidence on the fairness of the proceedings. The appellant's convictions were quashed.

Commentary

Formerly, s.74(1) of PACE rendered previous convictions of persons other than the accused admissible in criminal proceedings to prove that the person convicted committed the offence of which he was convicted, provided that this was "relevant to any issue in those proceedings". Subject to amendment by the Criminal Justice Act 2003, s.74(1) now renders previous convictions of persons other than the accused admissible in criminal proceedings to prove that the person convicted committed the offence of which he was convicted "if evidence of his having done so is admissible". Thus, it is submitted, in order to determine whether evidence of the previous convictions of a person other than the accused is admissible under s.74(1), it will now be necessary to determine whether evidence of the previous convictions is admissible under the bad character provisions of the Criminal Justice Act 2003 (which are considered in Chapter 13, below). Thus, if the evidence amounts to evidence of the bad character of the person convicted, it appears that the evidence will only be admissible under s.74(1) if evidence that the person convicted committed the offence of which he was convicted is admissible under one of the "gateways" created by s.100 of the 2003 Act (which relates to evidence of the bad character of persons other than the accused). If, however, the evidence either has to do with the alleged facts of the offence with which the accused is charged or is evidence of misconduct in connection of the investigation or prosecution of the offence with which the accused is charged, then, under s.98 of the 2003 Act, the evidence will not amount to evidence of bad character for the purposes of the bad character provisions of the 2003 Act and, it is submitted, its admissibility will be governed by the common law test of relevance.

9. THE HEARSAY RULE AND ITS COMMON LAW EXCEPTIONS IN CRIMINAL PROCEEDINGS

Key Principle: The admissibility of hearsay evidence in criminal proceedings is now governed by provisions of the Criminal Justice Act 2003 (CJA 2003) and a hearsay statement is, essentially, a representation of fact or opinion made by a person other than while giving oral evidence in the proceedings which is relied upon as evidence of a matter stated.

Maher v Director of Public Prosecutions 2006
The facts of this case are considered in Chapter 12, below.

Held: (QBD) The decision in this case is considered in Chapter 12, below.

Commentary
Scott Baker L.J. in the *Maher* case recognised that the admissibility of hearsay evidence in criminal proceedings is now governed by the statutory regime created by Chapter 2 of Part 11 of the CJA 2003. While the 2003 Act does not provide a definition of hearsay for the purposes of Chapter 2 of Part 11, Scott Baker L.J. adopted the definition of hearsay which the editors of *Archbold* 2006 had derived from ss.114(1) and 115 of the 2003 Act, namely, that hearsay is "any representation of fact or opinion made by a person otherwise than in oral evidence in the proceedings in question when tendered as evidence of any matter stated therein". It should be noted that s.121(2) of the 2003 Act, for the purposes of that section only, defines a "hearsay statement" as "a statement, not made in oral evidence, that is relied on as evidence of a matter stated in it." The s.121(2) definition must be read in conjunction with the definition of "statement", provided by s.15(2), as "any representation of fact or opinion made by a person by whatever means . . .", and the definition of "hearsay" which was derived by the editors of *Archbold* from ss.114(1) and 15 must itself be read in conjunction with s.115(3), which concerns the nature of those matters stated to which the provisions of Chapter 2 of Part 11 apply. Thus, as at common law, a statement may be made orally, in writing or by conduct (e.g. in *Chandrasekera v R.* 1937, the statement took the form of the victim of an attack, whose throat had been cut, nodding when asked whether it was the appellant

who had attacked her). The effect of s.115(3) is, essentially, to take implied assertions out of the ambit of the hearsay rule (see *Singh*, below).

Key Principle: **A statement made by a person who is not called as a witness is not hearsay evidence, and thus is admissible, if the purpose of the party who wishes to adduce evidence of the statement is merely to establish that the statement was made.**

Subramaniam v Public Prosecutor 1956
The appellant was found by the security forces to be in possession of ammunition and was charged with an offence of being in possession of ammunition without lawful authority. His defence was that he had been captured by terrorists and was acting under duress. At the accused's trial, the judge did not permit the appellant to give evidence of a conversation between himself and the terrorists.

Held: (PC) Evidence of a statement made by a person who is not called as a witness to a person who is called as a witness was inadmissible hearsay when the purpose was to establish the statement's truth but was not hearsay and was admissible where the purpose was to establish that the statement was made. Here, the terrorists might have made statements to the accused which, whether or not they were true, could have provided cogent evidence of duress. Thus, the appellant had not been permitted to give relevant and admissible evidence, and his appeal was allowed.

Commentary
The case demonstrates that at common law, where a witness was called to repeat a statement made by a person who was not called, the evidence was not hearsay evidence if it was relied upon merely to establish that the statement was made. The defence in *Subramaniam* were merely trying to establish that the terrorists had made threats to the accused which had reasonably caused him to apprehend instant death if he had not complied with the instructions given to him by the terrorists. Such evidence would not have been hearsay evidence, because the defence were not trying to establish that any statements made by the terrorists had been true,

but were merely trying to establish that the statements had been made and that the accused had believed them.

If the facts of the *Subramaniam* case arose today, under the hearsay provisions of the CJA 2003, the position would be the same, i.e. evidence of the threats would not be hearsay evidence and would be admissible without the necessity of identifying an applicable exception to the hearsay rule. This would be so because s.114 of the 2003 Act, which now governs the admissibility of hearsay evidence, applies to statements "not made in oral evidence" in criminal proceedings which are "admissible as evidence of any matter stated". While the threats which *Subramaniam* concerned were not made in oral evidence in the proceedings, the defence did not intend to rely upon those threats as "evidence of any matter stated", but merely intended to rely upon the fact that the relevant matters were stated, i.e. they merely intended to rely upon the fact that the threats were made.

Key Principle: **The combined effect of ss.114 and 118 of the CJA 2003 is to abolish the common law hearsay rules (other than the common law hearsay exceptions that s.118 preserves) and to replace them with a new statutory rule against hearsay that does not apply to implied assertions.**

R. v Singh 2006
The appellant was convicted of conspiracy to kidnap. At his trial, the prosecution had been permitted to adduce evidence of entries in the memories of mobile phones belonging to other conspirators to prove that the appellant was a party to the conspiracy.

Held: (CA) The combined effect of ss.114 and 118 of the CJA 2003 was to abolish the common law hearsay rules (other than the common law hearsay exceptions that s.118 preserves) and to create a new rule against hearsay which does not apply to implied assertions. On the facts of the *Singh* case, the telephone entries were not a "matter stated" but, rather, were implied assertions which were admissible because they were not hearsay. They were also admissible under the common law hearsay exception preserved by s.118(1)7 of the 2003 Act. Section 114(1)(d) provided a further route to admissibility.

Commentary
In *R. v Kearley* 1992, the House of Lords held that that the common law rule against hearsay applied to implied assertions just

as it did to express assertions. Thus, in *Kearley*, the House of Lords held that evidence of telephone calls to the appellant's house from persons asking to speak to the appellant and asking for drugs should not have been admitted to prove that the appellant was a supplier of drugs (even if the evidence was relevant for this purpose, which their Lordships thought it was not). Section 115(3) of the 2003 Act provides, however, that the hearsay provisions of the 2003 Act only apply to "a matter stated" if "the purpose, or one of the purposes, of the person making the statement appears to the court to have been" either "to cause another person to believe the matter" or "to cause another person to act or a machine to operate on the basis that the matter is as stated." Thus, implied assertions of the type which *Kearley* and *Singh* concerned fall outside the new statutory hearsay rule and, if relevant, are admissible whether or not an exception to the hearsay rule would be applicable. In fact, the Court of Appeal in *Singh* indicated that, had the telephone entries that the *Singh* case concerned been hearsay statements, the common law hearsay exception that s.118(1)7 of the 2003 Act preserved (i.e. the rule of law under which a statement made by a party to a common enterprise is admissible against other parties as evidence of the matters stated) would have been applicable or, alternatively, the court could have admitted the entries in the exercise of its inclusionary discretion under s.114(1)(d) of the 2003 Act. In relation to the decision of the House of Lords in *Kearley*, the Court of Appeal in *Singh* indicated that evidence of the requests for drugs that the *Kearley* case concerned would now be admissible to prove that there was a ready market for the supply of drugs from the appellant's house, the jury being entitled to infer that an occupier had the intention to supply drugs.

For another example of the application of s.115(3) of the 2003 Act see *R. v Isichei* 2006, which is considered in Chapter 12, below.

Key Principle: **Hearsay evidence is admissible in criminal proceedings under the common law hearsay exception preserved by s.118(1)4(a) of the CJA 2003 where the hearsay statement was made by a person whose mind was so dominated by an unusual, startling or dramatic event at the time when he made it that the possibility of concoction or distortion may be disregarded.**

R. v Andrews 1987

Donald Andrews and Peter O'Neill were charged with the murder of Alexander Morrow. O'Neill pleaded guilty to manslaughter and testified for the prosecution at Andrew's trial. O'Neill testified that Andrews had stabbed and robbed Morrow at the door of Morrow's flat. Apart from other evidence, including forensic evidence and evidence that Andrews was in possession of property stolen from Morrow's flat, the prosecution also adduced evidence of a statement made by Morrow in the presence of witnesses a few minutes after the stabbing, Morrow having stated that he had been attacked by "Peter O'Neill" and "Donald" (though one witness thought that he had said "Donovan"). The prosecution submitted that this hearsay evidence was admissible under the *res gestae* doctrine, the trial judge ruled that the hearsay evidence was admissible and the Court of Appeal dismissed Andrew's appeal.

Held: (HL) When hearsay evidence was tendered under the *res gestae* doctrine, the primary question for the judge was whether the possibility of concoction or distortion could be disregarded. In answering the question, the judge was required to consider whether the event was sufficiently unusual, startling or dramatic to dominate the declarant's thoughts such that the statement was an instinctive reaction to the event, the declarant having no real opportunity for reasoned reflection. The statement had to be so closely associated with the event that the declarant's mind was still dominated by the event when he made the statement. Where there were special feature relating to the possibility of concoction or distortion (e.g. malice on the part of the declarant against the accused), the judge had to be satisfied that, in the circumstances, there was no possibility of concoction or distortion. Where special features gave rise to the possibility of error (e.g. evidence that the declarant had been drinking excessively) the judge was required to consider whether the possibility of error could be excluded. Where the judge admitted the hearsay evidence, the judge was required to make clear to the jury that it was for them to decide what was said, that they must be sure that the witnesses were not mistaken, that they must be satisfied that the declarant did not concoct or distort and (where special features related to the possibility of mistake) the attention of the jury was to be drawn to the special features. The trial judge's approach concerning the admissibility of the evidence had been impeccable and, consequently, the House of Lords dismissed Andrews' appeal.

Commentary

The statement which the *Andrews* case concerned was clearly a hearsay statement because Morrow did not make it while giving oral evidence in the proceedings (he could not do so, as he was dead) and it was tendered by the prosecution as evidence of the truth of the facts that Andrews had asserted. The *Andrews* case concerned one of a number of common law exceptions to the hearsay rule which may be described as forming the "*res gestae* doctrine", a statement admissible under such a hearsay exception being admissible as "forming part of the *res gestae*". The relevant common law hearsay exception is now preserved by s.118(1)4(a) of the CJA 2003, which preserves the rule of law under which a hearsay statement is admissible if it was "made by a person so emotionally overpowered by an event that the possibility of concoction or distortion can be disregarded". The *Andrews* case confirmed that, as had been held to be the case by the Privy Council in *Ratten v R.* 1971, a statement may be admissible under this limb of the *res gestae* doctrine even though its making was not precisely contemporaneous to the occurrence of the event. Rather, their Lordships recognised that approximate contemporaneity is sufficient provided that the declarant's mind was still sufficiently dominated by the event when he made the statement. Thus, a statement may be admissible under this preserved common law hearsay exception even though it was made after the commission of the criminal acts has ceased.

The Privy Council in *Ratten* indicated that, in order for a hearsay statement to be admissible under this hearsay exception, it is necessary for there to be some evidence of the declarant's involvement in the relevant events other than the statement itself, otherwise the statement could render itself admissible, though it was accepted that in reaching its decision the court would be entitled to take the statement into account. Upon the facts of *Ratten*, the statement had taken the form of a request for the police made by a hysterical woman to a telephone operator from a house in which a shooting took place shortly afterwards (the wife of the accused being killed, the accused relying upon the defence of accident). The Privy Council held that there was ample evidence of the close connection between statement and shooting, they being closely associated in place and time, the statement being made in a call for the police and the caller using a hysterical tone of voice. The Privy Council indicated that the fact that the statement was made in a call for the police and the hysterical tone of voice showed that it "was being forced from the victim by an overwhelming pressure of contemporary event".

It is worth noting that if the facts of *R. v Andrews* were to arise today, Morrow's statement might also be admissible either under s.116 of the CJA 2003 (which relates to statements made by unavailable witnesses) or under the inclusionary discretion to admit hearsay evidence which was conferred upon the criminal courts by s.114(1)(d) of the 2003 Act.

Key Principle: **The fact that the maker of a hearsay statement is available to testify does not as a matter of law prevent the prosecution from adducing the hearsay evidence under the *res gestae* doctrine without calling the maker, but this may be a matter for the exercise of the court's exclusionary discretion under s.78 of the Police and Criminal Evidence Act 1984.**

Attorney General's Reference (No.1 of 2003) 2003

The accused was charged with non-fatal offences against the person against his mother. The prosecution believed that the accused's mother would give untruthful evidence in order to clear the accused. Thus, the prosecution decided not to call the accused's mother but, rather, to adduce evidence of statements made by her, implicating her son, at the time when her injuries were sustained. The prosecution submitted that the evidence was admissible as forming part of the *res gestae* but the judge held that, since the accused's mother was available to testify for the prosecution, the hearsay evidence was inadmissible. The prosecution offered no evidence against the accused, and not guilty verdicts were entered.

Held: (CA). Once hearsay evidence fell within the *res gestae* hearsay exception it was admissible even if the maker of the hearsay statement was available to give evidence. The correct procedure would have been for the judge to have accepted that the hearsay evidence was admissible but to have considered, under s.78 of PACE, whether admitting the evidence would have had such an adverse effect on the fairness of the trial that it ought not to have been admitted. The judge might well have concluded that this would have been the case if the purpose of the prosecution was to adduce the hearsay evidence without giving the defence an opportunity to cross-examine the maker of the hearsay statement.

Commentary

The House of Lords in *R. v Andrews* 1987 (considered above) indicated that where the declarant was available to testify, they would deprecate attempts by the prosecution to rely on the *res gestae* doctrine so as to avoid having to call the declarant, as this would deprive the defence of the opportunity to cross-examine the declarant. The Court of Appeal in the present case held that where the prosecution attempt to do so this does not render the hearsay evidence inadmissible as a matter of law (i.e. it does not prevent the hearsay evidence from being admissible under the *res gestae* doctrine) but that, in such circumstances, the court may well find it necessary to exclude the hearsay evidence in the exercise of its exclusionary discretion under s.78 of PACE.

Key Principle: **Hearsay evidence is admissible in criminal proceedings under the common law hearsay exception preserved by s.118(1)4(b) of the CJA 2003 where the statement accompanies and explains a relevant act.**

R. v McCay 1990

A witness to a "glassing" in a public house attended an identification parade and identified the accused by saying "It is number 8". At the accused's trial for wounding with intent to cause grievous bodily harm, the witness could not remember the number of the person that he identified. The police inspector who had conducted the identification parade was permitted to tell the jury that when the witness had made his identification he had said "It is number 8".

Held: (CA). The judge had properly admitted the evidence because the statement had accompanied a relevant act and had been necessary to explain the relevant act. In asserting that the assailant was number 8 the witness had been explaining his contemporaneous physical and intellectual activity of making the identification. The relevant act had been the physical activity of looking at the suspect combined with the intellectual activity of recognising the suspect.

Commentary

The case concerns the common law hearsay exception preserved by s.118(1)4(b) of the CJA 2003, which preserves the rule of law under which a hearsay statement is admissible if it "accompanied an act which can properly be evaluated as evidence only if considered in conjunction with the statement". The hearsay exception forms part of the old "*res gestae*" doctrine. Essentially, this old hearsay exception renders admissible statements whereby a person explained their contemporaneous acts. Perhaps the Court of Appeal in the *McKay* case stretched the ambit of the old hearsay exception somewhat in treating the statement as one which explained the witness's act. If the facts of the *McKay* case occurred today, however, it should be noted that one of the new hearsay exceptions created by s.120 of the 2003 Act renders statements identifying or describing an object, a person or a place admissible in criminal proceedings, provided that the witness testifies that, to the best of his belief, he made the statement and it states the truth.

Key Principle: **Hearsay evidence is admissible in criminal proceedings under the common law hearsay exception preserved by s.118(1)4(c) of the CJA 2003 as evidence of the existence of a contemporaneous physical sensation but is not admissible under that hearsay exception as evidence of the cause of the physical sensation.**

Amys v Barton 1912

On October 18, 1910, Amys was driving the engine of a threshing machine in his employer's field when a wasp allegedly stung him. Subsequently, he told a doctor who attended him in consequence of a pain in his leg, that he had been stung by a wasp on the 18th while he was threshing wheat. After his death, his widow brought a claim under the Workmen's Compensation Act 1906 and the judge, having admitted the doctor's evidence that Amys had told him that he had been stung by a wasp on October 18, held that the accident had arisen out of Amys' employment.

Held: (CA). There was no evidence that the accident had arisen out of Amys' employment. So far as the statement made by Amys to the doctor was concerned, the rule was that statements as to bodily or mental condition were admissible but that statements as to the causes of bodily or mental conditions were not admissible. Thus, the statement should not have been admitted.

Commentary

The case concerns one of two common law hearsay exception preserved by s.118(1)4(c) of the CJA 2003, which preserves the rule of law under which a hearsay statement is admissible if it "relates to a physical state". The hearsay exception forms part of the old "*res gestae*" doctrine. Essentially, under this hearsay exception, statements made by a person concerning their contemporaneous physical sensations are admissible as evidence of the existence of the sensation. As the *Amys* case demonstrates, however, such statements are not admissible under this common law hearsay exception as evidence of the existence of the sensation.

It should be noted that while the *Amys* case was a civil case, this common law hearsay exception, like the others considered in this chapter, no longer exists in civil proceedings. Rather, the evidence in the *Amys* case would now be admissible in civil proceedings under the general hearsay exception created by s.1 of the Civil Evidence Act 1995 (see Chapter 10, above). Indeed, in civil proceedings, hearsay evidence concerning a person's physical sensation may be admissible under s.1 the 1995 Act not merely as evidence of the existence of the sensation but also as evidence of its cause.

Should evidence of physical sensation be tendered in criminal proceedings, while such evidence would not be admissible as evidence of the cause of the sensation under the hearsay exception preserved by s.118(1)4(c), it should be noted that the Criminal Justice Act 2003 created a variety of new statutory exceptions to the hearsay rule which are not restricted in this way. Thus, for example, such a statement might now be admissible in criminal proceedings as evidence of the cause of the sensation either under s.116 of the 2003 Act (which relates to statements made by unavailable witnesses) or under the inclusionary discretion to admit hearsay evidence which was conferred upon the criminal courts by s.114(1)(d) of the 2003 Act.

Key Principle: **Hearsay evidence is admissible in criminal proceedings under the common law hearsay exception preserved by s.118(1)4(c) of the CJA 2003 as evidence of the existence of a contemporaneous state of mind.**

R. v Moghal 1977

Sadigha and Moghal, her lover, were jointly charged with the murder of Sadal, Sadhiga's former lover. Separate trials were ordered. Sadigha was tried first and was acquitted, her defence having been that while she had been present, she had taken no part in the murder. Moghal, whose defence was that he had merely been an unwilling spectator to a murder performed by Sadigha, was then tried and convicted. At Moghal's trial, the judge had excluded evidence of statements made by Sadhiga to police officers subsequent to the murder concerning her state of mind prior to the murder. Moreover, defence counsel had formed the view that the judge would not permit him to adduce evidence of a tape recording of a family conference several months before the murder in which Sadigha had stated that she intended to kill Sadal.

Held: (CA). The state of mind and feeling of Sadhiga before and at the time of the murder were relevant, but hearsay evidence of a person's state of mind or emotion was only admissible where the hearsay statements related to the person's contemporaneous state of mind or emotion. While contemporaneousness was a question of degree, what Sadhiga had said to the police officers was too long after the event to be admitted as evidence of her state of mind before and at the time of the murder. Sadhiga's state of mind at the time of the family conference was also relevant and, since the tape recorded statements were statements of her contemporaneous state of mind at the time of the family conference, they were admissible. The judge had never been required to make a ruling as to the admissibility of the tape recording, however, so, technically, the absence of the tape recording from evidence had not resulted from an error of law.

Commentary

The case concerns one of two common law hearsay exceptions preserved by s.118(1)4(c) of the CJA 2003, which preserves the rule of law under which a hearsay statement is admissible if it "relates to . . . a mental state (such as intention or emotion)". The hearsay exception forms part of the old "*res gestae*" doctrine. Essentially, this hearsay exception renders statements of a person's contemporaneous mental state admissible in criminal proceedings. The *Moghal* case demonstrates, however, that the common law exception does not render admissible statements whereby a person narrates a past, non-contemporaneous, state of mind. While the ambit of this common law hearsay exception (like the other common law hearsay exception preserved by s.118(1)4(c) of the 2003 Act and the hearsay exception preserved by s.118(1)4(c)) is limited by the somewhat flexible concept of contemporaneity, it should be noted that had the facts of the *Moghal* case arisen today, both the statement made by Sadhiga at the family conference and her statements to the police following the murder would potentially have been admissible under the inclusionary discretion to admit hearsay evidence which was conferred upon the criminal courts by s.114(1)(d) of the 2003 Act.

Key Principle: **Where a witness viewed the commission of an offence via a video recording made by a CCTV system, evidence of what they saw was not hearsay evidence.**

Taylor v Chief Constable of Cheshire 1987

The appellant was convicted of the theft of a packet of batteries from a shop. A video recording of the theft made by a CCTV system had been erased by security officers before the trial but police officers were permitted to give evidence of what they had seen when they had viewed the recording before it was erased.

Held: (QBD) For the purpose of admissibility, there was no effective distinction between directly viewing the commission of an offence, viewing it via the monitor of a CCTV system or viewing it via a recording made by the system. The evidence is not hearsay evidence but, rather, is direct evidence of what was seen to be happening in the relevant place at the relevant time.

Commentary

At common law, a photograph or video recording of a place, a person or an event was not hearsay evidence but, rather, was "real evidence", i.e. evidence that the court could see for itself. Thus, had the video tape that the *Taylor* case concerned been available, the jury could have watched the commission of the offence for itself, no question of hearsay arising. It would, of course, have been necessary for the prosecution to establish that the recording was made at the relevant place at the relevant time and, moreover, it would have been for the jury to determine the weight of the evidence by reference to factors such as the quality and duration of the recording, etc. While the recording was not available, the Divisional Court in *Taylor* held that a witness who viewed the commission of an offence via a video recording equated with one who viewed it live either through the monitor of a CCTV system or in person, the weight of the evidence depending upon factors such as the clarity and duration of the recording, etc.

The hearsay provisions of the CJA 2003 apply to "statements" as defined by s.115(2) of the 2003 Act, i.e. to representations of fact or opinion made by a *person*. Consequently, while a video recording of a person making a statement could fall within the hearsay rule as it exists under the 2003 Act (just as it could have amounted to a hearsay statement at common law), as was the case at common law, a video recording of the commission of an offence which is not relied upon as evidence of matters stated by someone on the recording will not fall within the hearsay rule as that rule now exists under the new 2003 Act statutory regime.

Key Principle: **Printouts, etc. produced by machines did not fall within the common law hearsay rule if the content of the printout did not depend upon information that had passed through a human mind.**

R. v Spiby 1990

The accused was convicted of an offence concerning the importation of cannabis. At the accused's trial, the prosecution had been permitted to adduce evidence of telephone calls from the hotel room of a Mr Zoabir in France to the appellant's home and his club. The evidence had taken the form of printouts which had been produced by a computer in the hotel which, for billing purposes, had recorded information including the number of the room in the hotel from which a call was made, the date, time and duration of the call and the telephone number to which the call was made.

Held: (CA) the evidence was real evidence, not hearsay evidence, because the content of the printout did not depend on anything that had passed through a human mind.

Commentary

At common law, evidence produced by a machine did not fall within the hearsay rule if the machine in producing its printout or other form of output (e.g. a reading on a screen) had not relied upon information that had passed through a human mind. Under the hearsay provisions of the CJA 2003, such printouts, etc. continue to fall outside the hearsay rule because the hearsay provisions of the 2003 Act apply to "statements" as defined by the 2003 Act, i.e. to representations of fact or opinion made by a *person*. Thus, if the facts of *Spiby* arose today, the printouts that the case concerned would still not be hearsay evidence.

At common law, printouts, etc. produced by a machine did fall within the hearsay rule if they contained information that had been implanted by a human (e.g. where, as in *R. v Coventry Justices ex parte Bullard* 1992, information concerning poll tax payments was implanted into a database by humans). Under the hearsay provisions of the Criminal Justice Act, such printouts will no longer be hearsay evidence because, like printouts produced by machines which do not rely upon information that has been implanted by a human (i.e. information that has passed through a human mind), they do not fall within the s.115(2) definition of a "statement". Unlike printouts of the latter type, however, a printout produced by a machine that relied upon data implanted by a human will only be admissible under the 2003 Act if the requirements of s.129(1) are satisfied. The effect of s.129(1) is that a representation of fact that was not made by a person but which depends for its accuracy upon information supplied directly or indirectly by a person will only be admissible if it is proved that the information so supplied was accurate.

10. CIVIL EVIDENCE ACT 1995 (THE CEA 1995)

Key Principle: **Where hearsay evidence is admitted in civil proceedings, s.4 of the CEA 1995 requires the judge, when estimating the weight of the hearsay evidence, to have regard to any circumstances from which an inference can reasonably be drawn as to its reliability or otherwise.**

Solon South West Housing Association Ltd v James 2004
The case concerned a possession order that the judge had made against the appellants in favour of the respondents on the grounds of non-payment of rent, breach of other obligations and "conduct causing or likely to cause a nuisance or annoyance to a person residing, visiting or otherwise engaging in a lawful activity in the community". In reaching his decisions to make and not to suspend the possession order, the judge had considered both the oral evidence of witnesses who were called to give evidence and the hearsay evidence of witness who were not called to give evidence, some of the witnesses whose hearsay evidence was relied upon not being identified because they were afraid both to give evidence against the appellants and to be named.

Held: (CA) Under s.4 of the CEA 1995, the availability of the maker of a hearsay statement went to the weight of the evidence and not to its admissibility, though the court did possess the power under the Civil Procedure Rules 1998 to exclude hearsay evidence. Under s.4 of the 1995 Act, a judge could decide that hearsay evidence that he had admitted was not worthy of weight and, consequently, there was little if any difference between asking a judge to exclude hearsay evidence and asking a judge not to rely on hearsay evidence that he had admitted. In relation to the anonymous witnesses, the judge in the instant case had, with minor exceptions, confined himself to the evidence of those witnesses who were in fear. In relation to the identified witnesses who had not been called (and in relation to some of the unidentified witnesses who were, in fact, identifiable), the appellants could have required the witnesses to attend for cross-examination, but the appellants had not made any applications under CPR 33.4. The hearsay evidence was largely contemporaneous with the events to which it related, some of it was corroborated by the oral evidence of other witnesses and some of it was confirmed by the evidence of the appellants themselves. Fear was clearly a factor that the judge was entitled to consider when determining the weight of hearsay evidence, otherwise the interests of the public and of landlords could not be properly protected. The judge's starting point and primary concern had been the oral evidence and he had concluded that the hearsay evidence was consistent with the pattern that the live evidence had established.

In reaching his decision, the judge had taken the European Convention on Human Rights into account. Reference to the decision of the House of Lords in *R. (on the application of McCann) v Manchester Crown Court* 2002 demonstrated that the admission of hearsay evidence in civil proceedings under s.1 of the CEA 1995 did not cause any general problems under the European Convention on Human Rights. The issue was whether the way the judge addressed the hearsay evidence and the weight that the judge attached to the hearsay evidence had been appropriate and fair, and the Convention appeared to add little to the proper application of the s.4 discretion. The exercise of this discretion by the judge had been appropriate and fair, the judge having approached the matter correctly and in a way which did not adversely affect the fairness of the proceedings.

Commentary
Unless excluded by some other rule of evidence or made or proved by an incompetent witness, hearsay evidence is now generally admissible in civil proceedings under s.1 of the CEA 1995, though the civil courts do now possess discretion to exclude admissible evidence under the Civil Procedure Rules 1998 (CPR 32.1). Section 4 of the CEA 1995 concerns the weight of hearsay evidence that is admitted in civil proceedings. Section 4(1) requires the court to have regard to any circumstances from which an inference can reasonably be drawn as to the reliability or otherwise of hearsay evidence when estimating its weight, and s.4(2) invites the court to consider a number of specific matters such as whether it would have been reasonable and practicable to have produced the maker of the hearsay statement as a witness and the contemporaneity of the hearsay evidence.

Article 6 of the Convention guarantees the right to a fair trial and Art.6(3)(d) specifically guarantees the accused in criminal proceedings the right to examine or have examined the witnesses against him. The House of Lords recognised in *R. (on the application of McCann) v Manchester Crown Court* 2002, however, that Art.6(3)(d) does not apply in the context of civil proceedings. Moreover, even though parties to civil proceedings are entitled to a fair trial under Art.6(1) of the Convention, the Court of Appeal in *Solon* recognised that Art.6 adds little to s.4 of the 1995 Act. It should be noted, however, that where civil proceedings, such as committal proceedings for civil contempt of court, are classified as criminal proceedings for the purposes of Art.6 of the European Convention on Human Rights, Art.6(3)(d) of the Convention will be applicable. This does not mean, however, that the admission of hearsay evidence in such proceedings under s.1 of the CEA 1995 will automatically give rise to a violation of Art.6(3)(d) of the European Convention on Human Rights (*Daltel Europe Ltd v Makki* 2006). For the approach of the English courts when considering whether admitting hearsay evidence in criminal proceedings violates Art.6(3)(d), see *R. v Sellick* 2005, which is considered in Chapter 12, below.

Key Principle: **Where a party to civil proceedings asserts that the maker of a hearsay statement adduced by another party was not competent at the time when he made the statement, the burden of proof is borne by the former party.**

C v C 2001

The case concerned the breach of a non-molestation order under the Family Law Act 1996. Under the order, among other matters, the appellant was not to harass or pester his wife, from whom he was separated, by making allegations about her sexual activities. When the appellant's ten-year-old daughter was collected by her mother (the appellant's wife) following a visit with the appellant, the appellant's daughter told her mother that the appellant had said that she (the mother) was a prostitute who slept with men for money. The appellant was arrested, bailed, and when the matter came before the county court, the appellant was sentenced to eight weeks' imprisonment. The appellant's daughter was not called as a witness in the proceedings, the judge having admitted hearsay evidence of what the appellant's daughter had said to her mother.

Held: (CA) The proceedings were civil proceedings and, consequently, hearsay evidence was admissible under s.1 of the CEA 1995. Section 5(1) of the 1995 Act provided that hearsay evidence was not admissible in civil proceedings if it was shown to consist or be proved by means of a statement made by a person who was not competent as a witness when he made the statement. The competence of a child in civil proceedings was governed by s.96 of the Children Act 1989, a child being competent if the child could understand that it was his duty to speak the truth and the child had sufficient understanding to justify his evidence being heard. The wording of s.5 of the 1995 Act made clear that where a party asserted that the maker of a hearsay statement was not competent, the burden of proof lay on the party who made the assertion. This had not been done in the county court and, moreover, bearing in mind the age of the appellant's daughter and the fact that she was doing well at school, it would have been difficult for the appellant to have discharged the burden of proving that his daughter was not competent when she made the statement. Rules of court made under s.3 of the 1995 Act permitted a party to civil proceedings to call the maker of a hearsay statement adduced by another party, but only with the leave of the court. The judge, recognising that the appellant's daughter was only ten years old, that if she were called she would have to give evidence for one of her parents against the other and that it was reasonable for her mother not to put her daughter in such a difficult position, decided that the appellant's daughter should not be called to give evidence. The Court of Appeal indicated that the appellant did not seriously challenge either the relevance of the considerations that the judge had taken into account in the exercise of her discretion or the exercise of the judge's discretion and, consequently, the issue concerning the admissibility of the hearsay evidence was disposed of in favour of the respondent.

Commentary
Section 5(1) of the CEA 1995, which concerns the competence of the maker of a hearsay statement in civil proceedings, is similar in effect to s.123 of the Criminal Justice Act 2003, which, essentially, concerns the competence of the maker of a hearsay statement which is tendered in criminal proceedings under ss.116, 117, 119 or 120 of the 2003 Act. It should be noted, however, that under the 2003 Act, unlike the 1995 Act, the burden of proof lies on the party who seeks to adduce the hearsay evidence.

The rule of court permitting a party to call the maker of another party's hearsay statement with the court's permission for cross-examination on the hearsay statement is now to be found in the Civil Procedure Rules 1998, the relevant rule being CPR 33.4.

Key Principle: **Where a witness to civil proceedings refuses to attend for cross-examination on a hearsay statement, the court should not automatically exclude the hearsay evidence in the exercise of its exclusionary discretion.**

Polanski v Conde Nast Publications Ltd 2005

The appellant was bringing proceedings in libel against the respondents. The appellant was a fugitive from the USA, he having pleaded guilty 28 years earlier to unlawful sexual intercourse with a 13-year-old girl but having fled from the USA before being sentenced. At the time when he brought the libel proceedings he was living in France and could not be extradited from France to the USA but had he come to the United Kingdom to attend the libel proceedings he would have risked extradition to the United States. Thus, the appellant indicated that he would not attend the trial to give oral evidence but, rather, wished to give evidence, under CPR 32.3, by video link. Eady J. directed that the appellant could give evidence by video link but the Court of Appeal discharged the judge's order. The Court of Appeal also indicated that if the appellant had sought to adduce his evidence as hearsay evidence and the respondents had applied for permission to cross-examine him on the hearsay statements the court would have been bound to allow the respondents' application and if the appellant did not attend for cross-examination the court would have been bound to exclude the hearsay evidence.

Held: (HL) As between the parties, Eady J. had rightly made the order, the Practice Direction supplementing CPR Part 32 indicating that the judgment was to be made on cost saving and whether ordering video conferencing would "be likely to be beneficial to the efficient, fair and economical disposal of the litigation". The issue was, however, whether the order would have brought the administration of justice into disrepute. The order would not have significantly prejudiced the respondents, as cross-examination could have taken place adequately by VCF but, rather, would have been more likely to prejudice the appellant by lessening the impact of his evidence. Refusing the order would have gravely handicapped the appellant, because his oral evidence would not have gone before the jury. A fugitive was entitled to invoke the assistance of the civil courts in protecting his civil rights. Thus, the judge had been right to exercise his discretion so as to make the VCF order, and the appeal was allowed. In relation to the hearsay issue, the court possessed discretion to exclude evidence under CPR 32.1 but if a VCF order had been refused and the accused had not attended for cross-examination on his hearsay evidence the court should not have automatically excluded the hearsay evidence, it being appropriate to make such an order only where, exceptionally, the interests of justice (i.e. the overriding objective of the Civil Procedure Rules 1998) so required. Rather, the rationale of the CEA 1995 was that in general hearsay evidence should be admitted and the court should then attach appropriate weight to it.

Commentary

The rule of court permitting a party to call the maker of another party's hearsay statement with the court's permission for cross-examination on the hearsay statement is now to be found in the Civil Procedure Rules 1998, the relevant rule being CPR 33.4. CPR 32.1 gives the civil courts discretion to give directions concerning the issues in relation to which they require evidence, the nature of the evidence they require and the way in which the evidence is to be placed before the court and empowers the court both to exclude otherwise admissible evidence and to limit cross-examination. Section 4 of the CEA 1995 requires the civil courts, when estimating the weight of hearsay evidence, to have regard to any circumstances from which an inference can reasonably be drawn as to its reliability or otherwise.

Key Principle: **Where a party who wishes to adduce evidence of the contents of a document neither has the original nor a copy in court, oral secondary evidence may be admissible to prove its contents.**

Masquerade Music Ltd and others v Springsteen 2001

In the context of a copyright action, the respondent was required to prove that he had title to the copyrights that the proceedings concerned. In order to do so, the respondent was required to prove that, in 1972, the assignment of copyrights from partnerships to limited companies had been in writing and had been signed on behalf of the partnerships, as required by s.36(3) of the Copyright Act 1956. The respondent did not produce the written assignments but, rather, adduced evidence to the effect that following inquiries the agreements could not be found. The judge permitted the respondent to adduce oral secondary evidence of the existence and contents of the written assignments from a lawyer who had been instructed to transfer the assets from the partnerships to the companies and from one of the original partners. On the basis of the secondary evidence, the judge, on the balance of probabilities, held that that assignments had been in writing and had been signed on behalf of the partnerships.

Held: (CA) Where a party sought to admit secondary evidence of the contents of a document it was for the court to decide what weight should be attached to the evidence in the circumstances of the case. If the party could readily have produced the document then, in the absence of special circumstances, it might be expected that the court would refuse to admit the secondary evidence on the basis that it was worthless. In contrast, where the party genuinely could not produce the document then, in the absence of special circumstances, it might be expected that the court would admit the secondary evidence, attaching to it such weight as was appropriate in the circumstances. Where the circumstances fell between these two extremes, it would be for the court to determine what weight should be attached to the secondary evidence. Thus, the admissibility of secondary evidence depended upon whether any weight was to be attached to it, which was a matter for the court to determine in the circumstances of the case before it. Upon the facts of the *Springsteen* case, the judge had been fully justified in admitting the secondary evidence.

While the respondent could have taken further steps to locate the assignments, he had not been under an obligation to make a search, the only requirement having been to provide a reasonable explanation for their non-production, failing which the court would probably have refused to admit the secondary evidence. Since the appellants had not alleged impropriety or bad faith on the part of the respondent, and there was no suggestion that the claimant's attempts to find the assignments had not been genuine, the judge had been entitled to admit the secondary evidence on the basis that the respondent did not

have the secondary evidence with him in court and could not
have done so without difficulty.

Commentary
Section 8 of the CEA 1995 provides that, in the context of civil
proceedings, where a statement in a document is admissible, the
statement may either be proved by producing the original document or by producing a copy, the document or copy being
authenticated in a manner approved by the court. Section 133 of
the Criminal Justice Act 2003 makes equivalent provision in the
context of criminal proceedings. Thus, had the respondent in
Springsteen had either the original assignments or a copy thereof
with him in court, the contents of the documents could have been
proved under s.8 of the 1995 Act. Where a party who wishes to
prove the contents of a document neither has the original nor a
copy in court, however, s.8 of the 1995 Act (like s.133 of the 2003
Act in the criminal context) will be of no assistance. Rather, in
such circumstances, the court may, at common law, permit the
party to adduce oral secondary evidence of the documents contents, i.e. the judge may permit the party to adduce the evidence of
a witness who read the document.

11. CONFESSIONS AND IMPROPERLY OBTAINED EVIDENCE

Confessions

The admissibility of confessions in criminal proceedings is governed by s.76(1) of the Police and Criminal Evidence Act 1984 (PACE) which provides that:

> "In any proceedings a confession made by an accused person may be given in evidence against him in so far as it is relevant to any matter in issue in the proceedings and is not excluded by the court in pursuance of this section".

Admissibility under s.76(1) is subject to the operation of s.76(2) (exclusion on the basis of oppression under s.76(2)(a) or on the basis of unreliability under s.76(2)(b)).

Key principle: **A confession made by an accused person and used as evidence of the matters stated is a hearsay statement but potentially falls within the ambit of the hearsay exception created by s.76(1) of PACE provided it was wholly or partly adverse to its maker at the time it was made and the court is satisfied that it was made by the accused.**

R. v Hasan 2005

The defendant was charged with aggravated burglary and at trial relied upon the defence of duress. The defendant stated in his evidence in chief that both he and his family had been threatened with harm by a drug dealer with a reputation for violence if he did not carry out the burglary. The prosecution sought to adduce as evidence statements made by the defendant during an "off the record" interview with police officers. The statements were wholly exculpatory in relation to the defendant's involvement in the burglary and therefore did not constitute a confession at the time that they were made. The statements did however contain contradictions to the defendant's evidence in chief, notably, key facts including the dates upon which threats had been made to the defendant being after the date upon which the burglary occurred.

The judge gave leave for the prosecution to adduce evidence of the defendant's previous inconsistent statements in rebuttal of his evidence in chief. The judge ruled that because the statements were wholly exculpatory they did not constitute a confession and therefore did not fall to be excluded under s.76(2)(b) of PACE. The defendant was convicted and appealed to the Court of Appeal. The Court of Appeal quashed the defendant's conviction and held that when determining whether or not a statement is a confession (e.g. whether or not it is wholly or partly adverse to the defendant's case) the decision should be made when the statement is sought to be admitted as a confession. The Crown appealed the decision to the House of Lords.

Held: (HL) Overturning the decision of the Court of Appeal the House of Lords held that even if a statement that appears to be wholly exculpatory subsequently becomes adverse to its maker at some later date, the statement does not then become a confession. The question of whether or not a statement constitutes a confession is to be decided by looking at the statement at the time it was made, in light of the circumstances in which it was made and taking into account the intention of its maker.

Commentary
Section 82(1) of PACE defines a confession as including:

> ". . . any statement wholly or partly adverse to the person who made it, whether made to a person in authority or not and whether made in words or otherwise . . .".

The decision in *R. v Hasan* demonstrates that a statement will only constitute a confession if the statement was wholly or partly adverse to its maker at the time that it was made. There will be situations where a previously wholly exculpatory statement may become adverse to its maker at a later date (e.g. as a result of that person making inconsistent statements in oral evidence). However, this does not render the statement a confession unless it was in some way adverse to its maker at the time that it was made.

Key Principle: **Generally a confession made by a defendant is admissible only against its maker and not against a co-defendant.**

R. v Hayter [2005]

Three defendants were all charged with murder. The prosecution's case was that one defendant, Ryan had been paid by another defendant, Bristow, to kill Bristow's husband. The third defendant, Hayter, had allegedly acted as a middle man in finding someone willing to carry out the killing and arranging payment.

The prosecution's case against Hayter hinged on proving that Ryan had carried out the killing and that the killing had been on behalf of Bristow. The main prosecution evidence against Ryan was a confession based upon admissions he made to his girlfriend. All three defendants were convicted despite the fact that Hayter submitted he had no case to answer on the basis that admissions made by Ryan were not admissible against him. The judge held that if the jury were satisfied that Ryan had carried out the killing and that the killing had been organised by Bristow they could consider those facts when considering Hayter's guilt.

Held: (HL) The House of Lords agreed with the trial judge's (and with the Court of Appeal's) reasoning that the judge's decision did not erode the principle that a confession made by a defendant cannot be used against a co-defendant as the prosecution were not using Ryan's confession to challenge any part of the defendant's evidence. The jury was therefore entitled to take into account Ryan's guilt when deciding whether the defendant was guilty.

Commentary

Under s.76(1) of PACE, a relevant confession made by an accused person may be given in evidence against *him*, i.e. s.76(1) does not render the accused's confession admissible against his co-accused. It appears that the House of Lords in *Hayter* effectively sanctioned a minor amendment to the rule that a confession made by one co-defendant cannot be used against another. This amendment appears to be in line with s.74 PACE (see Chapter 8, above) which allows a conviction to be admitted to prove that a person committed an offence notwithstanding the fact that no other evidence has been tendered to prove they committed it. In *Hayter*, the House of Lords accepted that where defendants are tried together and the guilt of one defendant is relevant to the guilt of another, it would be anomalous to prevent the jury from taking into account any conclusions as to the guilt of a co-defendant when deciding the guilt of the other. Thus, while Ryan's confession was not admissible against Bristow, if the confession made the jury satisfied beyond reasonable doubt that Ryan was guilty, it was entitled to take its finding that Ryan was guilty, which was based on the confession, into account when deciding whether Hayter was guilty.

In general, however, the principle remains that a confession can only be admitted as evidence against its maker, though it is possible for a defendant to "adopt" a confession made by a co-defendant if he accepts that the confession made by a co-defendant, implicating the defendant, is true. In this case the co-defendant's confession also becomes the defendant's confession as it is wholly or partly adverse to his case and he has therefore, in effect, made his own confession which becomes admissible under s.76 (*R. v Christie* 1914; *R. v Gunnerwardene* 1951).

Key principles: **Mixed statements (statements partly adverse to their maker) which are admitted in evidence may be relied on as truth of the matters stated both in relation to the parts that are adverse to their maker and also in relation to those elements that are in his favour.**

R. v Sharp 1988

Police officers responding to reports of a burglary spotted the defendant near the scene running in the opposite direction. The police officers gave chase and the defendant got into his car and drove away at speed. The police officers followed the defendant again but eventually lost him. Three days later the defendant voluntarily turned himself in at a police station and gave a statement admitting that he was in the area at the time of the burglary but giving an innocent explanation as to why he was there.

The defendant was charged with burglary. During the trial the defendant remained silent and the statement he made to the police was admitted as a confession on the basis that it was a "mixed statement" and therefore one that was partly adverse to his defence. The judge directed the jury that it was entitled to rely on the parts of the statement adverse to the defendant as evidence of truth of the matters stated but that any exculpatory parts of the statement were not admissible and therefore could not be considered.

Held: (HL) Upholding the Court of Appeal's decision and quashing the defendant's conviction the court held that where a mixed statement is admissible as a confession the jury is entitled to consider the whole statement including any exculpatory statements made as evidence of the truth of the facts alleged by its maker.

Commentary

For the purposes of determining whether a statement is a confession statements can generally fall into one of three categories: wholly inculpatory statements which amount to a full admission of guilt and are "wholly adverse" to their maker. Wholly exculpatory statements are statements which, at the time they are made, are not in any way adverse to their maker and therefore are not admissible as confessions (see *Hasan* above). The final category, mixed statements, contain both inculpatory and exculpatory elements. Where a mixed statement is admitted in evidence the whole statement is admitted and the jury is entitled to consider both the inculpatory and exculpatory elements.

Key Principle: **When deciding whether a confession should be excluded under s.76(2)(a) PACE 1984, oppression should be given its ordinary dictionary definition.**

R. v Fulling 1987

In September 1981, the defendant Ruth Fulling made a claim to her insurance company for £5,665 to cover the cost of property stolen during a burglary from her flat in Leeds. The insurance company subsequently settled the claim for £5,212. Some years later in July 1985, the police came across information from a known criminal turned police informant that the burglary had in fact been staged to allow the defendant to make a fraudulent insurance claim.

The defendant was arrested and questioned by police. On the first day of questioning she was interviewed twice but exercised her right to silence and gave a no comment interview. She was interviewed again the following day, the interview being split into two parts with a break in the middle.

During her time in the police station the defendant became aware that her partner had been having an affair with another woman who was also being held at the same police station, in the cell opposite her, having been implicated in another crime by the same informant. The defendant confessed soon after finding this out, claiming in her oral evidence that she was distressed and "couldn't stand being in the cells any longer". After being convicted by a majority of 10 to 2 the defendant appealed on the basis that her confession had been obtained by oppression.

Held: (CA) The defendant's confession had not been obtained by oppression. There had been no evidence of impropriety on behalf of the police officers and in his judgment Lord Lane C.J. commented that the court would:

> "... find it hard to envisage any circumstances in which such oppression would not entail some impropriety on the part of the interrogator".

When deciding on whether or not a confession had been obtained by oppression, the word "oppression" should be given its ordinary dictionary meaning.

Commentary
Section 76(2) of PACE provides that:

> "If, in any proceedings where the prosecution proposes to give in evidence a confession made by an accused person, it is represented to the court that the confession was or may have been obtained—
>
> (a) by oppression of the person who made it; or
> (b) in consequence of anything said or done which was likely, in the circumstances existing at the time, to render unreliable any confession which might have been made in consequence thereof,
>
> the court shall not allow the confession to be given in evidence against him except in so far as the prosecution proves to the court beyond reasonable doubt that the confession (notwithstanding that it may be true) was not obtained as aforesaid."

When determining whether or not a confession has been obtained by oppression the court will look for a "causal link", e.g. did the oppression cause the confession to be made? If the answer is yes, then the confession is likely to be excluded under s.76(2)(a) of PACE. It is crucial to remember that s.76(2) provides that the legal burden of proving beyond reasonable doubt that a confession was not obtained by oppression is borne by the prosecution, it not being for the accused to prove that the confession was so obtained.

S.76(8) of PACE partially defines oppression as including:

> "... torture, inhuman and degrading treatment, and the use or threat of violence (whether or not amounting to torture)."

In *Fulling*, the Court of Appeal indicated that when determining whether a confession has been obtained by oppression it should be given its ordinary dictionary meaning which according to the Oxford English Dictionary is the:

". . . exercise of authority or power in a burdensome, harsh or wrongful manner; unjust or cruel treatment of subjects, inferiors etc; the imposition of unreasonable or unjust burdens."

Key principle: **When considering whether a confession was or may have been obtained by oppression the court is entitled to take into account the characteristics of the defendant.**

R. v Seelig 1992

The defendant was charged along with others with conspiring to contravene provisions of the Prevention of Fraud (Investments) Act 1958, it being alleged that they had induced shareholders in a company into entering into agreements by dishonestly withholding material facts. The defendant and his co-defendants had previously given evidence to an inquiry carried out by inspectors appointed by the Secretary of State for Trade and Industry. The prosecution sought leave to adduce evidence of adverse statements made by the defendant to the inspectors. The defendant argued that the confession evidence ought to be excluded under s.76(2)(a) of PACE upon the basis of oppression, the inspectors not having explained the full significance of Part XIV of the Companies Act 1985 (i.e. the fact that his incriminating answers could be used against him in subsequent criminal proceedings) to the defendant. The judge, taking into account both the fact that the defendant was an intelligent experienced merchant banker and the fact that Part XIV had been available for the defendant to read or to take advice on, held that the questioning had not been oppressive.

Held: (CA) The Court of Appeal agreed with the trial judge's decision and reasoning.

Commentary

This case can be contrasted with the case of *R. v Miller*; *R. v Parris* and *R. v Abdullahi* (see below) in which the Court of Appeal suggested that additional protection would have to be given where they were dealing with a suspect who had a very low IQ. In *Seelig*

because the defendant was intelligent and articulate and understood the consequences of any admissions made the confession had
not been obtained in consequence of oppression when applying
the test from *Fulling* (above).

Key Principle: **"Heavy handed" questioning may amount to
oppression.**

R. v Miller, Parris and Abdullahi 1993

Better known as the "Cardiff Three", the defendants were
jointly charged with the murder of Cardiff prostitute Lynette
White and were tried along with two others. Despite shortcom-
ings in the prosecution case including the evidence of the two
main prosecution witnesses being thoroughly discredited, the
absence of any forensic evidence linking the men to the crime
scene and the fact a white man with an injured hand was seen
running from the scene of the crime but that none of the men
eventually charged were white, the three defendants were
convicted.

The convictions largely hinged on admissions made by Miller
during interviews at the police station which implicated the
three men eventually convicted. Miller's confession was admitted by the trial judge under s.76(1) PACE after hearing portions
of the tape-recorded interviews. The three defendants appealed
against their convictions on the basis that the confessions should
have been excluded as they were obtained by oppression; Miller
a man who was borderline mentally handicapped having made
the admissions after denying his involvement in the offence
over 300 times.

Held: The confessions had been obtained by oppression and
would therefore be inadmissible under s.76(2)(a) PACE.
Although the legitimate purpose of interrogating a suspect was
to pursue a line of inquiry, the police officers conducting these
interviews (particularly taking into account the suspect's diminished mental capacity) had clearly overstepped the mark by
continuing to aggressively question the suspect after over 300
denials. The defendant had not been helped by the fact that
there was a solicitor present while the interviews were carried
out who had failed to intervene at any stage to prevent the
oppressive questioning.

Commentary

The case demonstrates that oppression does not need to take the form of torture, violence or threats of violence, etc. Rather, as was recognised by the Court of Appeal in *Fulling* (considered above), oppression can also take the form of "exercise of authority or power in a burdensome, harsh or wrongful manner; unjust or cruel treatment of subjects, inferiors etc; the imposition of unreasonable or unjust burdens." The questioning in the instant case clearly seems to have fallen within this definition. Moreover, the personal characteristics of the accused ("borderline mental handicap") were clearly of relevance when the court was determining the admissibility of the confession under s.76(2)(a) (see *R. v Seelig*, above).

Key principle: **The test of whether a confession should be excluded under s.76(2)(b) of PACE is whether the confession was or may have been obtained in consequence of anything said or done which was likely in the circumstances that existed at the time to have rendered unreliable anything the accused might have said in consequence of the thing said or done.**

R. v Harvey 1988

The defendant and her lesbian lover were arrested in connection with a murder after being present when the victim was stabbed to death. The defendant's lover confessed to the murder and the next day the defendant also confessed to the murder. The defendant was tried for murder after her lover retracted her confession. The defendant's lover died before the trial and there was a suggestion that the defendant, who was of low intelligence, had a psychopathic disorder and an alcohol problem, had confessed to protect her lover.

Held: The trial judge excluded the defendant's confession on the basis that he could not be sure beyond reasonable doubt that it had not been obtained in consequence of something said or done likely to render it unreliable, i.e. the confession made by her lover and in relation to the circumstances existing at the time, being the mental state of the defendant.

Commentary

In *Harvey*, the issue was whether the confession had or may have been obtained in consequence of a thing "said or done" (i.e. the confession made by the accused's lover, of which the accused was aware) which was likely in the circumstances that existed at the time (which included the accused's personal characteristics) to have rendered unreliable any confession that the accused might have made in consequence of the thing said or done. The burden of proof lay on the prosecution and the judge was not satisfied beyond reasonable doubt that the confession had not been so obtained.

Key principle: **Although denial of an accused's right to legal advice in contravention of s.58 of PACE *may* give rise to circumstances in which a confession should be excluded under s.76(2) or may be excluded under s.78 of the 1984 Act, the judge is not under a duty to exclude a confession if he is satisfied that the confession was not "obtained" in consequence of the breaches of the accused's rights.**

R. v Alladice 1988
The defendant was arrested on suspicion of having committed an armed robbery and was improperly denied access to a solicitor in breach of s.58 of PACE as the police feared a solicitor would advise him to stay silent and therefore prevent him from making any admissions in relation to the robbery. During the course of the police interview the defendant made a number of admissions, the trial judge admitted the defendant's confession and he was convicted. He appealed on the basis that his confession should have been excluded due to the fact he was denied access to a solicitor.

Held: (CA) The trial judge had properly admitted evidence of the defendant's confession. Although the judge could have excluded the confession on the basis that the defendant was denied legal advice he was right not to do so in this case. The defendant was aware of his right to silence and access to a solicitor would have made no material difference to whether or not he was likely to confess.

Commentary
So far as s.76(2) of PACE is concerned, the court will be looking for a causal link between the "thing said and done in the circumstances" and the confession. If it can be said that the thing

said or done to the maker of the confession caused them to confess then the courts will exclude the confession under s.76(2)(b), the prosecution bearing the burden of proving beyond reasonable doubt that this is not so.

R. v Alladice appears to suggest that more protection will be given to suspects who are unused to police station procedure or who for some reason have a problem comprehending their rights. Thus in *Alladice*, where the suspect was well aware of his right to silence and understood the implications of making admissions, the court did not exclude the confession despite denial of legal advice (see also *R. v Samuel*, below).

Key principle: **The "thing said or done" must be something said or done to the maker of the confession and not an internal decision or assumption made by them.**

R. v Goldenberg 1988
The defendant, a heroin addict, made admissions to police about his heroin supplier five days after his arrest. At trial it was submitted that the confession might have been unreliable as the defendant might have confessed in order to get bail and obtain more heroin.

Held: (CA) The thing "said or done" in order to induce the confession and therefore render it unreliable had to be something externally said or done to its maker and not some internal thing said or done by its maker. For this reason the judge had been right to admit evidence of the defendant's confession.

Commentary
If the courts were prepared to accept that things said or done by the accused himself were capable of resulting in the exclusion of confessions under s.76(2)(b), this would result in a situation in which the accused by his statements or conduct would potentially be capable of rendering his own police interview inadmissible on the basis of unreliability.

Key principle: **The wording of s.76(2) of PACE expressly states that when the court is considering excluding a con-**

fession under s.76(2) the court is not concerned with the truth
or falsehood of the confession.

R. v Crampton 1991

The defendant, a heroin addict, was convicted on charges of
allowing premises to be used for the supply of heroin and of
conspiracy to supply heroin. He appealed against his conviction
on the basis that a confession he made during an interview with
police should have been excluded under s.76(2)(b) or s.78 of
PACE on the basis that the confession was unreliable as he was
suffering heroin withdrawal at the time of the interview.

Held: The mere fact that the suspect had been going through
heroin withdrawal at the time of the interview did not render
his confession unreliable. A doctor had passed him fit to be
interviewed and the police had believed him to be so. In the
context of s.76(2)(b) "unreliable" referred to anything said or
done by the police which meant the confession could not be
"relied upon as truth", not whether the confession was actually
true.

Commentary

Section 76(2) is expressly worded to indicated that a confession
can be excluded under it "notwithstanding that it may be true".
When deciding whether or not a confession should be excluded
under s.76(2) the court is concerned with the circumstances in
which the confession was obtained and whether those circumstances mean the confession cannot be "relied upon as truth". In
determining whether a confession is admissible under s.76 of
PACE the judge is not required to consider whether the confession
is true or false, this being a question for the jury if the confession is
admitted.

Key principle: **Where admissions are made in an interview
and are subsequently excluded in pursuance of s.76(2)(a) or (b)
of PACE any admissions made in later interviews may also be
rendered inadmissible notwithstanding the fact that the later
interviews were conducted properly.**

R. v McGovern 1991

The defendant, a pregnant 19-year-old with a low IQ, was
arrested on suspicion of murder. The defendant's low IQ meant

she had difficulty understanding the police caution and there were breaches of the Codes of Practice of PACE. She was denied access to a solicitor, contrary to s.58 PACE, during her first police interview and subsequently made a number of admissions. The defendant was interviewed a second time, this time in the presence of a solicitor and again made a number of admissions. The defendant's confession was admitted at trial and the defendant was convicted of manslaughter.

Held: (CA) Failure to allow the defendant access to legal advice along with breaches of the Codes of Practice meant the defendant's first confession was likely to be unreliable and therefore should have been excluded by virtue of s.76(2)(b) of PACE. The fact that the defendant had made admissions in the first interview was likely to have an effect on how the defendant would react in the second interview. Therefore the court could not be satisfied beyond reasonable doubt that admissions made in the second interview had not been made in consequence of the admissions made in the original excluded interview and therefore the second confession would also be excluded.

Commentary
The Court of Appeal again demonstrated that additional protection would be required for persons with a low IQ or diminished mental capacity. In all cases where admissions have been made in an interview that is then excluded the court will need to look closely at any admissions made in later interviews to determine whether or not there has been a "causal link" between earlier admissions and those subsequently made in later interviews, even if there is no suggestion that the later interviews were in any way conducted improperly. The fact that earlier admissions were made may be sufficient to render future confessions inadmissible if a "causal link" can be shown.

Key principle: **Where the sole issue is whether a confession was made by the accused or was fabricated a *voir dire* will not be required, but where the admissibility of a confession is in issue this will be an issue for the judge to determine on the *voir dire*.**

Ajodha v the State 1981
The appellant, on the basis of his signed confession, was convicted of murder. When the accused had given evidence at

his trial he had claimed that the confession was not his confession but that the police had forced him to sign a statement he had not read by beating him and threatening to beat him. The judge did not consider the admissibility of the confession.

Held: (PC) Appeal allowed. Challenges by the accused on the basis that he did not make a confession and on the basis that his confession was not voluntary were not mutually exclusive. Rather, where the accused denied that he was the author of the confession and asserted that he signed it under duress, the judge would hear evidence on the *voir dire* to determine the admissibility of the confession and if he admitted the confession the jury would then consider the authorship of the statement and the manner in which the accused's signature had been obtained. Thus, the judge in the instant case should have ruled on the admissibility of the confession.

Commentary

When a judge is required to consider the admissibility of a confession the judge does so "on the *voir dire*", i.e. during a "trial within a trial" at which the jury is not present. If the confession is excluded, the jury is not made aware of its existence. If the confession is admitted, it is then for the jury to decide whether the confession is true. As the Privy Council recognised in *Ajodha*, however, where there is no issue as to the admissibility of a confession and the sole issue is whether it was in fact made by the accused (i.e. where the accused asserts that the confession is a total fabrication), the issue is solely one for the jury and a *voir dire* is not required.

The concept of a "voluntary" confession, which the Privy Council referred to in *Ajodha*, was a common law concept which, essentially, was replaced by the concepts of oppression and unreliability which now exist under s.76(2) of PACE.

Key principle: **When cross-examined by the prosecution during the *voir dire*, the accused should not be asked whether his confession is true.**

Wong Kam-Ming v R. 1980

The appellant was convicted of murder. At his trial, the judge had ruled that the appellant's confession was inadmissible. The appellant had given evidence on the *voir dire*, in support of his assertion that his confession was not voluntary, concerning the police conduct while he was in custody and, when cross-examined during the *voir dire*, had admitted that he had been present when the crime was committed and had been involved in the attack during which the victim was killed. Subsequently, evidence of the admissions that the appellant had made when cross-examined during the *voir dire* was called by the prosecution during the trial, the judge ruling the evidence was admissible. When the defendant testified he was cross-examined in relation to the inconsistencies between his testimony during the trial and the evidence that he had given during the *voir dire.*

Held: (PC) Appeal allowed. When an accused was cross-examined during the *voir dire* he was not to be asked questions concerning the truth of his confession. Whether the confession was admitted or excluded, the prosecution were not entitled to adduce evidence of what the accused said during the *voir dire*. In *R. v Treacy* 1944 it had correctly been held that the accused could not be cross-examined by the prosecution on the contexts of an inadmissible confession. Similarly, where the accused's confession was excluded, the prosecution could not cross-examine the accused in relation to incriminating statements made by the accused on the *voir dire*. Where the confession was admitted, however, and the accused gave evidence concerning the reliability of the confession (rather than merely giving evidence in relation to the voluntariness of the confession) the accused could be cross-examined in relation to inconsistencies between his testimony during the trial and the evidence that he had given during the *voir dire.*

Commentary
The extent to which the principles laid down by the Privy Council in *Wong Kam-Ming* concerning the admissibility of confessions made during the *voir dire* remain valid now that the admissibility of confessions is governed by s.76 of PACE rather than by common law principles remains to be determined by the courts.

Key principle: **Where a jury considers that a confession was or may have been obtained either by oppression or in consequence of anything said or done which was likely to render it unreliable the jury is required to disregard it.**

R. v Mushtaq 2005

The appellant was convicted of conspiracy to defraud. At his trial, the defence had asserted that a confession that the accused had made to the police should be excluded under s.76(2) of PACE upon the ground that it was obtained by oppression but the judge admitted the confession. The judge had directed the jury members to the effect that it was for them to decide whether the confession was true but that if they were sure that it was true they were entitled to rely on it even if it had "been made as a result of oppression or other improper circumstances".

Held: (HL) Appeal dismissed. The Privy Council in *Lam Chi-ming v R.* 1991 had indicated that improperly obtained confessions are rejected not only because of their potential unreliability but also because a man cannot be compelled to incriminate himself and because of the importance in a civilised society that the police treat persons in custody properly. It was inconsistent with the purpose of s.76(2) of PACE to say that a jury was entitled to rely on a confession if it considered that it was or may have been obtained by oppression or any improper means. Rather, the logic of s.76(2) required the judge to direct the jury that it was required to disregard a confession if it considered that the confession was or may have been obtained by oppression or in consequence of anything said or done which was likely to render it unreliable. That this was the correct approach for the judge to adopt was confirmed by the right against self-incrimination which was implied into Art.6(1) of the European Convention on Human Rights. Under s.6(1) of the Human Rights Act 1998 it was unlawful for the judge or the jury (as a public authority) to act in a way which was incompatible with the Art.6(1) right against self-incrimination. Directing the jury as the judge had done was inviting the jury to act in a way which was incompatible with the Art.6(1) right, the direction itself being incompatible with that right. Upon the facts of the instant case, however, there had been no evidence either of oppression or of any other improper means and, consequently, neither the fairness of the appellant's trial nor the safety of the appellant's conviction had been affected.

Commentary

Where a judge considers that a confession was or may have been obtained either by oppression or in consequence of anything said or done which was likely to render it unreliable, the judge is required to exclude the confession under s.76(2) of PACE. If the judge admits the confession but the jury considers that the confession was or may have been obtained either by oppression or in consequence of any thing said or done which was likely to render it unreliable, the jury is required to disregard it. Whether or not there is any suggestion of oppression or unreliability, it is still for the jury to decide whether the confession is true.

Improperly Obtained Evidence

The discretion of the criminal courts at common law to exclude evidence tendered by the prosecution is preserved by s.82(3) of PACE. In addition, s.78 of the 1984 Act conferred a new and, apparently, wider, exclusionary discretion upon the criminal courts.

Key principle: **There is no common law defence of entrapment and, other than in the case of evidence obtained from the accused after the commission of the offence, the court does not possess discretion to exclude prosecution evidence at common law unless the probative value of the evidence is outweighed by its prejudicial effect.**

R. v Sang 1980
The accused was convicted of conspiring to utter counterfeit American banknotes. While the accused was in Brixton prison, he met another prisoner called Scippo who, unknown to the accused, was a police informer and an agent provocateur. Scippo told the accused that he knew of a safe buyer for forged banknotes and would arrange for this buyer to telephone the accused. The "buyer", who was in fact a police officer, telephoned the accused and arranged to meet him with the forged banknotes. The accused was arrested at the meeting. The accused argued that the judge had a discretion to exclude the prosecution evidence if satisfied that the offence was instigated by an agent provocateur.

Held: (HL) Appeal dismissed. The defence of entrapment was not known to English Law, and a judge did not possess discretion to exclude admissible evidence because the crime had been instigated by an agent provocateur. A judge in a criminal trial did possess discretion to exclude evidence if its prejudicial effect outweighed its probative value or if it took the form of evidence tantamount to a confession that was obtained from the accused after the commission of the offence by means that would justify the exclusion of a confession. It was not, however, part of the judge's role to discipline the police or prosecution concerning the way in which evidence was obtained, the concern of the judge not being with how the evidence was obtained but with how the prosecution used it at the trial.

Commentary

In *Kuruma v R.* 1955 the Privy Council indicated that, at common law, there was no rule of law that unlawfully, improperly or unfairly obtained evidence is inadmissible, the test of admissibility being one of relevance. The Privy Council recognised, however, that the court did possess discretion at common law to exclude evidence tendered by the prosecution where the strict rules of admissibility operated unfairly against the accused (for example, where evidence was obtained from the accused by a trick). In *Jeffrey v Black* 1978, the Court of Appeal, relying on *Kuruma*, recognised that the mere fact that evidence was obtained irregularly did not render it admissible, its admissibility depending upon its relevance, but that the court did possess discretion to exclude prosecution evidence if it would be unfair and oppressive to permit the prosecution to call it. The House of Lords in *Sang* was required to consider the ambit of this common law exclusionary discretion. More recently, in *Grant v the State* 2006, the Privy Council indicated that it may be possible to interpret *Sang* (see above) less narrowly but that, in any event, in the opinion of the Privy Council, the criminal courts possess an overriding discretion to exclude evidence which would put the accused at an unfair advantage or would unfairly deprive the accused of the ability to defend himself. The scope of the common law discretion appears, however, to be a matter of little practical significance in English Law, given the existence of s.78 of PACE (see below). In particular, it should be noted that, under s.78, the court is to have regard to all the circumstances, *including those in which the evidence was obtained*.

It should be noted that in *A v The Secretary of State for the Home Department* 2005, the House of Lords held that evidence obtained by torture is inadmissible at common law regardless of where in the world the torture took place and even though the torture was carried out by foreign officials. Thus, where evidence was obtained from a witness by torture in a foreign country without the involvement of the British authorities, it will be inadmissible in the English courts. Their Lordships recognised that it would take express provision in primary legislation to render evidence obtained by torture admissible.

Section 78 of PACE

The trial judge possesses a general exclusionary discretion in relation to all prosecution evidence under s.78 of PACE which provides:

> "(1) In any proceedings the court may refuse to allow evidence on which the prosecution proposes to rely to be given if it appears to the court that, having regard to all the circumstances, including the circumstances in which the evidence was obtained, the admission of the evidence would have such an adverse effect on the fairness of the proceedings that the court ought not to admit it."

Key Principle: **Significant or substantial breaches of requirements of provisions of PACE or the Codes of Practice may result in the exclusion of confessions under s.78 of PACE, and bad faith on the part of the police may render a breach significant and substantial which would not otherwise be so.**

R. v Walsh 1990

The defendant was arrested on suspicion of having committed robbery. The police officers who interviewed him denied him access to a solicitor and failed to record the interview or give the defendant a chance to verify its contents in breach of s.58 and Code of Practice C of PACE. The trial judge refused to exclude the defendant's confession under s.78 determining that the police officers had not acted in bad faith and that refusing the defendant access to a solicitor had not made the defendant more likely to confess. The defendant appealed against his conviction on the basis that evidence of his confession should have been excluded under s.78.

Held: (CA) Appeal allowed. The defendant's confession should have been excluded under s.78. The standards of fairness protected by s.78 had prima facie been breached by refusing the defendant access to a solicitor and the further breaches of Code C. Despite the fact that the Court of Appeal was satisfied that the police officers had not acted in bad faith they could not come to the conclusion that the breaches had had no effect on whether the defendant had confessed, it being uncertain whether the presence of a solicitor would have made a difference. Accordingly, the judge should have excluded the defendant's confession under s.78, and his conviction was quashed.

Commentary
In *Walsh*, the Court of Appeal recognised that admitting evidence obtained in the context of significant or substantial breaches of s.58 or of provisions of Code C would have an adverse effect on the fairness of the proceedings, but indicated that whether this would result in the evidence being excluded under s.78 would depend upon whether the adverse effect was such that justice required the exclusion of the evidence. Their Lordships also indicated that while bad faith on the part of the police may make a breach significant and substantial which would not otherwise have been so, good faith on the part of the police would not have the effect of rendering a significant or substantial breach less significant or less substantial.

Walsh can be contrasted with the decision made in *Alladice* (above). Although the facts of *Alladice* were very similar to those of *Walsh*, the defendant's confession was not excluded as the court was satisfied that the defendant was aware of his right to silence and that denial of legal advice made him no more or less likely to confess. As a result there was no danger that admitting the confession in those circumstances would have an adverse affect on the fairness of the proceedings. In *Alladice* the court appear to have placed significance on the fact that the defendant was an experienced criminal who had been arrested on a number of occasions and was well aware of his rights.

Key Principle: **The common law discretion identified by the House of Lords in *Sang* appears to be narrower than the s.78 discretion, but it seems that the criteria of unfairness are the same whichever discretion the court is relying upon.**

R. v Christou; R. v Wright 1992
A jewellery shop was set up by undercover police officers who used video-recording equipment to record people selling stolen goods to them. The defendants both made repeated sales of

stolen goods to the shop and were charged alternatively with burglary and handling stolen goods. They sought to have evidence of the undercover operation excluded either at common law or under s.78 of PACE, on the basis that the evidence had been obtained by trickery, or on the basis that the evidence was obtained in breach of Code of Practice C, i.e. that the defendants should have been cautioned in the shop. The trial judge determined that police had not "invited" a crime but had used deceit to obtain the evidence. The trial judge then determined that the operation and all of the evidence would have to be looked at in order to determine whether or not it would be admissible. The trial judge determined that as the evidence had been obtained after the commission of the crimes it would not prejudice the fairness of the proceedings to admit it, and also ruled that Code C did not apply. The defendants pleaded guilty and appealed.

Held: (CA) Appeal dismissed. The Court of Appeal agreed with the judge that whether a judge was exercising the s.78 discretion or the *Sang* common law discretion (which the judge had indicated was narrower than the s.78 discretion because the common law discretion only applied to evidence obtained from the accused after the commission of the offence), the criteria of unfairness were the same. Upon the facts of the instant case, the defendants had applied themselves to the trick rather than having had the trick applied to them, and not every trick that produced evidence resulted in unfairness. The exercise of exclusionary discretion by the judge could only be challenged if it was *Wednesbury* unreasonable, and this was not the case.

The purpose of Code C was to protect vulnerable suspects, usually when they were being questioned by police officers. It would generally be applied to ensure that police officers and suspects were on an equal footing. Code C did not apply in the instant case as the suspects and police officers had dealt on equal terms in circumstances in which the suspects had been unaware that they were dealing with police officers. The Court of Appeal did, however, state that it would be wrong for police officers to use such an operation simply to avoid the constraints of Code C and that in such circumstances the court would be able to exclude such evidence under s.78.

Commentary
It is not for an appellate court to impugn an exercise of judicial discretion merely because the court disagrees with the way in

which the discretion was exercised by the judge at first instance. Rather, the appellate court should only interfere where the exercise of discretion was "*Wednesbury* unreasonable" (*Associated Provincial Picture Houses v Wednesbury Corporation* 1948). This, essentially means, that the appellate court should only impugn the exercise of discretion below if it was so unreasonable that no reasonable judge would have exercised the discretion in that way, if the judge took legally irrelevant considerations into account in exercising the discretion or if the judge, in exercising the discretion, failed to take legally relevant considerations into account.

Key Principle: **Section 78 of PACE did not change the principle that there is no substantive defence of entrapment or agent provocateur. The fact that evidence was obtained by a trick, by entrapment or by an agent provocateur does not necessarily mean that the admission of the evidence would adversely affect the fairness of the proceedings.**

R. v Smurthwaite 1994
Two appellants jointly appealed against conviction for soliciting a person to murder. Both appellants had sought to have their spouses killed by contract killers who were in fact undercover police officers posing as contract killers. On both occasions police officers had secretly recorded conversations in which the appellants asked the officers to kill their spouses for money.

Both trial judges at first instance ruled that the tape-recorded evidence was admissible and declined to exercise their discretion under s.78 to have the evidence excluded. Both appellants appealed on the basis that the evidence was obtained by an "agent provocateur" and by way of a trick.

Held: (CA) *Sang* (see above) had made clear that English law recognised no substantive defence of entrapment or agent provocateur and that the courts did not possess discretion at common law to exclude evidence simply because it was unfairly or improperly obtained if its admission did not render the trial unfair. Section 78 had not altered the rule that there was no substantive defence of entrapment or agent provocateur. This did not mean, however, that entrapment, agent provocateurs or tricks were irrelevant to s.78, as s.78 permitted the court to consider "the circumstances in which the evidence was obtained", but entrapment, agents provocateurs or tricks should only result in exclusion under s.78 if, in the words of s.78, admitting the evidence "would have such an adverse affect on the fairness of the proceedings that the court ought not to admit it". In determining whether, in the exercise of his discretion, to admit the evidence of undercover police officers, the factors that the judge might consider included whether the officer had been enticing the accused to commit an offence that he would not have committed otherwise, the nature of the entrapment, if any, whether the evidence comprised admissions or whether it comprised the commission of an offence, how active or passive the role of the officer had been, whether there was an unassailable or strongly corroborated record of what had occurred and whether the officer had abused his role by asking questions that should only have been asked in accordance with Code C. In the instant case the recordings provided an accurate and unchallenged record of the offence being committed and had properly been admitted as evidence at the trials.

Commentary
This case is authority for the proposition that evidence should not be excluded simply on the grounds that it was unfairly, improperly or illegally obtained if its admission would not have an adverse effect on the fairness of the proceedings. Rather, when determining whether to exclude evidence under s.78 the courts should apply the test of whether admitting the evidence would have such an adverse effect on the fairness of the proceedings that it ought not to be admitted.

In *R. v Chalkley* 1998, the Court of Appeal indicated that the fact that evidence was obtained by unlawful or oppressive conduct will not necessarily mean that its admission is unfair. The position at common law (*Sang*) was that, other than in relation to confessions and evidence obtained from the accused after the commission of the offence, the court did not possess discretion to exclude evidence unless the way in which it was obtained had or might have affected its quality, and s.78 had not widened the common law rule in this regard. Section 78 was not to be exercised so as to express the judge's disapproval of the conduct by which the evidence had been obtained, the question being, rather, whether the admission of the evidence would be unfair to the accused.

In general, significant or substantial breaches of PACE will be taken as having had an adverse effect on the fairness of the evidence (see *Walsh* and *Samuel* above). Moreover, it seems that bad faith on the part of the police may render a breach significant and substantial which would not otherwise be so (see *Walsh*, above). Thus it does appear that the nature of the police conduct (e.g. disapproval of bad faith on the part of the police) may, in practice, be a factor which influences the court in the exercise of the s.78 discretion.

Key Principle: **Where evidence has been obtained through the use of an "agent provocateur" the usual procedure is to stay the proceedings as an abuse of process.**

R. v Loosely 2001

The defendant was charged with supplying heroin to an under-cover police officer. During the course of an authorised oper-ation against drugs in the area an undercover police officer had been given the defendant's name and telephone number and had been told that the defendant would be able to supply him with heroin. The defendant supplied the officer with a quantity of heroin in exchange for money and was arrested. The defen-dant argued that either the evidence should have been excluded under s.78 on the grounds of fairness or that proceedings should be stayed as the evidence constituted an abuse of process. The trial judge exercised neither discretion and admitted the evidence.

Held: (HL) While entrapment did not provide a substantive defence, there had been developments since *Sang* was decided and the court now possessed two remedies for entrapment. First, s.78 of PACE primarily concerned the procedural fairness of the trial but as Lord Taylor had recognised in *Smurthwaite*, the court was entitled to take into account factors such as whether the accused had been enticed to commit offences he would not otherwise have committed, the nature of the entrapment and how active the role of the police officer had been. Second, the court possessed jurisdiction to stay proceed-ings where there had been a serious abuse of process by the executive. The normal remedy for entrapment was the stay of proceedings but excluding evidence at the trial would often have the same result in practice. When the court was consider-ing an application to exclude evidence under s.78, the court was required to distinguish between an application on the ground that the accused should not be tried at all and an application on that of procedural fairness and where the accused based his application on both of these grounds the court would be required to reach a separate decision under s.78 in relation to each of them.

The approach of the English courts to entrapment was that it was necessary to balance the requirement that persons who commit crimes be convicted and punished against the requirement that there should not be an abuse of process, the courts emphasising the need to consider whether the accused was persuaded or pressurised into committing an offence that the person would not have committed or whether the accused freely took an opportunity which was presented to him to break the law. The approach of the English Courts was not inconsistent with the decision of the European Court of Human Rights in *Teixeira de Castro v Portugal* 1998, the principle stated in *Teixeira* being that the where the offence with which the accused is charged was incited or instigated by the police, the fairness of the trial under Art.6(1) of the European Convention on Human Rights is violated.

In this case the trial judge had been right not to exclude the defendant's evidence under s.78 or to stay proceedings as an abuse of process. The police officer had not done anything more than present himself as "willing customer". The defendant had chosen to take the opportunity and commit the offence and had not been forced or tricked into doing so by the police officer. The fact that the officer was part of an organised operation, set up due to reasonable belief that the drugs trade was active in the area was also taken into account as providing justification for his action.

Commentary

It appears that as a result of the decision in *Loosely* in cases where an "agent provocateur" has been used to cause or incite someone to commit a criminal offence the normal remedy will be for the court to grant a stay of proceedings in the exercise of its jurisdiction to prevent an abuse of process rather than excluding the relevant evidence in the exercise of its discretion under s.78 of PACE. Where there has been no stay of proceedings the accused may assert that the evidence should be excluded under s.78 though if this really amounts to an application to stay the proceedings the court should exercise the s.78 discretion in line with the principles that it would apply when considering whether to grant a stay of proceedings.

Key Principle: **The admissibility of unlawfully obtained evidence will not necessarily violate Art.6 of the European Convention on Human Rights even where the evidence was obtained in violation of Art.8.**

Khan v UK 2000

The applicant and his cousin arrived at Manchester airport on a flight from Pakistan and were arrested. The cousin was found to be in possession of heroin with a street value of £100,000. The applicant was released without being charged. Several months later, the applicant visited a friend in Sheffield. The friend was the subject of a separate police investigation and a covert listening device had been installed at his premises. The device recorded a conversation in which the applicant admitted being a party to the importation of the heroin. The applicant was arrested and charged on the basis of this evidence alone. At trial, the applicant argued that recording should be excluded under s.78 of PACE on the ground that it had been obtained in breach of Art.8 of the European Convention on Human Rights. The judge ruled that the evidence was admissible and the applicant subsequently pleaded guilty to the offence.

Held: (ECHR) The surveillance amounted to an interference with the applicant's rights under Art.8. As there was no statutory system in place at the time regulating the use of covert listening devices, the interference was not in accordance with the law. The admissibility of evidence was, however, primarily a matter for domestic law, the question for the European Court of Human Rights under Art.6 of the Convention being whether the proceedings as a whole had been fair (this included the way in which the evidence had been obtained). However, the proceedings as a whole were fair and there was no breach of Art.6. The Court noted in particular that the use of the listening device was not unlawful in the sense of being contrary to domestic criminal law at the time, the tape recording, while the only evidence against the accused, was very strong evidence and there was no risk of it being unreliable, that the admissions by the applicant were voluntary, that the applicant had the opportunity to challenge the authenticity and use of the recording and that the domestic courts had considered the admissibility of the evidence under s.78 of PACE and would have possessed discretion to exclude it had it given rise to substantive unfairness.

Commentary

While the admission of unlawfully obtained evidence may be capable of rendering a criminal trial unfair for the purposes of

Art.6 of the European Convention on Human Rights, it will not necessarily have this effect. The admissibility of evidence in English criminal proceedings is primarily a matter for English law and, under s.78 of PACE, the English courts possess discretion to exclude prosecution evidence the admission of which would have such an adverse effect on the fairness of the proceedings that it ought not to be admitted.

12. STATUTORY EXCEPTIONS TO THE HEARSAY RULE IN CRIMINAL PROCEEDINGS (OTHER THAN CONFESSIONS)

Key Principle: The admissibility of hearsay evidence under s.117 of the Criminal Justice Act 2003 (CJA 2003) depends upon satisfying the various requirements laid down by that section but the criminal courts now possess discretion to admit hearsay evidence, including multiple hearsay, under ss.114(1)(d) and 121(c) of the 2003 Act.

Maher v Director of Public Prosecutions 2006
The appellant was convicted of driving without due care and attention and failing to report an accident. Two witnesses had seen her reverse into a car in a car park, get out and inspect the damage and then drive off. One of the witnesses made a note of the appellant's registration number (YF51 SYR) and their contact details and left it under the wiper of the damaged car. The owners of the damaged car phoned the police and told them the registration number and a police clerk recorded the details in the police incident log. When interviewed by the police the appellant admitted being the driver of the car, being in the car park at the relevant time and reversing out of a space but denied that she was involved in a collision. By the time of the appellant's trial the note could not be found but the magistrates admitted the police incident log under s.117 of the CJA 2003.

Held: (QBD) The evidence was multiple hearsay, the registration number of the car having been transmitted from the witness who wrote the note to the owner of the damaged car who read it and then from the owner of the damaged car to the clerk who recorded the registration number in the police incident log. The first-hand hearsay was the owner of the damaged car saying that the witness who wrote the note had told her that the offending car was the car with the registration number YF51 SYR. The evidence was not admissible under s.117 of the 2003 Act because when the owner of the damaged car had transmitted the information to the police clerk she had not done so in the course of a trade, business, profession, occupation or office. Rather, the only route under the 2003 Act for admitting the first-hand hearsay was the s.114(1)(d) interests of justice test. In relation to s.121, which concerned multiple hearsay, the s.121(1)(a) and s.121(1)(b) multiple hearsay gateways were not available because, respectively, the statement was not admissible under ss.117, 119 or 120 and the parties had not agreed to its admission. Given the admissions that the appellant had made, the only issue was whether the witness who wrote the note had erroneously written down the wrong registration number or the number had been misstated in the line of communication to the police log, but both of these things were very unlikely. The witness who wrote the number down could have been cross-examined concerning the possibility of error on her part and the registration number recorded in the police incident log was identical to the registration number and description of a car that was seen by the witness in the car park, so it would have been extraordinary if there had been an error in transmitting the registration number to the police incident log. The possibility of error was so remote that there was an overwhelming case for the admission of the evidence. Had the magistrates had any concerns in relation to the reliability of the evidence they could have directed, under s.117(7), that it was not admissible under s.117 and, thus, the fact that they had admitted the evidence under s.117 suggested that they had not had such concerns. Thus, if the magistrates' attention had been drawn to ss.114(1)(d) and 121(1)(c) of the 2003 Act, it was inevitable that they would have admitted the evidence under those provisions, thus the appeal was dismissed.

Commentary

The Divisional Court in *Maher* recognised that under the new statutory hearsay regime created by the Criminal Justice Act 2003, hearsay is inadmissible unless it falls within one of the hearsay exceptions defined by the new legislation (i.e. by s.114(1) of the 2003 Act) and that s.121 of the 2003 Act imposes additional requirements relating to the admissibility of multiple hearsay. The hearsay evidence that the *Maher* case concerned was not admissible under s.117 of the CJA 2003 because while most of the requirements of that section were satisfied (i.e. oral evidence of the registration number would have been admissible, the witness who wrote the note had personal knowledge of the matters dealt with, the entry in the police incident log was created by the clerk while acting in the course of a trade, business, etc. and, while the police incident log had been created for the purposes of a criminal investigation, the witness who wrote the note could not reasonably have been expected to have any recollection of the registration number), one of the s.117 requirements was not satisfied, i.e. the owner of the damaged car through whom the information was supplied on its way from the witness who wrote the note to the police clerk did not receive it in the course of a trade, business, etc. If s.117 had applied, the hearsay evidence would, it appears, have been admissible under that section because s.117, where its requirements are satisfied, is capable of admitting multiple hearsay without recourse to s.121.

Other than where multiple hearsay is admissible under s.117 of the 2003 Act, the additional requirements imposed by s.121 will come into play where a party to criminal proceedings wishes to rely upon multiple hearsay. Essentially, s.121 permits a party to rely upon a hearsay statement to prove that an earlier hearsay statement was made in any of three situations, namely, if one of the statements is admissible under ss.117, 119 or 120 of the 2003 Act, if the parties agree that the later statement may be admitted to prove that the earlier statement was made or if the value of the evidence, taking the reliability of the statements into account, is so high that the interests of justice require the later statement to be admitted to prove that the earlier statement was made. No such agreement had been reached in the *Maher* case and none of ss.117, 119 (which concerns previous inconsistent statements) or 120 (which concerns previous consistent statements) were applicable, and so the admissibility of the multiple hearsay depended upon a combination of the inclusionary discretion to admit hearsay evidence in the interests of justice which was conferred upon the criminal courts by s.114(1)(d) of the 2003 Act and the discretion to permit a hearsay statement to be relied upon to prove that an earlier hearsay statement was made which was conferred upon the criminal courts by s.121(1)(c). The Divisional Court, taking into account the factors laid down by s.114(2) which the court is required to consider when exercising the s.114(1)(d) inclusionary discretion and recognising that, in the context of *Maher*, it was necessary to consider the s.114(1)(d) and s.121(1)(c) interests of justice criteria cumulatively, ruled that the magistrates would inevitably have exercised their discretion under s.114(1)(d) and s.121(1)(c) so as to admit the hearsay evidence.

Key Principle: **The hearsay provisions of the CJA 2003 preserve the common law rule that evidence is only admissible if it is relevant to an issue in the proceedings.**

R. v T 2006

The appellant was convicted of the indecent assault of his niece, the complainant. The appellant's father had also been interviewed by the police concerning allegations made by the complainant, had admitted the allegations against him and had been charged, but had died before the trial. The trial judge admitted the contents of the appellant's father's interview at the appellant's trial under s.116 of the CJA 2003.

Held: (CA) Section 114(3) of the 2003 Act made clear that the common law rules concerning relevance as a precondition of admissibility continued to apply. For the hearsay exception created by s.116 to apply to a hearsay statement, the statement had to be admissible if given in oral evidence by the witness. Relevance was a precondition of admissibility. The fact that the appellant's father had admitted abusing the complainant was not relevant to the issue of whether the appellant had abused her. The only purpose for which evidence of the appellant's father's interview could have been put before the jury was to establish that since the complainant had told the truth in relation to the appellant's father she had also told the truth in relation to the appellant, but the mere fact that she had told the truth on other occasions, even though in the same context, was not logically probative of her allegations concerning the appellant. It was not permissible to admit evidence merely to support the credibility of a witness. Thus, the judges ruling had been wrong, and the appeal was allowed.

Commentary

Section 114(3) of the CJA 2003 essentially provides that nothing in the hearsay provisions of the 2003 Act affects the exclusion of evidence of a statement on grounds other than the statement was not made in oral evidence in the proceedings. One of the conditions of admissibility of a hearsay statement under s.116 of the 2003 Act is that the oral evidence of the maker of the hearsay statement would be admissible in the proceedings as evidence of the matter stated. It is a fundamental principle of the common law that evidence (including the oral evidence of a witness) is not admissible if it is not relevant to an issue in the proceedings (i.e. if it is not logically probative or disapprobative of a fact in issue). The admissions made by the appellant's father were not admissible to prove that the appellant had abused the complainant because they were not relevant to that issue. Thus, since it is not permissible to adduce evidence merely to support the credibility of a witness, the evidence was not relevant to an issue in the proceedings and should not have been admitted.

Key Principle: **Where it is unclear whether or not a statement is a hearsay statement, the existence of the inclusionary discretion conferred upon the criminal courts by s.114(1)(d) of the CJA 2003 may make the judge's decision concerning the hearsay or non-hearsay status of the evidence less critical.**

R. v Isichei 2006

The appellant, whose first name was Marvin, was convicted of assault occasioning actual bodily harm and robbery. The prosecution case was that two female students had met three white men in a bar. They had also seen two black men in the bar. They had gone to a club but found it closed and one of the men had phoned someone he referred to prior to making the call as "Marvin", and the group then went to the "Press Club". The doorman would not let them in, so (according to one of the two students, but not the other) the man phoned "Marvin" again. A black man came out of the club and, after discussion with the doorman, the two students were allowed in but the three men were not. Inside the club the students saw the same two black men whom they had earlier seen in the bar. When the students left the club and were walking to the station, the two black men got out of a taxi and the complainants were assaulted and robbed. One of the students identified the appellant at a video identification procedure, the accused's defence being mistaken identification. The defence had sought to have the evidence that the white man referred to "Marvin" when he made the telephone call to find a club excluded upon the basis that it was hearsay evidence, but the trial judge admitted the evidence. The judge ruled that the evidence was not hearsay evidence because, in accordance with s.115(3) of the 2003 Act, the word "Marvin" was not a statement, as it had not been said for the purpose of causing a person to believe the matter stated. Moreover, the judge indicated that if this was incorrect, the evidence statement was admissible in the interests of justice under s.114(1)(d) of the 2003 Act.

Held: (CA) The judge may have erred in ruling that the statement was not a hearsay statement, though that required a semantically correct and highly artificial application of s.115(3) in the context of what to the speaker would have been an inconsequential part of the story. Why should the speaker have cared whether the others believed he was talking to someone called Marvin, the only interest of the rest of the group being whether they could find a club to go to. It was possible to infer that the speaker had spoken to Marvin, and if he had not had the purpose of causing others to believe that he was talking to Marvin, the evidence was even more probative than it would have been had he had this purpose. Whatever the position was re s.115(3), the statement was clearly admissible under s.114(1)(d), it being "part of the story of a common sense series of events".

Commentary

The Court of Appeal does not appear to have reached a firm conclusion concerning whether the statement made by the white man on the telephone was or was not a hearsay statement. Their Lordships do appear to have recognised, however, that there seems to have been little reason why the man would have had the purpose of causing the rest of the group to believe that he was speaking to a person called Marvin. Thus, it is submitted that the judge at first instance was entitled to conclude, under s.115(3) of the 2003 Act, that the matter stated was not one to which the hearsay provisions of the 2003 Act applied and, thus, did not fall within the new statutory hearsay rule that the 2003 Act had created. Re the nature and operation of s.115(3) of the 2003 Act see the commentary to *R. v Singh* 2006, in Chapter 9, above.

The Court of Appeal did not need to finally determine whether the statement made by the white man on the phone was or was not a hearsay statement because their Lordships were satisfied that the admission of the statement was in the interests of justice and, consequently, that it was admissible via the inclusionary discretion that s.114(1)(d) of the 2003 Act conferred upon the criminal courts. In practice, in consequence of the existence of the s.114(1)(d) discretion to admit hearsay in the interests of justice, it may well be that the courts will, in future, not be too concerned about drawing fine distinctions between evidence that falls within the hearsay rule and evidence that does not fall within that rule. Formerly, the drawing of a distinction between hearsay and non-hearsay evidence was at times critical, i.e. in circumstances in which if evidence was classified as hearsay, it did not fall within the ambit of an available exception to the hearsay rule and was, thus, inadmissible.

Key Principle: **When the court is considering whether hearsay evidence should be admitted in the interests of justice under s.114(1)(d) of the CJA 2003 the court should take into consideration the factors to which it is required to have regard by s.114(2), but the court is not required to investigate each factor or to come to an individual conclusion in relation to each factor.**

R. v Taylor 2006

The appellant was convicted of causing grievous bodily harm with intent. In their evidence in chief (which took the form of video-recorded interviews), two prosecution witnesses named the appellant as a participant in the attack to which the charges against the appellant related. One of the witnesses had been told the appellant's name by her (the witness's) boyfriend. The other witness had been told the appellant's name by the former witness (i.e. the latter witness's knowledge of the appellant's name was derived from double hearsay). The trial judge held that the references made by the witness to the appellant's name were admissible in the interests of justice under s.114(1)(d) of the CJA 2003 and, consequently, the video recordings were played to the jury without editing out the parts where the witnesses named the applicant. The fact that the latter witness's knowledge of the appellant's name was based on multiple hearsay only came out when the latter witness was cross-examined, and defence counsel invited the judge to consider the additional requirements of s.121 and to reconsider his original ruling, but the judge declined to reconsider his ruling.

Held: (CA) When deciding whether hearsay evidence was admissible in the interests of justice under s.114(1)(d) of the CJA 2003, it was not necessary for the court to undertake an investigation into, and reach a conclusion in respect of, each of the factors to which s.114(2) of the 2003 Act required the court to have regard. Rather, the court was required to consider the s.114(2) factors, and any other relevant factors, to assess their significance, and to exercise its judgment as to the admissibility of the hearsay evidence under the s.114(1)(d) inclusionary discretion in the light of such consideration. The trial judge in *R. v Taylor* had done so, and his judgment could not be effectively challenged. So far as the multiple hearsay issue was concerned, bearing in mind that the jury had already heard the hearsay evidence, it had been open to the judge to decline to reconsider his original ruling. There had been a considerable amount of other evidence against the appellant and there was no reason for regarding his conviction as unsafe, so his appeal was dismissed.

Commentary

If the judge in *Taylor* had been aware from the outset that the evidence of one of the witnesses was multiple hearsay, he would presumably have considered whether, under s.121(1)(c) of the CJA 2003, the value of the evidence was so high that the interests of justice required the later statement to be admissible for the purpose of proving that the earlier statement was made. Presumably, since the judge had ruled that the admission of the hearsay evidence was admissible in the interests of justice under s.114(1)(d) of the 2003 Act, he would have been likely to have ruled that it was in the interests of justice to admit the multiple hearsay. It is submitted, however, that the fact that hearsay evidence is multiple hearsay is a factor that can considerably affect its probative value, and that it would have been better if the judge had revisited his decision and justified it in terms of s.121(1)(c). What is, of course, crucial is that where such evidence is admitted, the judge gives the jury a clear direction concerning its potential weight.

––––––––––

Key Principle: **The case provides another example of circumstances in which the Court of Appeal held that hearsay evidence was admissible under the inclusionary discretion created by s.114(1)(d) of the CJA 2003.**

R. v GJ 2006

The accused was convicted of several counts of indecent assault on his stepdaughter; the offences had allegedly been committed about 20 years before the trial. The appellant's defence was that the allegations were false and had been invented by the complainant because, after her mother's death, she resented the appellant's presence in the family home. A witness who was a neighbour and family friend of the appellant and his deceased wife, the complainant's mother, testified that about 16 years before the trial, the complainant's mother had told the witness that the complainant had made allegations of sexual abuse against the appellant, that the complainant's mother had put the allegations to the appellant and that the appellant had admitted that they were true. The witness also testified that she had been present on occasions when the appellant had had arguments with the complainant's mother, during which the appellant had admitted that he had sexually abused the complainant. Further, the witness testified that during a car journey the appellant had told her that the complainant was threatening to tell the police what had happened.

Held: (CA) The Court of Appeal refused the appellant leave to appeal in relation to his ground of appeal that related to the admission of the witness's hearsay evidence because they did not consider that the ground was an arguable ground. At the trial defence counsel had accepted that the hearsay evidence was admissible under the Criminal Justice Act 2003 but had asserted that it should have been excluded under s.78 of PACE. Thus, the judge had given his ruling solely under s.78 of PACE. Consequently, the judge had not dealt with the factors that s.114(2) of the CJA 2003 required him to have regard to when considering the admissibility of hearsay evidence under s.114(1)(d) of the CJA 2003. The reason why the judge had not done so was obvious, however, i.e. the prosecution had not been required to make an application under s.114(1)(d) in consequence of the agreement that the evidence was admissible subject to the exercise of the s.78 discretion. The judge's ruling under s.78 had been carefully reasoned and was unimpeachable and had the judge been required to consider the s.114(2) factors he would have reached the same conclusion. Moreover, following the death of the complainant's mother, the hearsay evidence was probably admissible under s.16 of the 2003 Act.

Commentary

It is submitted that the Court of Appeal in R. v GJ appears, as in a number of the other recent cases on hearsay, to have been willing to accept that hearsay evidence was admissible under s.114(1)(d) of the 2003 Act without undertaking a detailed consideration of the provisions of the 2003 Act. This does not accord with the guidance given by Leveson J. in the Divisional Court in *Maher v Director of Public Prosecutions* 2006 where his Lordship indicated that the courts must analyse the precise provisions of the 2003 Act, ensure that the route by which hearsay evidence is admissible is correctly identified and, in the case of multiple hearsay, must do so in stages in order to test "each link in the multiple chain".

In *R. v GJ*, it is submitted that the witness's evidence that the complainant's mother had told her of a complaint made to the complainant's mother by the complainant and of an admission made by the appellant to the complainant was multiple hearsay. That being the case, it is submitted that the court should have considered both s.114(1)(d) of the 2003 Act and s.121, which imposes additional requirements in relation to the admissibility of multiple hearsay. Indeed, the courts suggestion that the evidence might have been admissible under s.116 of the 2003 Act, in consequence of the death of the complainant's mother, would face the problem that admissibility of one of the statements under s.116 of the 2003 Act, unlike ss.117, 119 or 120, does not satisfy the requirements of s.121(1)(a) of the 2003 Act. It is accepted, however, that if evidence of the complaint was admissible under s.120 of the 2003 Act as a recent complaint, evidence of the mother's statement to the witness might have been admissible under s.116 in which case the multiple hearsay requirement of s.121(1)(a) would have been satisfied because one of the statements would have been admissible under s.120. Alternatively, both of the hearsay statements might have been admissible in the interests of justice under s.114(1)(d) of the 2003 Act, in which case the multiple hearsay issue might have been satisfied via the interests of justice test laid down by s.121(1)(c) of the 2003 Act.

So far as the admission made by the appellant to the complainant's mother and proved by the witness was concerned, it is submitted that, in accordance with s.128(2) of the 2003 Act, this, being a confession, could only have been admissible if it would have been admissible under s.76 of the Police and Criminal Evidence Act 1984. Since there does not appear to be any suggestion that the admission was obtained by oppression or in consequence of anything said or done to the appellant that was likely to make any confession he might have made in the circumstances unreliable, however, it appears that his confession would have been admissible under s.76. This being the case, it is submitted that the statement made by the complainant's mother to the witness could have been admitted under s.116 or s.114(1)(d) of the 2003 Act and that the additional multiple hearsay requirement imposed by s.121 could have been satisfied via the s.121(1)(c) interests of justice test.

Key Principle: **The admission of hearsay evidence for the prosecution in criminal proceedings will not necessarily give rise to a violation of Art.6 of the European Convention on Human Rights even where it is the sole or decisive evidence against the accused.**

R. v Sellick 2005

The appellants were convicted of murder. The trial judge had admitted four hearsay statements under s.23 of the Criminal Justice Act 1988, two on the basis that their makers did not give oral evidence through fear and two on the basis that their makers could not be found, all reasonable steps having been taken to find them. The judge, under s.26 of the 1988 Act, had ruled that the admission of the hearsay evidence was in the interests of justice.

Held: (CA) The trial judge had properly exercised his discretion to admit the hearsay evidence. In relation to the witness who had been kept away by fear generated by the appellants or persons acting for them, their evidence had been important but had not been the sole or decisive evidence. The appellants could not complain that their Art.6 rights were infringed merely because those witnesses were not at the trial. In relation to the witnesses who could not be found, the evidence of one of the witnesses had not been important and, while the other had given important evidence it, again, was not the sole evidence. Rather, there was a great deal of circumstantial evidence and the powerful evidence of a (hostile) witness who had given oral evidence at the trial. Even if the evidence of the latter witness was decisive, the judge had been entitled to admit it because counter-balancing measures had properly been in place, i.e. the defence had been able to attack the credibility of the latter witness and the judge had given the jury appropriate directions concerning the weight of the hearsay evidence, including the disadvantages to the defence in not being able to cross-examine the witnesses. There had not been a violation of Art.6 of the Convention and, consequently, the appellants' appeal was dismissed.

Commentary

The *Sellick* case concerned provisions of the Criminal Justice Act 1988 that have since been repealed and, in part, replaced, by provisions of the CJA 2003. Essentially the former hearsay exception created by s.23 of the 1988 Act was an ancestor of that which currently exists under s.116 of the 2003 Act, both hearsay exceptions concerning the evidence of unavailable witnesses but s.116, unlike s.23 of the 1988 Act, encompassing oral statements as well as those made in documents. The 2003 Act does not contain a provision equating to s.26 of the 2003 Act which, in the context of ss.23 and 24 of the 1988 Act, imposed an interests of justice leave requirement in circumstances in which a hearsay statement had been prepared for a criminal investigation or criminal proceedings. In practice, however, where hearsay evidence is tendered under s.116 of the 2003 Act, a trial judge may exclude such evidence in the exercise of his exclusionary discretion under s.78 of PACE and, moreover, where the reason for the witness's unavailability is fear, the operation of s.116 is subject to the interests of justice leave requirement that is imposed by s.116(4).

Under Art.6(1) of the European Convention on Human Rights the accused is guaranteed the right to a fair trial and under Art.6(3)(d) the right of the accused to examine the witness against him or to have them examined is set out. The Court of Appeal in *Sellick* examined the relevant case law of the European Court of Human Rights. Their Lordships found that while the admissibility of hearsay evidence is primarily a question for domestic law, the normal position is that evidence must be given at a public hearing and in general the defence must be given an adequate opportunity to question witnesses, but their Lordships also found that the admission of hearsay evidence is not necessarily incompatible with Art.6, relevant considerations when determining the fairness of the trial for the purposes of Art.6 including the reasons why the admission of the hearsay evidence was held to be necessary, the nature of the measures taken to counterbalance any handicap to the defence, the quality of the hearsay evidence, its inherent reliability and the degree of caution exercised in relation to the hearsay evidence. Their Lordships held, however, that the decision of the ECHR in *Luca v Italy* 2006 was not authority for the proposition that regardless of the circumstances and the counterbalancing measures that were adopted, where the hearsay evidence of a witness who the defence have had no opportunity to question is the sole or decisive evidence against the accused, there will inevitably be a violation of Art.6. Rather, the Court of Appeal in *Sellick* held that even where hearsay evidence was the sole or decisive evidence against the accused, if the maker of the hearsay statement had been kept away by the accused or persons acting for him, the evidence was of good quality, the attention of the jury had been drawn to the witness's credibility and the jury were

clearly directed to exercise caution, the accused could not complain that Art.6(3)(d) had been infringed, because he had kept the
witness away himself, and the counterbalancing measures would
ensure that the trial was fair for the purposes of Art.6(1). Where it
was not clear, but was highly probable, that witnesses who could
not be found had been intimidated by or on behalf of the accused
there was, again, no absolute rule that admitting the witness's
compelling hearsay as the sole or decisive evidence against the
accused would automatically result in the infringement of the
accused's rights under Art.6.

Key Principle: **The admission of hearsay evidence for the
prosecution in criminal proceedings may be capable of giving
rise to a violation of Art.6 of the European Convention on
Human Rights.**

Crown Prosecution Service Durham v CE 2006

The respondent was charged with rape. The prosecution case
was wholly or mainly based on a video-recorded interview of
the complainant who the prosecution did not intend to call as a
witness. For the purposes of the hearsay exception created by
s.116 of the CJA 2003 the judge found that the complainant was
unfit to be a witness because of her bodily or mental condition
and that she would not give oral evidence through fear. The
judge refused to admit the hearsay evidence, however, under
s.116 of the CJA 2003. The prosecution appealed to the Court of
Appeal against the judge's ruling.

Held: (CA) Under Art.6(3)(d) of the European Convention on
Human Rights, the accused had the right to examine or have
examined the witnesses against him. Under s.6 of the Human
Rights Act 1998, it was unlawful for a court to act incompatibly
with a convention right. The European Court of Human Rights
(in *Luca v Italy* 2006), had held that Art.6 is contravened if the
accused's conviction is solely or decisively based on statements
made by a person whom the accused had had no opportunity to
examine or have examined. The Court of Appeal (*R. v Sellick*
2005) had held that this right is not an absolute right, that the
ECHR authorities had not considered the position where a
witness is kept away by fear induced by the accused and that
the court could take counterbalancing measures to allow such a

hearsay statement to be read. Upon the facts of the case, the sole or decisive evidence against the accused had been the hearsay evidence that had not been cross-examined and was untested. While the complainant was not giving evidence partly through fear, the fear had not been induced by the respondent, and admitting the hearsay would have been a breach of Art.6. Thus, the judge had exercised his discretion on correct principles, the exercise of discretion was not unreasonable or perverse, and the prosecution's appeal was dismissed.

Commentary

The hearsay exception created by s.116 of the 2003 Act applies to the evidence of witnesses who are unavailable because they are dead, unfit to attend due to their bodily or mental condition, outside the UK and it is not reasonably practicable to secure their attendance, cannot be found, all reasonably practicable steps having been taken to find them or do not give evidence through fear. The fear condition is subject to the leave of the court being given in the interests of justice under s.116(4), otherwise admissibility under s.116 is not a matter of judicial discretion though, as the Court of Appeal recognised in the *CPS* case, the admissibility of hearsay evidence for the prosecution under s.116 is subject to the exercise of the court's exclusionary discretion under s.78 of the Police and Criminal Evidence Act 1984. In the *CPS* case the judge, recognising that the hearsay evidence was the sole and decisive evidence against the accused and that it would have been difficult for the accused to have challenged the hearsay evidence if the complainant did not testify, held that it would be a violation of Art.6 of the Convention, and unfair for the purposes of s.116(4) of the 2003 Act, to admit the hearsay evidence and, consequently, properly exercised his discretion so as to exclude the hearsay evidence.

Key Principle: **The admission of hearsay evidence for the prosecution does not give rise to a violation of Art.6 of the European Convention on Human Rights in circumstances in which the maker of the original statement is available for cross-examination.**

R. v Xhabri 2005

The appellant was convicted of a number of offences, including false imprisonment, rape, threats to kill and control of prostitution through gain. The trial judge admitted evidence of statements made by the complainant to three witnesses, permitting the witnesses to give evidence of what they had been told by the complainant, and permitted a police witness to give evidence of statements made to him by two witnesses who had spoken to the complainant, the evidence being multiple hearsay because the two witnesses repeated to the police witness what they had been told by the complainant. The judge held that the hearsay evidence of three of the witnesses was admissible under s.120 or s.114 of the CJA 2003 or, in the case of the multiple hearsay, under s.121 of the 2003 Act.

Held: (CA) The evidence of the first three witnesses was admissible under s.120 of the CJA 2003, the requirements of s.120(7) appearing to have been satisfied. Even if the requirements of s.120 had not been satisfied, the judge had clearly possessed discretion to admit it in the interests of justice in the exercise of his discretion under s.114(1)(d) of the 2003 Act. There was a multiple hearsay element to the evidence of one of the three witnesses, but the judge could properly have held it admissible under s.21(1)(c) of the 2003 Act. In relation to the evidence of the police witness, the complainant's statement was admissible under s.120 of the 2003 Act and the additional requirements of s.121 re multiple hearsay were satisfied both via ss.121(1)(a) and 121(1)(c). It was not unfair to admit the police witness' evidence because, while the two witnesses who had spoken to him were not available for cross-examination, the complainant, who had provided the information that the two witnesses had relayed to the police witness, was available. While s.114 of the 2003 Act permitted the court to admit the hearsay evidence of witnesses who were not available for cross-examination, s.114 was not incompatible with Art.6 of the European Convention on Human Rights, the court possessing the power to exclude hearsay evidence under s.126 of the 2003 Act and, indeed, being under a duty to do so under the Human Rights Act 1998 in circumstances in which admitting hearsay evidence would infringe Art.6. There was no inherent inequality of arms in the hearsay provisions of the 2003 Act, because they applied equally to prosecution and defence. The admission of the hearsay evidence in *Xhabri* had not infringed Art.6. All of the hearsay derived from the complainant, who was available for cross-examination. Thus, the appeal was dismissed.

Commentary

The hearsay exceptions created by s.120 of the CJA 2003 relate to evidence of previous consistent statements made by persons who are called to give evidence, previous consistent statements forming part of the subject matter of Chapter 5, above. The hearsay exception to which s.120(7) relates, and which was applicable upon the facts of *Xhabri*, concerns the admissibility of complaints made at the first reasonable opportunity by the victims of offences with which the accused is charged. One of the ways in which the additional multiple hearsay requirement imposed by s.121 of the 2003 Act may be satisfied is by showing that one of the hearsay statements is admissible under s.120 of that Act. As has already been seen in the present chapter, ss.114(1)(d) and 121(1)(c) of the 2003 Act confer upon the criminal courts, respectively, discretion to admit hearsay evidence in the interests of justice and discretion to admit multiple hearsay in the interests of justice. The discretion to exclude hearsay evidence which was conferred by s.126(1) of the 2003 Act applies where the case for excluding the evidence, taking into account the danger that admitting it would unduly waste time, substantially outweighs the case for admitting it, taking its value into account. Section 126(2) preserves the power of the court to exclude evidence both under s.78 of the Police and Criminal Evidence Act 1984 and at common law. It is submitted that in circumstances in which the admission of hearsay evidence for the prosecution in criminal proceedings would violate Art.6 of the Convention, it is the exercise of the s.78 discretion rather than that of the s.126 discretion which would be appropriate, the former discretion relating to evidence the admission of which would adversely affect the fairness of the proceedings, the latter discretion relating to evidence of limited probative value, the admission of which would result in an undue waste of time.

Key Principle: **Where the case against the accused is based on unconvincing hearsay evidence, the judge may be required to stop the trial.**

R. v Joyce 2005

The appellants were convicted of possessing a firearm with intent to cause fear of violence. Three witnesses had made statements to the police identifying the appellants, but all three witnesses subsequently retracted their statements before the trial, indicating that they had made mistakes. At the trial, the evidence of the three witnesses was inconsistent with their police statements. One of the witnesses admitted making a previous inconsistent statement to the police. The other two witnesses were treated as hostile witnesses and their inconsistent statements (i.e. their police statements) were proved under s.3 of the Criminal Procedure Act 1965. The judge thus admitted the police statements as evidence of the matters stated under s.119 of the CJA 2003. The defence submitted that the hearsay evidence was so unconvincing that the judge should have directed an acquittal under s.125 of the 2003 Act, but the judge left the case to the jury.

Held: (CA) The shootings which the case concerned had taken place in daylight, the witnesses had known the defendants and had had unobstructed views of them, in the case of two of the three witnesses over a significant period of time. It stretched credulity to suggest that all three witnesses had made mistakes. It would thus have been astonishing if the judge had reached a different conclusion. The judge had properly directed the jury in indicating that the three options open to them were to accept a witness's police statement (if sure that it was true), to accept the evidence that a witness had given in court (if sure that it was true) or, in the light of the inconsistencies between the statement and the witness's testimony, to decide that they could not rely on any evidence emanating from the witness, and, thus, totally ignore it.

Commentary
Section 125 of the CJA 2003 applies in the context of trial on indictment. Under s.125, where the case against the accused is wholly *or* partly based on a statement that was not made in the proceedings and the evidence provided by the statement is so unconvincing that, given its importance to the case against the accused, the accused's conviction would be unsafe, the judge is under a duty either to direct an acquittal or, where he believes that there should be a retrial, to discharge the jury. Section 119 of the 2003 Act creates a hearsay exception under which previous inconsistent statements made by witnesses who give oral evidence in criminal proceedings are admissible where the witness either admits making the inconsistent statement or the statement is proved under ss.3, 4 or 5 of the Criminal Procedure Act 1865. (In relation to the proof of inconsistent statements under the provisions of the 1865 Act see Chapter 5, below.)

13.   EVIDENCE OF CHARACTER

Good Character

Key principle: **Evidence of the accused's good character is only admissible as evidence of the accused's general reputation and does not extend to specific examples of the accused's good character.**

R. v Rowton (1865)
The defendant was a schoolteacher charged with indecently assaulting a 14-year-old pupil. The defendant adduced a number of character witnesses who gave evidence that he was a man of good character giving regard to his general reputation and standing within the community. The prosecution sought to rebut this character evidence by calling another former pupil of Rowton who testified that:

> "I know nothing of the neighbourhood's opinion, because I was only a boy at school when I knew him; but my own opinion, and the opinion of my brothers who were also pupils of his, is, that his character is that of a man capable of the grossest indecency and the most flagrant immorality."

The trial judge admitted this evidence in rebuttal of the good character evidence adduced and the defendant was convicted.

Held: (CA) Evidence of an accused's character should be limited to evidence of his general reputation and does not extend to specific examples. The evidence called by the prosecution in rebuttal would therefore not be admissible as it was evidence of an individual opinion.

R. v Redgrave (1981)
The defendant was charged with importuning for immoral purposes. The case for the crown was that the defendant had committed sex acts in front of plain clothes police officers in a public convenience. At trial the defendant wished to adduce evidence that he was or had been engaged in a number of relationships with women by producing photographs and love letters to demonstrate his heterosexual tendencies. The judge refused to allow the defendant to adduce the evidence; the defendant was convicted and subsequently appealed.

Held: (CA) Applying *Rowton* (above) the Court of Appeal rejected the defendant's arguments and held that he was not entitled to adduce specific examples of previous heterosexual relationships. The court did, however, indicate that had the defendant been married or been in a single stable heterosexual relationship he would have been able to adduce evidence to show that he had a normal sexual relationship with his female partner.

Commentary
The decision in *Rowton* allows a defendant to adduce evidence of their good character only in the form of evidence relating to their general reputation. Although the decision in Rowton has never been overruled and therefore a defendant remains unable to adduce specific examples of their good character the courts have indicated, as in Redgrave above, a willingness to apply the law in a flexible manner. Hence the statement in Redgrave that someone in a stable relationship would be entitled to indicate that they enjoyed a healthy sexual relationship with their partner should that be relevant.

The Court of Appeal's decision in *Rowton* can now be read as relating only to the admissibility of evidence of good character as the provisions of Chapter 1 Part 11 of the CJA 2003 (considered below) deal specifically with the admissibility of bad character. Where evidence of bad character is admissible, however, the common law rule that bad character may be proved via reputation is preserved by ss.99(2) and 118(1) of the 2003 Act.

Key principle: **Evidence of the accused's good character is relevant both to his guilt and to his credibility.**

R. v Vye (1993)
The defendant, a 50-year-old man previously of good character, was tried and convicted of one count of rape by a majority verdict of 10 to 2. During the trial, the judge informed the jury that the defendant had a "clean record" but did not direct them as to its relevance. The defendant's defence was one of consent and he appealed on the basis that the jury should have been directed that his previous good character was relevant both to his guilt and to his credibility.

Held: (CA) The trial judge had made an error in failing to properly direct the jury as to how they could rely on the defendant's previous good character. The defendant's character was relevant both to his guilt (i.e. the likelihood that a man of 50 years' previous good character would have committed the offence with which he was charged) and to his credibility. In this case, the fact that the issue was one of consent made the defendant's good character particularly relevant. The jury would have been compelled to decide who was the more credible, the accused or the defendant, and it was therefore of "first importance" that the character direction should have been linked to credibility.

Commentary

The good character direction is split into two limbs: the first relating to credibility and the second to guilt (i.e. to propensity). The credibility limb of the direction attaches to the weight the jury is entitled to give to evidence that the accused gives in his defence. The guilt or propensity limb of the direction relates to the likelihood of the accused having committed the crime with which he is charged (i.e. to the unlikelihood that a man of good character would have done so).

Where the defendant either testifies or does not testify but relies on exculpatory parts of a mixed statement, the judge will be required to give a character direction to the jury both as to the credibility of the accused and to the likelihood or otherwise of his guilt.

Where the defendant does not testify and does not rely on exculpatory parts of a mixed statement there is no requirement that the judge gives the credibility limb of the good character direction as no issue of credibility will arise. The judge will still be required to give a direction about the relevance of the accused's good character as to his guilt (e.g. his likelihood or otherwise to have committed the offence).

Key principle: **Failure to give a good character direction may render a conviction unsafe. The trial judge retains a discretion not to give a direction as to the accused's good character in circumstances where he is satisfied that it would be an "insult to common sense" to do so.**

R. v Aziz 1995

Three defendants A, Y and T were jointly tried and convicted of fraudulent evasion of income tax and VAT using false invoices. A's defence was that he had been misled by one of the co-accused. Y and T admitted in oral evidence some misconduct relating to issues surrounding the invoices but denied acting dishonestly. Y also admitted making false mortgage applications and lying to customs officials. All three defendants were of previously good character and therefore sought good character directions.

A was given the propensity limb of the good character direction in relation to his likelihood to have committed an offence of the type with which he was charged. Y and T were both given the credibility limb of the good character direction in relation to the weight to be given to their evidence. The defendants appealed and their convictions were quashed by the Court of Appeal.

Held: (HL) A trial judge possessed a residual discretion not to give good character directions in relation to a defendant who had no previous convictions where the giving of such directions would be "an insult to common sense" (e.g. where the accused had no previous convictions but admitted involvement in serious criminal activity during the trial). Alternatively, a judge might be able to give the jury a "fair and balanced picture" by giving good character directions but qualifying them. In the present case all three defendants were entitled to be given both limbs of the good character direction, on that basis the Court of Appeal had correctly quashed their convictions and the appeal was dismissed.

Commentary

A person of good character is entitled to receive both limbs of the good character direction relating to both their propensity to commit offence of the type with which they are charged and their credibility. Failure to properly direct the jury as to the accused's good character could potentially lead to a conviction being deemed unsafe if a properly directed jury may have come to a different decision.

Where the accused gives evidence of his good character but there is also evidence of bad character, e.g. previous convictions or admissions made by the accused during the trial, this may result in the judge not giving, or qualifying, the good character directions.

Bad character

Key Principle: **Section 98(a) and (b) of the CJA 2003 provide a definition of bad character for the purposes of Chapter 1 Part 11 of the 2003 Act. .**

R. v Edwards and Rowlands 2005

Edwards and Rowlands were jointly charged with conspiracy to supply a class A drug, namely ecstasy. The prosecution case was that Rowlands had gone to visit his brother-in-law, Edwards, who was confined to a wheelchair following a serious car accident. Undercover police officers witnessed Rowlands remove something from the boot of his car and enter Edwards' house. Shortly after police raided the property and found two bags containing a large quantity of ecstasy tablets, £2,830 in cash and latex gloves containing traces of Edwards' DNA and ecstasy. Both men were arrested and following a search of Rowlands' house police discovered a live 8mm cartridge, Rowlands was then also charged with possession of ammunition without a certificate.

At trial the firearms offence was severed from the indictment and the judge allowed cross-examination of Rowlands regarding the discovery of the cartridge which Rowlands explained he had found buried in his back garden. Both defendants were convicted and appealed on a number of grounds (see *Edwards* below). One of the grounds upon which Rowlands appealed was that the evidence of bad character relating to the firearms offence should not have been admitted because it was not evidence of bad character as it "had to do with the alleged facts of the offence".

Held: (CA) The wording of s.98(a) of the CJA 2003 "has to do with the alleged facts of the offence" was quite widely drawn and therefore covered the discovery of the cartridge in this case, which had been the subject matter of a count which had originally been joined in the same indictment. Thus, it was not necessary to consider the admissibility of the evidence under s.101 of the 2003 Act, though where evidence fell within s.98(a) or (b) it could be admissible other than under the bad character provisions of the 2003 Act. It was, however, difficult to see what relevance the evidence had to the jury's verdict.

Commentary

Section 98 of the CJA 2003 provides that:

"References in this Chapter to evidence of a person's 'bad character' are to evidence of, or of a disposition towards, misconduct on his part, other then evidence which:

(a) has to do with the alleged facts of the offence with which the defendant is charged, or
(b) is evidence of misconduct in connection with the investigation or prosecution of that offence."

For the purposes of the CJA 2003 "misconduct" is defined under s.112 of the 2003 Act as the commission of an offence or other reprehensible behaviour.

Evidence of the accused's bad character is only admissible under "gateways" created by s.101 of the 2003 Act. Here, however, the evidence did not amount to evidence of bad character, due to the operation of s.98(a) of the 2003 Act, and thus its admissibility was not governed by s.101 of the 2003 Act. Thus, it is submitted, the admissibility of the evidence should, subject to the exercise of the PACE s.78 exclusionary discretion, have depended upon the common law test of relevance (*R. v Manister* 2005).

Key Principle: **It was doubtful whether the mere making of an allegation could amount to bad character for the purposes of s.100(1).**

R. v Bovell 2005
The appellant became angry when he was refused credit by a local shopkeeper. He returned to the shop with his girlfriend, who was carrying a golf club. An altercation ensued during which the shopkeeper was stabbed three times in the leg. The appellant claimed that he had been hit from behind. While he was slumped over, he heard a knife drop. He picked it up and waved it in front of him intending only to frighten. He claimed that he did not intend to stab the victim and that he had picked up the knife in order to defend himself. The defence was refused leave to adduce evidence of the shopkeeper's previous convictions for handling stolen goods and robbery, both of which dated back to 1993. Following trial, it emerged that the robbery involved the use of a knife by the shopkeeper. It also emerged that the shopkeeper had been charged with wounding with intent in 2001.

Held: (CA) The judge's decision regarding the 1993 robbery might have been different if he had known about the use of the knife. However, it was unlikely that the judge would have admitted the evidence of the 2001 allegation.

Commentary

The Court doubted whether the making of an allegation was capable of being evidence within s.100(1) (which provides "gateways" relating to the admissibility of bad character of persons other than the defendant). In the present case, the Court's doubts were increased because the allegation had in fact been withdrawn. Where such an allegation was to be admitted, it would necessarily involve an excursion into satellite matters and this should be discouraged. The Court stressed the importance of all parties having access to information about bad character within good time. To this end, it was important that the time limits concerning the giving of notice were complied with.

It should be noted that authorities under s.101 of the 2003 Act (e.g. *R. v Edwards and Rowlands* 2005) have suggested that evidence of allegations may be admissible.

Key Principle: **The fewer the number of previous convictions and the further the distance in time, the less likely they are to establish a propensity to commit offences of the kind charged. Offences of dishonesty do not, of themselves, demonstrate a propensity to be untruthful.**

R. v Hanson 2005

A bag containing £600 cash was stolen from a bedroom above a public house. The appellant had been drinking in the public house that afternoon and had been allowed behind the bar into a private kitchen to make up a bottle for his child. There was a stairway leading from the kitchen allowing access to the bedroom. The Crown's case was that the appellant was the only person who had an opportunity to enter the bedroom at the relevant time. The appellant's previous convictions for offences of dishonesty were admitted as being relevant to an important matter in issue between prosecution and defence, namely whether the appellant had a propensity to commit offences of the kind charged.

Held: (CA) Although the judge should have looked at the convictions individually and convictions for handling stolen goods and aggravated vehicle taking were not, without more, indicative of a propensity to burgle or steal, the appellant had numerous convictions for burglary and theft from a dwelling which were properly admissible. The appeal was dismissed.

Commentary
This is one of the earliest decisions under the bad character provisions and contains a number of important principles of general application. Their Lordships began by observing that the purpose of the new law was to assist in the evidence based conviction of the guilty, without putting the innocent at risk of conviction by prejudice. Their Lordships hoped that bad character applications would not be made as a matter of routine and that the prosecution would have regard to the circumstances of each individual case in deciding whether to make an application. It appears that bad character applications should not be used to bolster a weak prosecution case.

Section 101(1)(d), one of the seven "gateways" (as the courts have referred to them) under s.101 dealing with the admissibility of the defendant's bad character, allows evidence of bad character to be adduced where it is relevant to an important matter in issue between prosecution and defence. Section 103(1) provides that matters in issue for the purposes of s.101(1)(d) include the question whether the defendant has a propensity to commit offences of the kind with which he is charged, except where that makes it no more likely that he is guilty of the offence; and the question whether he has a propensity to be untruthful. Without prejudice to other methods of so doing, propensity to commit offences of the kind as the offence with which the accused is charged may be proved by evidence of his conviction for an offence of the same description (e.g. previous convictions for theft where the accused is charged with theft) or an offence of the same category (e.g. the theft category which the Home Secretary has prescribed as including theft, robbery, burglary etc.). Section 103(3) provides that this method of establishing propensity to commit offences of the kind with which the accused is charged may not be adopted where the court regards it as unjust. More-over, under s.101(3), the court must not admit evidence under gateway (d) or gateway (g) where, upon a defence application, it appears that admitting the evidence would have such an adverse effect on the fairness of the proceedings that it ought not to be admitted.

The following principles emerge from *Hanson*:

1. Although there is no minimum number of events necessary to demonstrate a propensity, the fewer the number of previous convictions, the less likely it is that evidence of propensity can be established.

2. The judge should always consider the strength of the prosecution case. Where there is little other evidence against the defendant, it is likely to be unjust to admit previous convictions.

3. Old convictions are likely to adversely affect the fairness of proceedings unless they share some special feature with the current offence.

4. Dishonesty and untruthfulness were two separate issues. Previous convictions for dishonesty were only likely to show a propensity to be untruthful where a defendant pleaded not guilty and gave an account at trial which the jury disbelieved or where the offence itself involved a propensity for untruthfulness, for example by the making of false representations.

5. The Crown will need to decide whether to rely upon the fact of the conviction or also upon the circumstances of it. If the latter, the circumstances and the manner in which they are to be proved should be set out in the application.

6. Section 103(2) provides that propensity to commit offences of the kind charged may be established (without prejudice to any other way of doing so) by evidence of conviction for an offence in the same category. Their Lordships held that it was important to consider each individual conviction, even where the previous convictions fall into the same category as the offence charged. In Hanson itself, for example, the court doubted whether previous convictions for aggravated vehicle taking, handling stolen goods and robbery were properly admissible on a charge of burglary.

7. In any case involving evidence of bad character, the judge should warn the jury that the fact that a defendant has a propensity to commit offences of the kind charged or a propensity to be untruthful does not mean that he committed the present offence or has been untruthful in the present case. The specimen direction on bad character should be followed closely.

Key Principle: **Evidence of a defendant's propensity to commit offences need not be limited to evidence that he has previous convictions for offences of the same category.**

R. v Weir 2005
The defendant was convicted of sexual assault on a girl under the age of 13. The victim was a friend of the defendant's daughter. The victim claimed that the defendant had touched her vagina over her nightclothes during a sleepover at his house. She also claimed that he had previously exposed himself to her on five occasions and that once, when he had taken her swimming, he had looked into the cubicle while she was getting changed and then given her £3. The defendant denied the offence and denied any previous improper behaviour. The trial judge admitted the defendant's previous caution for taking an indecent photograph of a child. The defence argued that as the taking of an indecent photograph of a child did not fall in the same category as sexual assault according to the Criminal Justice Act 2003 (Categories of Offences) Order 2004, the caution should not have been admitted.

Held: (CA) Section 103(2) of the CJA 2003 provided that a defendant's propensity to commit offences of the kind with which he was charged might (without prejudice to any other way of doing so) be established by evidence that he had been convicted of an offence of the same category as the one with which he was charged. The word "may" and the phrase "without prejudice to any other way of doing so" showed that propensity could also be demonstrated in other ways. The judge was entitled to admit the caution.

Commentary
Weir shows that evidence of propensity is not limited to evidence of previous convictions. Previous cautions, or even offences that an accused has asked to be taken into consideration at sentence, may be admissible. The Court of Appeal also held that even where the Secretary of State has prescribed categories of offences, evidence of propensity need not be confined to evidence of previous offences within the same category as the offence charged. Perhaps surprisingly, the Court did not appear to have been invited to consider whether a single caution for an offence that was four years old was capable of demonstrating propensity (see *R. v Hanson* above) or whether it was capable of having such an

adverse effect on the fairness of the proceedings that the court ought to have excluded it under s.101(3).

Key Principle: **Evidence of an accused's bad character is admissible under gateway 101(1)(c) if it is important explanatory evidence.**

R. v Chohan 2005

The defendant was charged with robbery, possession of an imitation firearm while committing a Sch.1 offence and possessing an imitation firearm with the intent to cause fear of violence. The circumstances of the offence were that while the defendant was in the home of an 89-year-old man, he threatened the man with an imitation firearm and took his wallet. He was chased by some of the victim's neighbours and threatened them with the imitation firearm in order to escape.

The primary evidence to be adduced by the prosecution was from a witness who knew the defendant and had identified him as running from the scene of the crime. The witness knew the defendant well as he had been supplying her with heroin for a considerable period of time. The prosecution wanted to adduce evidence of the defendant's bad character in the form of the defendant's supply of heroin to the witness in order to establish the accuracy of the identification. The judge acknowledged that he would have to give the jury a *Turnbull* warning in relation to the identification evidence (see *R. v Turnbull* in Chapter 3 above) and to ask them to look for supporting evidence. As a result he admitted evidence of the defendant's character in the form of his heroin dealing so that the jury could properly understand the context of the identification.

Held: (CA) The trial judge had properly admitted the defendant's bad character under gateway 101(1)(c) as it was important explanatory evidence of the accuracy of the witness's identification.

Commentary

Evidence of the accused's bad character is admissible under gateway (e) where it is important explanatory evidence, i.e. where the court or jury would find it difficult or impossible to understand other evidence without it and its value for understanding the case as a whole is substantial (s.102).

Key Principle: **Section 101(1)(e) of the CJA 2003 allows the admission of evidence of a defendant's bad character where it has substantial probative value in relation to an important matter in issue between a defendant and a co-defendant.**

R. v McLean 2005

Two men (M and S) were charged with wounding another man, O, with intent to cause him grievous bodily harm. M was also charged with wounding G, again with intent to cause GBH. M denied involvement in the first attack and claimed that in relation to the second incident he was acting in self-defence. S claimed that both attacks had been carried out by M and that M had a propensity for violence. The trial judge rejected an application by the crown to have M's previous convictions for violence admitted under gateway 101(1)(d) in an attempt to demonstrate his propensity to commit offences of the type with which he was charged. Subsequently the trial judge admitted evidence of M's previous convictions under gateway 101(1)(e) on the basis that they were relevant to an important matter in issue between the two co-accused. M was convicted and appealed against the decision on the basis that having decided not admit his previous convictions under gateway (d) it was perverse for the judge to then admit them under gateway (e).

Held: (CA) Dismissing the appeal, the Court of Appeal determined that it was entirely proper for the trial judge to admit the defendant's convictions under gateway (e). Although the two defendants were not running "cut-throat" defences, their respective versions of events were different. In such a circumstance M's previous convictions for violence were therefore of substantial probative value to a matter in issue that existed between the two co-defendants.

Commentary

Evidence of the accused's bad character is admissible under gateway (e) where it has substantial probative value in relation to an important matter in issue between defendant and co-defendant.

Key Principle: **Evidence of bad character to correct a false impression under gateway 101(1)(f) is only admissible where the false impression created is about the defendant.**

R. v Pickstone 2005

The appellant had a previous conviction for indecent assault of an 11-year-old girl in 1993. He met his wife before that conviction and they subsequently had three children. In 2002, the children were placed in foster care as a result of concerns on the part of the social services. In 2004, the oldest child complained that the appellant had sexually assaulted and raped her. The appellant was interviewed and claimed that the child was making up the allegations in order to secure his removal from the family home, so that she could leave foster care and move back in with her mother. At his trial, the prosecution applied for leave to adduce evidence of the 1993 conviction under gateways (d), (f) and (g). The trial judge admitted the evidence under (d) and (g).

Held: (CA) The judge's conclusions as to gateways (d) and (g) were correct. The passage of time did not make the admission of the evidence under gateway (d) unjust. The appellant's allegations were an attack on the complainant's character, making the evidence admissible under gateway (g). In asserting that the complainant wanted him removed from the family home, gateway (f) was not activated because this was not a false impression "about the defendant".

Commentary

Evidence of the accused's bad character is admissible under gateway (f) where it is evidence to correct a false impression given by the defendant and under gateway (g) where the defendant has made an attack on another person's character. The operation of gateway (g) is subject to s.101(3) (see the commentary to *Hanson*, above).

Key Principle: **Evidence of bad character is admissible under s.101(1)(g) of the CJA 2003 where the defendant has made an attack on another person's character.**

R. v Edwards 2005

On the April 30, 2004, the defendant was stopped by two police officers while driving a motor vehicle. After searching his car, the officers attempted to arrest the defendant upon which he became violent and a scuffle ensued in which both the defendant and the officers sustained minor injuries. The defendant was arrested and taken to the nearest police station. At the police station he voluntarily handed over a lock-knife. He was charged with two counts of common assault and with having a bladed article in a public place.

At trial the prosecution sought to adduce evidence of the accused's bad character in the form of previous convictions for burglary and robbery under s.101(1)(d) for the purposes of questioning the defendant's credibility. However, due to the age of the offences (having occurred some 13 years beforehand), the trial judge refused to admit them on the basis of their adverse effect on the fairness of the proceedings. During the course of the trial the defence mounted a "severe" attack on the prosecution witnesses. The prosecution thus made a new application to admit the defendant's bad character under s.101(1)(g). The defence argued that the defendant's convictions should be excluded under s.101(3) due to their age and potential prejudicial effect but the recorder rejected this argument and admitted them on the basis that the jury were entitled to be made aware of them in light of the sustained attack on prosecution witnesses.

Held: (CA) The trial judge had properly admitted the defendant's previous convictions under s.101(1)(g). In light of his sustained attack on the prosecution the court felt that it would have been misleading to the jury had they not been informed of the defendant's previous convictions.

Commentary
The case demonstrates that, in relation to the application of the s.101(3) fairness test, it may be unfair to admit evidence under gateway (d) but yet may be fair to admit the same evidence later in the trial under gateway (g).

Key Principle: **Evidence of bad character is not limited to evidence of a defendant's previous convictions. The common law principles governing the admissibility of similar fact evidence in criminal proceedings are no longer relevant to evidence of bad character.**

R. v Somanthan 2005

Following the breakdown of her marriage, the complainant began to attend a Hindu temple at Thornton Heath where the defendant was a priest. She alleged that he visited her home twice and raped her on each occasion. The defendant denied the offences in interview. He denied that he had had any problems in his previous post as a priest in Tooting. The defendant claimed that the allegations had been made because a section of the community wanted to blacken the name of the temple and, in his defence statement, he suggested that the complainant was not a witness of truth and had an ulterior motive. At trial, the trustee of the temple in Tooting gave evidence that the defendant had been dismissed from his post as a result of his behaviour and attitude towards women. The trial judge also permitted two young women to give evidence that the defendant had made sexual advances towards them at a time when they were emotionally vulnerable. The defendant called seven character witnesses to say that he had never behaved inappropriately towards female worshipers.

Held: (CA) The evidence was admissible under gateway (d) to show propensity notwithstanding that it would not have been admissible under the old principles governing the admissibility of similar fact evidence. The evidence was also admissible under gateway (f), to correct a false impression given by the defendant in interview. The attack on the complainant's character would also admit the evidence under gateway (g). The probative value of the evidence was such that the judge was correct not to exclude it under s.101(3).

Commentary

Obiter comments in *O'Brien v Chief Constable of South Wales Police* 2005, suggested that common law similar fact evidence principles might still be relevant when considering evidence of bad character under the Criminal Justice Act 2003. In *Somanthan*, the Court of Appeal confirmed both that evidence of bad character was not confined to evidence of a defendant's previous convictions and that "enhanced probative value" was not required. On the facts of *Somanthan*, the Court held that the evidence was properly admitted under all three gateways.

Section 105(6) only admits evidence under gateway (f) if it goes no further than necessary to correct the false impression. In *Somanthan*, the Court held that the evidence of the defendant's behaviour in Tooting and his behaviour towards the two young women was admissible because the defendant had given the impression that he was a priest who had always behaved properly towards women in the past.

Section 101(3) directs the court not to admit evidence under gateways (d) or (g) if, on application by the defendant, it appears that its admission would have such an adverse effect on the fairness of the proceedings that the court ought not to admit it. It appears from *Somanthan* that where trial counsel does not apply to exclude the evidence under s.101(3), a judge should encourage the making of such an application if appropriate. The Court held that s.101(3) requires the judge to conduct a balancing exercise and it appears that the probative force of the evidence sought to be adduced will be relevant.

Evidence of Bad Character in Civil Proceedings

Key Principle: **Evidence of bad character may be admissible at common law in civil proceedings as "similar fact evidence" where it is relevant and its admission would not be unfair or oppressive to the other side.**

Mood Music v De Wolfe 1976
The plaintiffs' were the holders of copyright in a musical work. The defendant in the case supplied a piece of music for use in a television play which was very similar to the plaintiffs' piece of music which was subject to copyright. The plaintiffs contended that the defendant had copied their piece of music whereas the defendant, although acknowledging that the two pieces were similar, argued that any similarity was merely coincidental.

In support of their claim the plaintiffs sought to rely upon evidence that on three separate occasions in the past the defendant had produced other musical works similar to musical works in which the copyright was held by another party. The judge admitted this evidence and judgment was given in favour of the plaintiffs. The defendant appealed on the basis that the evidence should not have been admitted.

Held: (CA) The courts had the power to admit "similar fact evidence" in civil proceedings providing it was of "sufficient probative weight" to justify its admission and that to admit it would not be unfair or oppressive to the other side. In this case where the question to be decided was had the defendant copied the work of the claimant or was it merely a coincidence that the two pieces sounded the same, evidence that the claimant had copied works in the past would clearly have a high probative value. The evidence had been properly admitted and the appeal was dismissed.

O'Brien v Chief Constable of South Wales Police 2005

The claimant was convicted of murder until his conviction was quashed 11 years later by the Court of Appeal. Upon his release the claimant commenced civil proceedings against the Chief Constable of South Wales Police for misfeasance in public office and malicious prosecution. His claim was that the police officers investigating his case had intentionally "framed" him for the offence. The claimant served notice that he intended to adduce evidence to show that named police officers connected with the investigation of his offence had acted with similar impropriety in relation to other investigations.

The judge ruled that the evidence was admissible as similar fact evidence and also that he retained a power to exclude the evidence under his case management powers. In this case the judge decided not to exercise that discretion and to admit the majority of the evidence. Judgment was given for the claimant and the decision was upheld in the Court of Appeal, who in fact decided that the court should have admitted all of the evidence. The defendant Chief Constable appealed to the House of Lords.

Held: (HL) When deciding whether to admit similar fact evidence into civil proceedings the test was whether the evidence was relevant, i.e. whether the evidence had probative value in relation to an issue in the proceedings. In this case the evidence of past misconduct by officers involved in the investigation of the offence clearly went to the heart of the case and was of a high probative value, it therefore fell to be admissible.

Commentary

The House of Lords in *O'Brien* recognised that, under rule 32.1 of the Criminal Procedure Rules 1998, the court possesses the power to exclude admissible evidence and to limit cross-examination. In determining whether to admit such evidence, the judge should ensure that the probative value of the evidence justifies the risk of unfair prejudice, if any, that its admission gives rise to and should consider the need for proportionality and expedition and whether admitting the evidence would give rise to side issues that would unbalance the trial. To adopt the wording of Lord Denning in the earlier *Mood Music* case, the admission of the evidence must not be "oppressive or unfair".

INDEX

LEGAL TAXONOMY
FROM SWEET & MAXWELL

This index has been prepared using Sweet and Maxwell's Legal Taxonomy. Main index entries conform to keywords provided by the Legal Taxonomy except where references to specific documents or non-standard terms (denoted by quotation marks) have been included. These keywords provide a means of identifying similar concepts in other Sweet & Maxwell publications and online services to which keywords from the Legal Taxonomy have been applied. Readers may find some minor differences between terms used in the text and those which appear in the index. Suggestions to *taxonomy@sweetandmaxwell.co.uk*.

(all references are to page number)